The Scots

Iain Finlayson

——— ✳ ———

THE SCOTS

Constable · London

First published in Great Britain 1987
by Constable and Company Limited
10 Orange Street, London WC2H 7EG
Copyright © 1987 by Iain Finlayson
Set in Linotron Ehrhardt 11 pt by
Rowland Phototypesetting Limited
Bury St Edmunds, Suffolk
Printed in Great Britain by
St Edmundsbury Press Limited
Bury St Edmunds, Suffolk

British Library CIP data
Finlayson, Iain
The Scots.
1. Scotland – History
I. Title
941.1   DA760

ISBN 0 09 466400 5

This book is for MAY and BETH FINLAYSON

Contents

Illustrations

The Edinburgh Festival Fringe Club (*Chris Hill*)
The Highland Games in Canada (*Agent General of the Province of Nova Scotia*)

There is nothing that I am prouder of than that I am a Scotsman, and, I may add, a Scotch peasant too; for where on all the earth is there a country that can be compared with Scotland in every noble thing that elevates a nation? And where is there a class of human beings to be found like her peasantry? They are not only an honour to the land they live in but a credit to the whole world . . . He would be a writer of pith indeed who could praise the Scots too much and one of matchless impudence who could revile them.

The Scottish Gallovidian Encyclopaedia: John MacTaggart, 1824.

Acknowledgements

For the ready loan of books and timely advice, I'd like to thank Mr John Reid. To Dr Anne Smith I owe thanks for so much generous friendship that particular acknowledgement of her encouragement of this book is but a token of a greater gratitude.

I also wish to thank Robin Baird-Smith and Prudence Fay of Constable, Tom Stewart and Ann Rittenberg of Athenaeum, and Deborah Rogers for their enthusiasm and patient attention to the development of *The Scots*. They were as stout-hearted and discerning as the subjects of this book.

I gratefully acknowledge the following writers and publishers, for extracts quoted from their work: Moray McLaren for *Return to Scotland* (Duckworth) and *The Scots* (Penguin); Alan Bold and Longman for *Modern Scottish Literature*; Leslie Fiedler and Jonathan Cape for *Love and Death in the American Novel*; Paul Theroux and Hamish Hamilton for *The Kingdom by the Sea*; Colm Brogan and Frederick Muller for *The Glasgow Story*; Edwin Muir for *Scottish Journey* (Heinemann) and the poem quoted on pages 46–7, from his *Collected Poems* (Faber & Faber); Trevor Royle and Macmillan for *The Macmillan Companion to Scottish Literature*; Compton Mackenzie and Chatto & Windus for *Hunting the Fairies*; T. W. H. Crosland and Grant Richards for *The Unspeakable Scot*; Bil Gilbert and Atheneum for *Westering Man*; T. C. Smout and Collins for *A Century of the Scottish People* and *A History of the Scottish People*; Ann Barr and Peter York, and the

Ebury Press for *The Sloane Ranger Handbook*; Andrew Campbell and Roddy Martine, and Wolfe Publishing for *The Swinging Sporran*; Charles Kightly and Thames & Hudson for *Folk Heroes of Britain*; Neil McCallum and James Thin for *A Small Country*; David Daiches and André Deutsch for *Glasgow*; Christopher Harvie and Edward Arnold for *No Gods and Precious Few Heroes*; Keith Webb and Molendinar for *The Growth of Nationalism in Scotland*; James Campbell and Weidenfeld & Nicolson for *Invisible Country*; Steve Bruce and Mainstream Publishing Co. for *No Pope of Rome*; Hugh MacDiarmid for 'The Dour Drinkers of Scotland' (MacGibbon & Kee) and *Aesthetics in Scotland* (Mainstream Publishing Co.); Harry Lauder and D. C. Thomson for *Ticklin' Talks*; William Power and Faber & Faber for *My Scotland*; The Cluny Press, in association with the E. A. Hornel Trust, for *The Scottish Gallovidian Encyclopaedia*; Faber & Faber for *Memoirs of a Modern Scotland*, edited by Karl Miller, from which essays by the following authors are quoted – Muriel Spark, Charles McAra, Tom Nairn, Arthur Marwick, George Scott-Moncreiff, Karl Miller, George Mackay Brown and Alastair Reid; Putnam and Sir R. H. Bruce Lockhart for *Scotch*; John Wain for his Introduction to James Hogg's *The Private Memoirs and Confessions of a Justified Sinner* (Penguin); and Cedric Watts and Laurence Davies, and the Cambridge University Press for *Cunninghame Graham: A Critical Biography*.

I am grateful also to the following writers and the publications in which their quoted work appeared: Anne Smith (the *Scotsman*); Lady Abdy (*Harpers & Queen*); Nicholas Coleridge (*Harpers & Queen*); Miles Kington and Alan Coren (*The Times*); Jack Maclean (the *Glasgow Herald*); Rennie Owen and Douglas Lowe (the *Glasgow Herald*); Prof. Norman Stone (the *Sunday Times*); Alistair Dunnet (the *Scotsman*); Alan Bold (the *Scotsman*); Alastair McLeod (the *Scotsman*); Stuart Hood (the *Listener*); and to several leader-writers on the *Glasgow Herald*.

I.F.
1987

A cautionary foreword

THERE have been many histories and studies of Scotland and the Scottish people. This is neither a history nor a scientific, anthropological study. I do not attempt to track the progress of any chain of historical events or to trace the development of Scottish institutions except in so far as they illuminate the Scottish character and help account for the origin and evolution of aspects that seem to me interesting, notable, and peculiar to that character.

There is matter for dispute on every page. This will be a partial, opinionated portrait by a Scot of his fellow-countrymen as they have presented themselves. I write as a single, male, middle-class, middle-aged, Lowland Presbyterian Scot who has spent most of the past sixteen years in exile in England. The views expressed will have been filtered through my own psyche. Since that is profoundly Scottish, they will be understandable – if not always agreeable – to the Scots. I do not dissociate myself from any praise or criticism I may give them. I do not disclaim my complicity in the national psychology or my collusion with its fantasies. If I criticize, I do not blame; if I praise I do not condone. The Scots are accustomed to wag the finger at themselves or clap themselves on the back – they have little need of anyone to do it for them.

This book is largely about the invention, development, and

perpetuation of Scottish national myths. To identify and attempt to account for these myths is not necessarily to devalue them – it may well be to reinforce them. In the process of psychoanalysis, personal myths are not easily shattered – the personality tenaciously guards its myths by all and any means against attempts to change or subvert them. They are personal defences against reality, and the process of coming to terms with them is slow and, often, anxiety-making. But psychoanalysis has joys as well as agonies: one of the great pleasures is making connections, of recognizing the effect one thing has on another, perceiving the nexus intuitively and spontaneously, as a sudden illumination, rather than by a process of logic. Hugh MacDiarmid named this 'satori'.

As I wrote this book, I was aware of connections. Material in one chapter suddenly gave rise to a connection with material in another – the book began to take shape as a whole, rather than as a series of chapters dealing with individual aspects of the Scottish national character. For this reason, the material may seem to some readers to be discursive and to refer back, again and again, to matters already discussed or remarked. The nature of the Scots, I might plead, has largely dictated the form of the book: critics who perceive a sinful inner chaos will not be deceived; those who perceive a natural progression from one topic to another will recognize that some attempt has been made to impose order upon the chaos. Disorderly order is, after all, a form of order that anyone who has even partly succeeded in knowing his own character will recognize.

I have frequently adopted the published views of fellow-Scots where they appeared to coincide with my own, and rallied them to my support. These commentators will forgive me, I hope, if I have inadvertently presented their words out of context or given them emphases that were never intended. My interpretations of fact and opinion are wholly my responsibility.

I

———— ✳ ————

A small country:
pride, poverty and prejudice

A T a London dinner party a few years ago, the talk turned
to bloodstock – our own. National characteristics were
discussed over the smoked cod's roe, paternity over the pheasant,
until the talk developed into conversational one-upmanship as to
who among the eight guests could claim the best blood. Russian
and French were both acceptable, but those of us with a claim to
undiluted Scottish blood came out top of the ethnic table. It was
considered a little *déclassé* to have veins filled only with English
ichor, or that was at least the implication since none of the guests
thought it worth bragging about. Grandparents and great-
grandparents were summoned from the Steppes, pressed into
service from Paris, introduced from Ireland, and conjured from
Caledonia. The yeomen of Old England gibbered, ghostlike and
ghastly, from the wrong side of the Solway, denied their blood.

Those who have little reason to think much about, far less
disparage, their origins in England are – somewhat unconsciously
– envious of the Scots. Perhaps the English feel rather deracinated: 'You have somewhere to go back to,' remarked an English
artist. 'It's not my fault I was born in Epsom and brought up in
Croydon. I have the suburbs, but you have another country. You
come down here, make your fortunes, and head back, eventually,
behind the Wall, having raped and pillaged.' No doubt this was

intended innocently and humorously, but the words betrayed an atavistic anxiety about the invasion of Scottish barbarians who combined the finesse of Machiavelli and the aggression of Attila the Hun, sticking their long noses into politics and business, their sticky fingers in the till, and their rude penises into English-women, before making off with their booty behind the border. The Scots are still thought of as reivers and raiders, however polished their shoes, manners, and accents. The ineradicable image of the Scot furth of Scotland is of an opportunist.

The Scots are perceived to be, generally, a prideful, poor, prejudiced and xenophobic people who continue traditions that are mostly alien to those of the English. The Scots are mainly concerned to resist being assimilated into an English culture. A certain pride, national or personal, is inevitable. However much that pride may appear ridiculous, petty, or arrogant, it is just as often worthy, self-sacrificing, noble, and touching. Always, it rests firmly on the past, a past that is endlessly and energetically debated by the Scots who seek truth, morality, instruction, or support from it. It deeply influences and partly forms the national consciousness, and is ingrained in individual, personal awareness.

The Scots are beset by Scottish history: they cherish it, but have no use for it. They are a product of a more than usually vivid history and culture. They are traditionalists, but also a forward-looking people, adept at inventing, advancing and disseminating the arts and sciences of the modern civilization we take for granted. They love to wallow in the glories and bewail the catastrophes of the past while dealing with a difficult present and a problematical future. The Scots readily and ably assimilate the new while they busily and meticulously embellish the old. It goes almost without saying that the interpretation of the past is a subject that animates the Scots like no other, and it is a brave man who will attempt publicly to state his own version. He can expect flat denial and disagreement on all sides from his fellow country-men. Should a stranger, a non-Scot, attempt an analysis of the Scots, he will be faced not with sniper fire but a solid phalanx of artillery from the Scots standing, for once, shoulder to shoulder. The personal element will become subsumed in a collective defence of patriotism, national prejudices, and the desire to maintain the old myths. The Scots are their own history, a history kept alive like a flame by a nation of guardians who, all too often, are consumed by it.

The rules by which the Scots are self-governed are, like the British Constitution, unwritten, but have been evolved through long experience and confirmed by precedent as surely as any decision of the Court of Session. These traditions are, to put it mildly, complex. Though Scotland is a small country and its population does not exceed that of London, it is divided within itself to an almost unimaginable degree. 'It has no unity except upon the map,' declared Robert Louis Stevenson. 'Two languages, many dialects, innumerable forms of piety, and countless local patriotisms and prejudices, part us among ourselves more widely than the extreme east and west of that great continent of America.' Yet, when any convention is threatened, poverty, patriotism and a fierce independence of mind and territory often unite to repel the threat. Scotland may be little, but she is fierce. It has always been so: according to Gibbon, 'The native Caledonians preserved in the northern extremity of the island their wild independence, for which they were not less indebted to their poverty than to their valour.'

There has been change, of course, over the centuries, but in general any attempt to subvert the Scots has been subtly vitiated by the Scottish determination to adapt necessary change within the native tradition. That tradition has become glamorized – since it is becoming more and more irrelevant in the modern world, it alters its character to become a mystique. If we are to define the Scots, in the words of the poet Cleveland, as 'a nation epidemical', and Scotland as a nation with its roots in Scottish soil but rampant in its growth, extending its influence by spreading its people like seeds windblown to the corners of the earth, we must recognize some dilution of Scottish traditions as they were in reality in Scotland and a corresponding vigorous development of traditions immortalized and ameliorated by myth. However rough the transplantation, the Scottish seedling will normally accommodate itself to unfamiliar, often positively hostile, territory. It will keep many of its characteristics, against all the odds.

Even when Scottishness degenerates into a suitable subject for amusing dinner-party conversation, that drop of Scottish blood is cherished like a certificate of respectability, a ticket of admission to an ancestry with a distinctive, archaic culture, rich in tradition, implying a glamorous strain of the Celt in the characters of many who have never seen Scotland or met an indigenous Scot. The Scots have achieved much, but they have often achieved their greatest fame and successes furth of the old country. The benefits of their genius have too often passed Scotland by, and what the Scots in Scotland are left with, in their decline, are the legends represented by the touristic, trumpery fetishes of lochs and bens, crags and glens, kilts and claymores, haggis and Highland whisky, porridge and pipers.

The result, in Scotland, has been a sharp division between Scot and Scot, an ideological battle between, on the one hand, the camp of Sir Harry Lauder and, on the other, the lieges of the poet Hugh MacDiarmid. It is quite as much a political as an aesthetic conflict, and it enrols some mighty guns on either side. It is a continuing war between sentimental patriotism and proud nationalism. It is a struggle for the hearts, minds, and souls of the Scots. Moray McLaren has described the Scots as 'a small family in the congregation of Europe, a family that has for a millennium struggled with varying success to establish and preserve its corporate, as well as what might be described as its individual, individuality.' The family has its internecine conflicts, but generally it will not break ranks against an outside threat to its shaky cohesion. It is domestic dispute, rather than outside violence, that most threatens it.

Scotland has always considered itself a country unique in its contribution to the wider world. In its history and cultural traditions, the Union with England has often been perceived as a limited benefit. The Scot prefers to think of himself as a

European. This view is occasionally strengthened by the regard of others – even by whimsical Englishmen who are now and again obliged to admit the Scottish genius: Horace Walpole declared Scotland to be 'The most accomplished nation in Europe, the nation to which, if any one country is endowed with a superior partition of sense, I should be inclined to give the preference in that particular.' He was much influenced, in this opinion, by the achievements of eighteenth-century Scots in philosophy, litera-ture and science. The Scots may, perforce, be British, but they are not English. This is a matter of the most consuming importance to the Scots, and of perfect indifference to the English.

The Scots will complain bitterly when they are lumped, with-out a thought, together with their immemorial antagonists. Though they take some care to respect the touchy feelings of the Scots, the media will now and again describe Great Britain or the British as England or the English. To the English, the injured pride of the Scots thus annihilated is incomprehensible. The English took the Union in their stride as implying no diminution of England. The national identity of the Scots as Scots persists: abroad (that is, south of the border), a Scot will more often than not describe himself as Scottish rather than British, no matter the designation on his passport. He is, of course, British – but first of all he is a Scot. Hugh MacDiarmid, in his essay 'Satori in Scotland', defined his sense of being Scottish somewhat in the negative – as though part of the experience of being Scottish was a feeling of being not-English. This is probably more common than is generally supposed.

2

* * *

The Caledonian Antizyzygy:
the divided Scot

IMMEDIATELY that indispensable word 'nevertheless' may be introduced. Writing in *Memoirs of a Modern Scotland*, in 1970, Muriel Spark breaks off in mid-essay to remark:

> I am reminded how my whole education, in and out of school, seemed even then to pivot around this word. I was aware of its frequent use. My teachers used it a great deal. All grades of society constructed sentences bridged by 'nevertheless.' It would need a scientific study to ascertain whether the word was truly employed more frequently in Edinburgh at the time than anywhere else. It is my own instinct to associate the word, as the core of a thought-pattern, with Edinburgh particularly. I can see the lips of tough elderly women in musquash coats taking tea at MacVittie's, enunciating this word of final justification, I can see the exact gesture of head and chin and gleam of the eye that accompanied it. The sound was roughly 'niverthelace' and the emphasis was a heartfelt one. I believe myself to be fairly indoctrinated by the habit of thought which calls for this word. In fact I approve of the ceremonious accumulation of weather forecasts and barometer-readings that pronounce for a fine day, before letting rip on the statement: 'Nevertheless, it's raining.' I find that much of my literary composition is

based on the nevertheless idea. I act upon it. It was on the nevertheless principle that I turned Catholic.

'Nevertheless' is a dramatic word (the Scots are a dramatic people) to tumble empires or reputations. It is a word to bridge, neatly, the two parts of a sentence in which white, if not precisely proved to be black, is at least declared to be so. 'Nevertheless' is a word to make the unconvincing irrefutable and to nullify the indisputable. It is a word to thwart any inconvenient argument. Generally, it prefaces an irony, an impossibility or a paradox. 'It would be unfair, however,' says Moray McLaren of the Scots, in *Return to Scotland*, 'to leave the impression ... that we are a cantankerous race whose main intellectual pleasure lies in dis-agreement. This is very far from true. The Scot, in his attitude towards his own past, is animated less by the spirit of opposition than by loyalties to ideas and persons with whom he feels personally connected.' Nevertheless – loyalty demands, some-times, that the indefensible must be defended, and somehow one's own principles and those being defended, if clearly contra-dictory, must be reconciled even at the cost of argument that is plainly spurious. In such a case there can be a profound pleasure in such an intellectual challenge, surpassing mere sophistry, which reaches an unassailable truth beyond pure reason.

Holding two contradictory ideas in perfect – or, more usually, imperfect – tandem is a heroic stance. The worst of Dr Jekyll's faults, as Jekyll himself admitted, 'was a certain impatient gayety of disposition, such as has made the happiness of many, but such as I found it hard to reconcile with my imperious desire to carry my head high, and wear a more than commonly grave counten-ance before the public. Hence it came about that I concealed my pleasures; and that when I reached years of reflection, and began to look around me and take stock of my progress and position in the world, I stood already committed to a profound duplicity of life.' James Boswell, to a lesser degree, suffered the same dilem-ma: '*spero meliora*,' he wrote at the end of his life; 'I hope for better things.' He hoped, at least, to repress the worse and assert the better part of his character that would lead him to greater things than he considered he had yet achieved. An Englishman like wicked Jack Wilkes had no such compunction; he blazoned such irregularities as he was guilty of. Jekyll, however, 'from the high views that I had set before me, I regarded and hid them with an almost morbid sense of shame. It was thus rather the exacting nature of my aspirations than any particular degradation in my faults that made me what I was, and with even a deeper trench than in the majority of men, severed in me those provinces of good and ill which divide and compound man's dual nature.'

The Caledonian Antizyzygy, a term coined by the literary critic G. Gregory Smith, may also be described as the Antithetical Mind. Its literary *locus classicus* is to be found in Robert Louis Stevenson's *Dr Jekyll and Mr Hyde*, and the psychologist R. D. Laing has drawn attention to it in his book, *The Divided Self.* In exhibiting 'myriad-mindedness', Hugh MacDiarmid believed he was being fundamentally Scottish. The holding of opposing or paradoxical viewpoints is not a trait unique to the Scots, but it is among the Scots that contradiction becomes apotheosized.

> Perhaps in the very combination of opposites [*wrote G. Gregory Smith*] – what either of the two Sir Thomases, of Norwich and Cromarty, might have been willing to call 'the Caledonian Antizyzygy' – we have a reflection of the contrasts which the Scot shows at every turn, in his political and ecclesiastical history, in his polemical restlessness, in his adaptability, which is another way of saying that he has made allowance for new conditions, in his practical judgement, which is the admission that two sides of the matter have been considered. If therefore Scottish history and life are, as an old northern writer said of something else, 'varied with a clean contrair spirit,' we need not be surprised to find that in his literature the Scot presents two aspects which appear contradictory. Oxymoron was ever the bravest figure, and we must not forget that disorderly order is order, after all.

Jekyll is an extreme example of the Scottish Antizyzygy, and a picture, painted luridly, of his creator's, Robert Louis Stevenson's, own feelings about himself as a 'shameless Bohemian haunted by duty'. Stevenson's alleged failure of artistic nerve, said to have given the moralist the triumph, is attributed to a conflict between wicked energy and virtuous impotence. But, emphasizes Stevenson in the words of Jekyll, 'I was in no sense a hypocrite; both sides of me were in dead earnest . . . I saw that, of the two natures that contended in the field of my consciousness, even if I could rightly be said to be either, it was only because I was radically both.' D. B. Wyndham Lewis describes Stevenson as a 'Calvino-Agnostic', and certainly Stevenson was brought up in an atmosphere, in the family home in Edinburgh in the mid-nineteenth century, of strict Calvinist piety against which he rebelled but which nevertheless left its ineradicable mark on his psychology. *The Strange Case of Dr Jekyll and Mr Hyde* was published in 1886, sixty-two years after publication of *The Private Memoirs and Confessions of a Justified Sinner* by James Hogg.

In his introduction to the Penguin edition of that book in 1983, John Wain pointed out that Hogg's remarkable novel 'has an intensely Scottish flavour'. Aside from its particular historical period detail, 'its characters exhibit a psychology and a motivation very rarely to be met with among the English.' The story is based on the concept of predestination, a Calvinist tenet. 'The relatively easy-going and pragmatic English mind has never welcomed such harsh logic,' remarks Wain, 'with its attendant possibilities of cruelty and suffering. The Scottish mind, by contrast, has.' In Hogg, says Wain, 'the visionary and down-to-earth seemed to co-exist as naturally as they did in the mind of Burns,' and enabled Hogg to create the character of Robert Wringhim who falls victim to the subtle wiles of the Arch-Fiend through pride in being one of the elect. Since Wringhim is not predestined to damnation, his worldly actions cannot imperil his safe reception into the ranks of the saved after death. He despises, with pity and contempt, the creatures of this world who, indiscriminately damned, grovel on the earth with no hope, despite every good action, of salvation. He is open to seduction by evil. But dimly he perceives that he might equally have opted for good. It is within his power to be either – or both. But like Jekyll he finds that evil is the stronger lure. And like Jekyll he is not hypocritical. Wringhim can believe that his actions are not open to judgement, either in this world or the next. Good and evil, therefore, can be said to have no real meaning for Wringhim: he is free to act as he pleases.

Blanchard, remonstrating with Wringhim, declares: 'Religion is a sublime and glorious thing, the bond of society on earth, and the connector of humanity with the Divine nature; but there is nothing so dangerous to man as the wresting of any of its principles, or forcing them beyond their due bounds: this is of all others the readiest way to destruction. Neither is there any thing so easily done.' The Scots are adept at breaking bounds, but here speaks the moderate man, the man ill-disposed to fanaticism in any form. 'There is not an error into which a man can fall,' continues Blanchard, 'which he may not press Scripture into his service as proof of the probity of.'

The most celebrated student of Calvinist doctrine in Scottish literature, who presses Scripture into praise of himself and damnation of others, is Burns's Holy Willie, one of the self-styled elect. *Holy Willie's Prayer* is a masterpiece of self-deception:

> O Thou, who in the heavens does dwell,
> Who, as it pleases best Thysel,
> Sends ane to heaven, an' ten to hell,
>   A' for thy glory,
> And no for ony gude or ill
>   They've done afore Thee!
>
> I bless and praise Thy matchless might,
> When thousands Thou hast left in night,
> That I am here afore Thy sight,
>   For gifts an' grace
> A burning and a shining light
>   To a' this place.
>
>   . . .

When frae my mither's womb I fell,
Thou might hae plungèd me in hell,
To gnash my gums, to weep and wail,
   In burnin' lakes,
Where damned devils roar and yell,
   Chain'd to their stakes.

Yet I am here a chosen sample
To show Thy grace is great and ample;
I'm here a pillar o' Thy temple,
   Strong as a rock,
A guide, a buckler, and example,
   To a' Thy flock.

     . . .

But yet, O Lord! confess I must,
At times I'm fashed wi' fleshly lust:
An' sometimes, too, in warldly trust,
   Vile self gets in;
But Thou remembers we are dust,
   Defil'd wi' sin.

     . . .

Lord, bless Thy chosen in this place,
For here Thou hast a chosen race:
But God confound their stubborn face,
   An' blast their name,
Wha bring Thy elders to disgrace
   An' public shame.

     . . .

But, Lord, remember me an' mine
Wi' mercies temporal an' divine,
That I for grace an' gear may shine,
   Excell'd by nane,
And a' the glory shall be Thine,
   Amen, Amen!

'I go too much to extremes,' declared Moray McLaren. 'I do not really understand the English genius.' The genius, he meant, of compromise in matters great and small. In *Return to Scotland*, he looked upon the less attractive face of Edinburgh in 1930 and was taken aback not just by squalor but by his own reaction to it: 'I was also depressed by my own disgust, for I disapproved of myself for being excited by romantic and colourful squalor, and then being so easily repelled by the more drab side of the same thing.' A middle-class Scot, from a prosperous family, like Stevenson, McLaren enjoyed the idea of bohemianism, while simultaneously feeling there was something not quite right about it, something distasteful with which he had not succeeded in coming fully to terms. 'Though I love luxury and subtlety of mind,' he admitted, 'I am always trying to contrast with them the crude colouring and manners which the life of the poor people produces.' There is, in this, not only a conscious effort to encompass all and every mental capacity and variation, but equally a sense of guilt that occasionally, by squalor or crudity, he is naturally repelled. But guilt is a matter to be dealt with separately. And there is, in his statement about 'luxury and subtlety of mind' and 'the crude colouring and manners' (the bridging word 'nevertheless' haunts the sentence), a determination to experience, without prejudice or condescension, another reality. The Caledonian Antizyzygy crosses all barriers of race, sex, class or education. Nothing, ultimately, is – or should be – foreign to the Scot. He should be mobile in every direction – up, down, or sideways.

The Scot, to travel between Glasgow and Edinburgh, has to travel sideways, at least geographically. There is an hour's journey by train, forty miles' distance, and a world of difference, between Scotland's principal cities of the west and east coasts. Put at its most basic, Glasgow is a great commercial – and has been until recently a great industrial – city, while Edinburgh is a city of long-established and rich professional lawyers, bankers and accountants. Each has its own dyed-in-the-wool partisans, though the Scottishness of both, however distinct the type to the Scots, appears more or less interchangeable to aliens, including the English. Jane, Lady Abdy, in 1983, 'arrived at Glasgow. Once a giant among cities, now ringed with sad, deserted skyscrapers of the 1950s. A few splendours remain: the Co-operative Exchange is a Roman town hall of the 1880s, built in Tennent time, and now sadly alone amongst derelict warehouses. I stayed at the Western Club: I want to live there. In the prettiest square of 1830 Glasgow, with a library in the middle like the Maison Carré at Nîmes, the Club is pure heaven: charming rooms, a segregated floor for the "ladies". Breakfast (anything you wish) is ordered by teatime the day before.' Lady Abdy continued on to Edinburgh where she found Jenners (a large and rather grand Princes Street department store) 'the same haven as the Western Club, unchanged in *politesse* of staff, and that gorgeous security of tea cakes and tartan.' Lady Abdy is perceptive, sensitive, and keenly appreciative of the best that, distinctively, Scottish, English, French, and other European cultures have to offer. If she can find the same civilized warmth of welcome, courtesy of manners, grace in architecture and comfort in scones that both cities have to offer, then there is pleasure to be found that is representative of Scotland as a whole.

Both cities have flourished, according to their particular genius. Edinburgh is regarded as a city whose finest hour was the eighteenth century, while Glasgow's grandest period is considered to have been the nineteenth. They have existed forever in uneasy harness, economically and socially complementary but – towards one another – uncomplimentary and deeply suspicious. Their traditional rivalry persists, and is a reflection of the division that exists in the Scottish character. For all her elegance and lofty-mindedness, Edinburgh is a reserved, plain, cautious and thrifty city. She is more Lowland, in these respects, than Highland. Glasgow is, though acquisitive, an expansive, extravagant, romantic, less tight-laced city and, being on the western side of the country, partakes more of the Highland character. Indeed, it was to Glagow rather than to Edinburgh that the Highland clansmen naturally gravitated. The clan chiefs and their families, however, when they became grander and more sophisticated, mostly spent their social seasons in Edinburgh, a Hanoverian city: Burns described Edinburgh in the eighteenth century as 'heavenly Hanoverianism'.

To contrast Edinburgh and Glasgow it is instructive to listen to Alan Coren, editor of *Punch*:

> Know what's wrong with the Duke of Edinburgh? . . . What's wrong is that there isn't a Duke of Glasgow as well. I mean, the Duke of Edinburgh represents the Edinburgh side of things very well – the formality, the dryness, the wryness – but what about the Glasgow side of things? At the Cup Final you should have the Duke of Edinburgh clapping politely in one seat and the Duke of Glasgow standing up next to him, waving his tartan scarf and screaming himself hoarse. At state occasions you should have the coach of the Duke of Glasgow with Radio 1 going full blast inside and the occasional empty beer bottle being thrown out of the window.

Coren catches, vividly and pungently, the contrast between the two styles of the cities and the two sides of the Scottish character, the austere Athenian and the barbarian berserker.

Edinburgh, according to Robert Louis Stevenson, has 'one of the vilest climates under heaven.' He left it for England, America, and Samoa. Muriel Spark left it for America and Italy. She writes, in *What Images Return*, that:

> Edinburgh is the place that I, a constitutional exile, am essentially exiled from. I spent the first eighteen years of my life, during the 1920s and 1930s there. It was Edinburgh that bred within me the conditions of exiledom; and what have I been doing since then but moving from exile into exile? It has ceased to be a fate, it has become a calling . . . Most Edinburgh people, of my generation at least, must have been brought up with a sense of civic superiority. We were definitely given to understand that we were citizens of no mean city. In time, and with experience of other cities, one would have discovered the beautiful

uniqueness of Edinburgh for oneself as the visitors do. But the physical features of the place surely had an effect as special as themselves on the outlook of the people. The Castle Rock is something, rising up as it does from pre-history between the formal grace of the New Town and the noble network of the Old. To have a great primitive black crag rising up in the middle of populated streets of commerce, stately squares and winding closes, is like the statement of unmitigated fact preceded by 'nevertheless'. In my time the society around it generally regarded the government and bureaucracy of Whitehall as just a bit ridiculous. The influence of a place varies according to the individual. I imbibed, through no particular mentor, but just by breathing the informed air of the place, its haughty and remote anarchism. I can never now suffer from a shattered faith in politics and politicians, because I never had any.

Edinburgh's anarchistic tradition is well-established: Stevenson gives the examples of David Hume who 'ruined Philosophy and Faith, an undisturbed and well reputed citizen' of Edinburgh, and the literati of the city who formed 'an academy of gilt unbelief and artificial letters' to which Burns 'came from the plough-tail'.

Their heads full of cynicism, the citizens seemed to Stevenson to go 'thronging by, in their neat clothes and conscious moral rectitude, and with a little air of possession that verges on the absurd'. No less absurd, and no less real, is the Glasgow drunk's famous and unassailable belief that, in his cups, 'Glasgow belongs to me.' Colm Brogan, in *The Glasgow Story*, says that, 'Glasgow may have the reputation of being a reliable whisky-producer because it also has the reputation of being an enthusiastic whisky-consumer.' There are just as many drunks in Edinburgh, of course, but the legend will have it that Argyle Street in Glasgow is the spiritual and spiritous home of all Scottish drinkers. Edwin Muir in *Scottish Journey* thought that the 'public flaunting of degradation is one of the things which distinguish the Scottish from the English slums.' He was talking of the notorious

Glasgow Gorbals, now partly cleaned up but replaced in spirit by high-rise tower blocks like the Red Road flats. 'Probably it arises from a last-ditch sentiment of justice. To publish one's degradation is a moral protest. The London slums are dreary; but the Glasgow slums always hold a sense of possible menace; they take their revenge on the respectable and the rich if in nothing else by compelling them to grow a still thicker hide of insensibility and suppression.' Glasgow bawls out its complaints agin the government and other established bodies, against anyone and anything the Glaswegians consider to be oppressors, while the Edinburghers, deeply radical not in Glaswegian outrage but in Edinburghian unbelief, have nothing to shout about in their cups since they never expected justice or fairness and, consequently, have made suitable provision against exploitation and attack. Edinburgh is unshockable and cannot generally be taken by surprise. Glasgow is constantly being caught on the hop and continually vocal in its astonishment and outrage at the duplicity of its apparent enemies. The difference between Edinburgh and Glasgow is not unlike the difference between the wise and foolish virgins – and who but a moralist should say which is better? All Scots being more or less moralists will, of course, have their obdurate opinion, and will be, as ever, in this as in all matters, divided.

The Scot contrives effortlessly to contain his contradictions. 'It is a quintessential feature of Scottish thought to encourage the clash of ideas in order to achieve . . . "a distinctive blend of the secular and the sacred,"' asserts the modern Scottish poet Alan Bold, citing the example of the poet Hugh MacDiarmid whose perplexing 'personality exhibited a contrariness that confused him until he was able to elevate it into a literary principle that served him for a long creative lifetime.'

'The Scot,' declared G. Gregory Smith, 'is not a quarrelsome man, but he has a fine sense of the value of provocation, and in the clash of things and words he has often found a spiritual tonic.' That is to say, the Scot is a more complete man than most – he recognizes the diversity of his character. He does not attempt to suppress or deny his 'shadow' side (as a Jungian psychotherapist might term his baser nature) but harnesses it to his finer qualities, holding both in tandem as Plato's charioteer directs his horses, in order to achieve his essential balance. Like Hugh MacDiarmid, the Scot often comes to rest 'whaur extremes meet', and on that knife-edge he is completely at home, his contradictions comfortably coalesced in harmonious – though often improbable – resolution. His capriciousness, his dogmatism, his genius for rushing to a logical extreme is accountable to an early stage of the Scot's search for balance. In order to rest at the meeting of extremes, he must first energetically explore the polar opposites of his character, march perilously out on a limb, first in one direction, then in another. A man cannot be expected to reconcile opposites if he has not first discovered what they are and experienced them, testing their (and his) limits. But, at the last, the Caledonian Antizyzygy is a form of integration of the self rather than a mere confusion and conglomeration of contradictions roughly bundled together. There may be easier, less aggressive methods of achieving integration, but the Scot was (and is) never a man to take the smoother path.

MacDiarmid is the prime modern example of the Caledonian Antizyzygy. But Scottish literature is full of the most ample evidence that he has predecessors, fictional or otherwise. Among them must be numbered, and ranked very high, James Boswell, Dr Samuel Johnson's biographer, whose naïveté in the conduct of his own life is well documented – not least by himself. The Caledonian Antizyzygy often implies an apparent absurdity, since the balance a man achieves for himself may be plainly, to others, eccentric. Boswell, time and again, with the facts of a matter staring him full in the face, was able, with no obvious effort, to assemble the constituent parts of a problem into an alternative pattern, another reality, to justify his acting apparently in flat contradiction of common sense. But, like all Antizyzygysts, he acted always, however improbably, in utter sincerity, more often than not in the rational belief that what he was doing was proper, making up his rationale later. He had, in my view, considered the matter fully, assembled the facts to his own liking, and acted too precipitately upon the resultant conviction – often to his considerable confusion and disadvantage. Yet eccentricity achieves its own peculiar balance, and eccentricities are often necessary for a man's mental health – many Scots have been, or are, eccentric in a mild, quirky fashion: others are whipped along by an eccentricity stemming from motives that shape and direct their entire being. It is a difference of degree, merely, in preserving a Scot's equilibrium. Once that precarious balance has been achieved, he may safely assume that not he, but everyone else, is strange or misguided. Unlike the English who make a virtue of compromise, 'the Scottish character has a thoroughness, or in other words an inability to know when to stop,' remarked Edwin Muir. The Scots have never been afraid to proceed to a logical extreme and there take their last stand.

3

*

Two nations:
Highland and Lowland Scots

COMMENTING on *Kidnapped* by Robert Louis Stevenson, the American literary critic Leslie Fiedler dwells on the relationship between David Balfour and Alan Breck:

> David must measure the Scoundrel against himself, and the more unwillingly come to love that which he must disapprove. Here good and evil are more subtly defined, more ambiguous: pious Presbyterian and irreverent Catholic, solid defender of the status quo and fantastic dreamer of the Restoration – in short, Highlander and Lowlander. Scotland divided against itself. It is the Lowlander that Stevenson *was* who looks longingly and disapprovingly at the alien dash, the Highland fecklessness of Alan through the eyes of David (was not Stevenson's own mother a Balfour?); but it is the Highlander he *dreamed* himself (all his life he tried to prove his father's family were descended from the banned Clan MacGregor) that looks back. The sombre good man and the glittering rascal are both two and one; they war within Stevenson's single country and in his single soul.

If it is not enough that the Scot should be divided within himself, it is little wonder that the country itself is divided, not only east and west, but north and south. The one complements the character of the other – an interesting synchronism.

The Highland Line runs diagonally across Scotland from the tip of Buchan in the north-east to the Mull of Galloway in the south-west, parallel escarpments extending across Scotland that effectively divide the country in geographical character. It comes as a surprise to most people to learn that Glasgow is closer to the Highland Line than Edinburgh, and that the island of Arran, off the coast of Ayrshire, is the south-western tip of the Grampian Highlands. Aberdeen is not a Highland city. The Highland Line is as significant a division as the Mason-Dixon Line in the United States of America in its delineation of northern and southern attitudes. The division, in post-Reformation times and after the Union of 1707, was religious and political as much as geographical, adding fresh peat to the fire of an older, more generalized distaste of southerners for northerners. It is hardly an exaggeration to describe the revulsion Lowlanders felt for Highlanders as a species of apartheid. For their part, Highlanders were no less scornful of Lowland Scots. The Lowlanders initially took their cue from the ancient Romans and left the heathenish Highlanders to themselves. The Highlanders, oblivious of, or indifferent to, great events beyond their mountain ranges and their ken, including the discovery of America, the Union of the Crowns and of the Parliaments, lived more or less contentedly in clachans, groups of huts held by individual families owing final allegiance only to their clan chief, who in turn owed allegiance, in practice, to no man but himself (and only in theory to the King) as head of his extended family of clansmen and women.

Highlanders were, to Lowland eyes, light-handed with property not their own (the concept of property and its ownership was stronger in the south than in the north); disinclined to become 'civilized' (they knew little of urban life and nothing of being employed by a master in commerce or industry); idle (they were not disposed to 'better' themselves through sustained work); and above all they continued in the faith of their forefathers as Papists, devoted to the Old Faith and the Old King. They were Jacobites almost to a man. The Lowlander, so secure in his contempt, was irritated beyond measure by the refusal of Highlanders to be moved by the lure of glittering prizes and their reluctance to abandon their traditional way of life or to move with the times. The theory of the superiority of the 'noble savage', evangelized by Rousseau, fell on stony Lowland ground. But the Highlanders could not hold their borders forever against the tides in the affairs of Scotland that engulfed them after the Union of 1707. Political expediency, after the failure of the 1715 and 1745 rebellions, revolutionized the life of the Highlanders. For their support of Prince Charles Edward Stuart, they were treated more or less indiscriminately as traitors to the Hanoverian Crown. The Gaelic language, the bagpipes, the kilt, every manifestation of a distinct, and therefore antithetical, culture was proscribed by George II. Jacobites were hunted down by the troops of the Duke of Cumberland, the laws of the country were wholly disregarded by the furious Hanoverians, and the Highlands were put under the boot of the British. A way of life already threatened by General Wade's roads and bridges, was virtually extinguished, the clans were broken up, and after 'the Killing Time' there was a hundred-year period of utter disorientation. Lowland Scots had not been idle: the blame for the extirpation of Highland life cannot be laid solely at the door of the English – too often, they were aided and abetted by the active connivance and collusion of Lowland Scots.

There then followed the brutal and insensitive catastrophe of the Clearances in the late eighteenth and early nineteenth centuries, which more than decimated the Highland population by prompting the exodus of emigrant Scots to Canada, Australia, New Zealand and the United States of America. The general consensus seems to be that the revenge taken against the Highlanders after 1745, and the subsequent Clearances, merely telescoped an inevitable process whereby the Highlanders would have been irresistibly lured south, and the Lowlanders would have been unable to resist intruding into the Highlands. That the inevitable occurred so sharply, providing no long period of natural assimilation during which the best might have been more perfectly preserved, is regrettable. The battle of Culloden and the Clearances were followed by a third disaster. The old clan chiefs, overthrown, were succeeded by chieftains to whom Highlanders still remained doggedly and traditionally loyal, but who owed their survival to the goodwill of London. To maintain or reinforce their position, these chiefs generally found it expedient to remove themselves to London to be near the Court, where they were supported in some style by rents and gifts from their clans. Once in London, not unlike French courtiers who found provincial life stifling and unsophisticated, they lost the taste for life in the Highlands, among their own people, and many sold the lands of their clans to purchasers wishing to use their estates for sport. 'Scott and Queen Victoria were probably the two people most responsible for this last disastrous phase,' was the opinion of Edwin Muir. 'Scott sent the tourist wandering over the Highland hills, and Queen Victoria built Balmoral. The net result of these two innocent actions was to turn the Highlands into a huge game preserve covered with fences and dotted with notices making the pedestrian a trespasser.'

Among the exiled clansmen and their families, the Highlands lived in the hearts of its uprooted people. The sentimental, well-nigh maudlin *Canadian Boat Song* gives tearful voice in its verse to the keening, yearning sense of loss that is still felt by descendants of the Scottish Diaspora.

> From the lone shieling of the misty island
> Mountains divide us and the waste of seas;
> Yet still the blood is strong, the heart is Highland,
> As we, in dreams, behold the Hebrides.

And so on for several sad stanzas. Under certain conditions, usually induced by drink, it is virtually impossible for a Scot not to be moved near to tears by a sensitive rendering of this poem – even in Scotland. It should, by rights and by modern standards, be laughable. In sober fact it is immensely moving, laying bare old wounds and inspiring emotional despair as comforting as a poultice. This, and other songs in the same mode, give rise to what Compton Mackenzie irritatedly referred to as 'the Lone Shieling complex', a psychological condition akin to the innocent state of mind of those who believe in Peter Pan's Never-Never-Land, the creation of another Scot, the playwright and novelist J. M. Barrie.

In the twentieth century many well-intentioned efforts have been made to vitalize the Highlands. The near-fortuitous oil boom off the East coast and the Shetland and Orkney Islands has done most to bring prosperity, though not to the delight of everyone concerned with the long-term interests of the Highlands. Yet another temporary natural resource, some say, has been again diverted for the enrichment of England: but this is largely a Nationalist, political claim and should be assessed in a wider context. It has, however, a narrow appeal for the Scots.

The first sustained attempt to import industry into the Highlands was made by a Bolton soap manufacturer, William Hesketh Lever, Viscount Leverhulme. In 1918, he bought the island of Lewis as 'a delightful home'. But the itch to make a profit was irresistible – he looked around him and saw a community subsisting on crofting and fishing. Speaking of the Shetland Isles, Hugh MacDiarmid commented, 'It is, indeed, impossible to eke out a decent living in the Shetlands by crofting alone. That is the difference between the Orkneys and the Shetlands. The Orcadian is a farmer with a boat; the Shetlander is a fisherman with a croft.' Lord Leverhulme considered the way of life of the natives to be uneconomic and the people themselves to be sadly backward, still speaking the Gaelic tongue which, he thought, 'stands in the way of civilization of the natives making use of it,' and still working by methods notably cost-inefficient. To rid the folk of Lewis of their crofts and their fishing boats would be a mercy and, besides, would render them eager to find alternative employment supplied by Lever himself. He was, by his own lights, a sincere philanthropist, a kind and well-disposed man who thought he knew best what was good for Lewis. He fully intended to raise productivity and prosperity, and genuinely despised the sporting aristocracy and bourgeoisie who used the Highlands and Islands for sport.

Leverhulme built factories and villas and held out material rewards – all of which the Lewis islanders decisively rejected, preferring their crofts and their boats. Leverhulme's incomprehension was profound and complete. He could never understand the philosophy of those to whom he had offered so much. In the event, Port Sunlight deteriorated and other financial interests so slumped that the English benefactor was obliged to cut his Highland losses.

The philanthropist was succeeded by quangos – committees that came and went: first, the Highlands and Islands Advisory Panel, succeeded by the Highlands and Islands Development Board. Commissions and Consultative Panels have earnestly debated the 'problem' of the Highlands and Islands – which not only remains unaltered but somewhat difficult to identify. That there is a 'problem' no Committee doubts – what it is, and how it may best be solved, remain questionable. It is a 'problem' that involves the Highlanders and Islanders themselves who are probably the last people in Europe, it has been said, who consider that development is possible without change.

Highlanders are not amenable to development, perhaps because they are disinclined to shed their past and no method of development founded on that past has yet been devised by a committee or a commission, try though they may have. The Highlanders themselves are thought to be 'at fault', since they are not amenable to the Lowland ethos – what has come commonly to be known as the 'Protestant work ethic'. To this extent, the old words of Lord Belhaven come floating back from the days of the debate about the Union in 1707: 'We want neither men nor sufficiency of things to make a nation happy: all depends upon management . . . Yet I see our ancient Mother Caledonia sitting in the midst of our senate, like Caesar, waiting for her own children to strike the fatal blow.' The children, the Highlanders, have no desire to be efficiently 'managed'.

'*We want neither men nor sufficiency of things to make a nation happy . . .*' But what nation, and what makes it happy? The Highlanders want less, generally, while the Lowlanders want considerably more. Moray McLaren in *The Scots*, published in 1951, analyses the Highlanders' character with some subtlety, claiming that they march to a different tempo than the rest of the British, that their apparent idleness is in fact due to a different concept of time. That concept, as McLaren explains it, appears to be akin to the 'mañana' concept of Spaniards and Mexicans (though a Highlander, reminded of that word, remarked: 'There's nae such emergency here') or the unhurried pleasure Southern Europeans take in fully coming to grips with the multiple details and full implications of a question before feeling able to deal with it or to dismiss it as fatuous and hardly worth the trouble of having had to be bothered with it. Time, in the Highlands, takes care of all things and by tomorrow a question may have resolved itself or, if not, have become quite another matter requiring further consideration. The Highlander, says McLaren, 'can be really lazy, that is to say negatively indolent in a mentally costive kind of way without the positive pleasure of true relaxation.' The Highlander is brave, is supported by a religious or spiritual temperament that saves him from despair (though he can put up a good imitation of that condition), because he is convinced 'that the eternal values will somehow put things right in eternity'. People of the mountains and those who live by the ocean are peculiarly prone to this sort of faith in the slow, underlying movements of nature that heal all things and reshape them according to ineffable laws that tend towards the balance of all things. Their apparent apathy, therefore, can be explained and excused by the Highlanders' sense of fatalism. As McLaren puts it: 'his greatest temptation when faced by crude, cruel material, men and circumstances, over which even his bravery cannot, or does not seem likely to, prevail, is to withdraw too easily into an inner world of his own thoughts, inactive, dignified, and doomed.'

The Highlander cherishes his freedom like nothing else, but McLaren points out that his inability to harbour malice, to take his revenge cold, like a civilized man, militates against his very survival in the world. He is quick to anger, and just as quick in the cooling of it. The Highlander not only forgives, he also, occasionally and fatally, forgets. He has been an easy prey for those who have considered him an anachronism and an inconvenience. In attack he is strong, in defence he is weak. Edwin Muir quotes Eckermann talking to Goethe about Wellington's Scottish Highlanders: 'I saw them in Brussels a year before the battle of Waterloo. They were men! All strong, nimble, and free as if they had come straight from the hand of God. They carried their heads so freely and gaily and marched so lightly, swinging along with their bare knees, that you would have thought they had never heard of original sin or the primal curse.' Muir says, of this proud, civil, dignified, gay people that their 'numbers have been thinned, their mode of life degraded, by a series of objective calamities. They have kept through all these changes their courtesy, their dignity, and one might almost say their freedom, for that seems to exist independently of any service, however menial, which they may render. But these qualities are bought at the expense of the disdainful recognition which a proud people feels in acknowledging defeat, a resignation so profound that it can treat its conqueror with magnanimity, while keeping him at his distance. Whether this is a good quality or a bad one I do not know, but in any case it is an extraordinary one.'

The tough struggle for existence, the ability to survive on very little and to be glad of that little without wishing to acquire more, the independence and self-sufficiency that the Highlands bred in its people is threatened, says George Mackay Brown, by 'the fatal blessing of prosperity'. He senses 'a growing coldness' in the people of the Highlands and Islands as the material world engulfs them and they become more acquisitive; and this is perhaps true of other hitherto inaccessible cultures throughout the world to which the values of 'civilized' society have been brought by, generally, well-meaning missionaries of the consumer society. It is the last and most wounding attack upon a society that for generations has been ill-used. A vigorous society without defences has been eroded and will, like any other defenceless species, die. 'For two hundred years,' says Moray McLaren, the Highlander 'has been consistently and remorselessly attacked by means of weapons he cannot resist economically, politically and socially. He has been wounded in his most vulnerable parts, his pride, his loyalty and his love for the land . . . The attack on him has been ferocious, and his temperament has been peculiarly susceptible to that form of attack. His circumstances and his temperament have doomed him.'

With the eclipse of the Highlander, an ironic though well-intentioned interest in him has arisen, almost in direct proportion to that decline. With a vestige of remorse, and a desperate attempt to salvage what has been lost, the elements of Highland culture are studied and cultivated by Lowlanders and North Americans anxious to repossess the traditions, skills and customs of a people dispersed and all but destroyed. It is an acquisitive urge, and no sooner has a dead or dying tradition been disinterred than it is petrified, given a coat of gay paint, and promulgated or sold to consumers. 'The Highlands are very much on Scotland's conscience today,' wrote Moray McLaren in 1951. Like an imp of the perverse, they still nag. Like a ghost, they still haunt the imagination. There have been international proposals to turn the Scottish Highlands into a great national park, though what will remain of it once the acid rain and drifting nuclear fallout have done their worst, it is difficult to say. The *National Geographic* magazine in 1984 warned that famous beauty spots such as Loch Lomond are being 'loved to death' by tourists. Holiday-makers cause log-jam hold-ups on Highland roads regularly every summer, and footpaths thoughtfully marked, such as the West Highland Way, take a terrific pounding from the boots and sports shoes of marching townsfolk eager to walk with ease through rugged country. Development which attempts to preserve is at least one partial solution to the Highlanders' wish for development without change, but what the Highlanders never really reckoned with was the impact of too many people who will, inevitably, by their very presence, change what they have come to admire and enjoy. Each tourist despises and wishes to escape from every other tourist, of course. But they are the last invaders – first the sheep, then the sporting guns, now the people.

There are not so many Highlanders left in the Highlands. They have, through necessity, infiltrated south of the Highland line or emigrated abroad. Unlike the Lowlanders, the Highlanders move only because they must. They are loyal to their homes: 'they are not', points out Moray McLaren, 'an imperially-minded or expansionist people.' The Highlanders are not aggressive, but preservationists and conservatives. They admit little need for change, but when change is forced upon them they will adapt by, if necessary, adapting the land to which they are forced in order to render it more amenable to their taste. Like Poles in exile, the Highlanders form Highland Societies to which others, including some Lowlanders, are drawn, and membership will also include those who are not themselves Highlanders but who are sympathetic towards the Highlanders both at home and in exile. Lowlanders, by contrast, are not clannish outside Scotland. The Irish, the Chinese, the English, West Indians, and other nationalities tend to clump together when they find themselves foreigners in a strange land. But the Lowland Scot is independent-minded: he makes his name, fortune, or whatever he sets out to achieve, on his own.

The Scot abroad is assumed to be one of two types: either he is a Lowlander and thought to be 'dour, unimaginative, cautious, reliable and, if not exactly dull, good company only in a dry sardonic fashion, a master of understatement and in his general character to be compounded of the austere grey colours of the North.' If his origin is Highland, he is expected to conform to a type that is 'high-spirited, gay and melancholy by turns, something of a savage and something of a poet; and any moments of quietness or abstraction in his behaviour will be put down to a touch of "feyness". He is visualized at home as being draped in tartan and existing against a background of great natural beauty or in an eternal mist.' Moray McLaren neatly extracts the meat from both halves of the cracked nutshell into which the Scots may be conveniently crammed. The Lowlander's character fits him, of course, to be an accountant or a lawyer, a banker or a builder. The Highlander's more unpredictable character probably marks him as a poet or novelist, a soldier or a salesman – probably, these days, an advertising man. 'Roughly speaking,' says McLaren, 'the dry and cautious element in our character is Lowland and the more picturesque is Highland.' Put together, they are a combination to conjure with. While the Highlander pulls the glamour over your eyes, the Lowlander sells you a used car. While the Lowlander works out the bill and takes your credit card, the Highlander persuades you it will actually go.

If the Highlander is open to caricature, the Lowlander is no less a target for humorous cliché. The Lowlander is popularly supposed to be a grim realist, a hard-headed, hard-hearted, hard-fisted fellow who cracks a smile only when he finds a sixpence lying, unaccountably disregarded, in the street. The Aberdonian is a particularly maligned figure in this respect. Paul Theroux, in *The Kingdom by the Sea*, published in 1983, caused great offence to Aberdonians by some ill-tempered observations made during his brief stopover in Aberdeen while on his journey round the coast of Great Britain. Aberdeen 'had certainly been affected by the influx of money and foreigners.' Theroux is referring to the economic effect of the offshore oil industry on Aberdeen. 'I guessed that in the face of such an onslaught the Aberdonians had found protection and solace by retreating into the most unbearable Scottish stereotypes. It was only in Aberdeen that I saw kilts and eightsome reels and the sort of tartan tight-fistedness that made me think of the average Aberdonian as a person who would gladly pick a halfpenny out of a dunghill with his teeth.' This was not well received by the local media. Neither was the remark that Aberdeen 'had all the extortionate high prices of a boom town but none of the compensating vulgarity. It was a cold, stony-faced city. It did not even look prosperous. That was some measure of the city's mean spirit – its wealth remained hidden. It looked over-cautious, unwelcoming and smug, and a bit overweight like a rich uncle in dull sensible clothes, smelling of mildew and ledgers, who keeps his wealth in an iron chest in the basement. The windows and doors of Aberdeen were especially solid and unyielding; it was a city of barred windows and burglar alarms, of hasps and padlocks and Scottish nightmares.'

In all this, Aberdeen was not unusual, thought Theroux: 'It was fully-employed and tidy and virtuous, but it was just as bad as any of the poverty-stricken places I had seen – worse, really, because it had no excuses. The food was disgusting, the hotels over-priced and indifferent, the spit-and-sawdust pubs were full of drunken and bad-tempered-men – well, who wouldn't be bad-tempered? And it was not merely that it was expensive and dull; much worse was its selfishness. Again it was the boom town ego. Nothing else mattered but its municipal affairs.' The Highlanders at least maintain a guarded courtesy, but it is generally, regrettably, true that Lowlanders are a graceless lot, austere and somewhat joyless in their pleasures. It is difficult for a Lowlander to relax, to take pleasure without guilt either on his own behalf or on behalf of others. Dr Anne Smith, in her weekly column in the *Scotsman*, explained that 'beyond the shadow of a doubt, it will be found the Knox Syndrome is at the root of all our major national afflictions, from tooth decay to alcoholism.' The chief symptom of the Knox Syndrome, which she happily labelled the 'Knoxplex', she identifies as 'a distrust of pleasure, so profound as often to be mistaken for religious paranoia'. Her argument is rich and subtle, and will sound strange to anyone but a Lowland Scot who will recognize it instantly. But not only the Lowland Scots are infected – those of the Free Church of Scotland, in the Highlands and Islands, are not excepted. What Dr Smith has to say goes double for them.

Briefly, if we are enjoying ourselves and haven't recently suffered, we tend to look nervously over our shoulders, fearing the Hound of Heaven as Sir Henry did the ditto of the Baskervilles. For we know surely that if we haven't suffered before pleasure, we shall inevitably suffer immediately after it. The victim of Knoxplex is convinced that he is only truly alive when he is suffering, or working (one and the same thing, usually). He has invented his own means of coping with this, though.

We cope with Knoxplex in four ways. Some hope to cheat the Hound by pretending that their pleasures are in themselves painful duties. This manifestation of the disease was first noted by the poet Burns in the eighteenth century, and succinctly defined by him as 'unco guidness'. Some convert their pleasure into pain. Again this was noted by the Bard –

'See Social-life and Glee sit down
All joyous and unthinking.
Till, quite transmogrify'd, they're grown
Debauchery and Drinking.'

– leading to overweight, heart-disease, cirrhosis of the liver, bronchitis . . .

The third group are simpler in their approach. Immediately after experiencing pleasure they spare the Lord effort by punishing themselves. It is a peculiarly Protestant response to procure absolution without confession. Football hooligans provide a clear-cut example. Before and immediately after leaving the stands they ensure that they receive a punitive wound, bruise or at the very least, pneumonia. The fourth group offer the most serious symptoms, however. They simply eschew pleasure of any kind altogether, accepting that it is by definition sinful. They work all the time.

It is difficult if not impossible to find a cure for this at present. Perhaps budding Scottish Freuds have been deterred by the example of their predecessor, the Bard, who appears to have drunk and fornicated himself to death in his heroic effort to save the nation from the baneful influence of what a young relative recently described to me as 'the soorfaced auld boy wi' the bannet in New College.' [*The statue of John Knox*] Inter-marriage with Italians seems to be the only hope, at present, of a cure, but it is rightly seen by many as a somewhat extreme remedy (and a shame for the Italians).

The lives of the Lowland Scots have been shaped by their environment every bit as much as the Highlands made the Highlanders. If there is something large, grand, dignified, timeless, impenetrable, secret, and romantic about the Grampian and Western Highlands, there is something austere about the Lowlands that manifests itself in many ways, not least in the character of the land, the architecture and the spirit of the people. If the sorrows of the Lowlands are different in kind and character to those of the Highlands, they are not less keenly felt. The Lowlands contain the industrial heartland, the commercial centres, much of the fertile agricultural land and most of the population of Scotland. Glasgow possesses a good deal of magnificent Victorian and Edwardian architecture; Edinburgh has its classical eighteenth-century New Town and the earlier Old Town. Aberdeen is built of granite which, though grey and depressing when the skies are cloudy, sparkles in sunlight. Some towns in Galloway, the Borders, and at the gateways to the Highlands, are pretty; but the general aspect of a small Scottish Lowland town or village is predictably plain, grey, and resolutely dour. As Edwin Muir wrote:

> This is a difficult land. Here things miscarry
> Whether we care, or do not care enough . . .
> Sun, rain, and frost alike conspire against us:
> You'd think there was malice in the very air . . .
> We are a people; race and speech support us,
> Ancestral rite and custom, roof and tree,
> Our songs that tell of our triumphs and disasters
> (Fleeting alike), continuance of fold and hearth,
> Our names and callings, work and rest and sleep,
> And something that, defeated, still endures –
> These things sustain us. Yet there are times
> When name, identity, and our very hands,
> Senselessly labouring, grow most hateful to us,
> And we would gladly rid us of these burdens . . .
> We have such hours, but are drawn back again

By faces of goodness, faithful masks of sorrow,
Honesty, kindness, courage, fidelity,
The love that lasts a life's time. And the fields,
Homestead and stall and barn, springtime and autumn.
(For we can love even the wandering seasons
In their inhuman circuit.) And the dead
Who lodge in us so strangely, unremembered,
Yet in their place. For how can we reject
The long last look on the ever-dying face
Turned backward from the other side of time?
And how offend the dead and shame the living
By these despairs? And how refrain from love?
This is a difficult country, and our home.

The difficult country of Lowland Scotland at once obliges the Scots to work to get at its riches, constantly biting at the soil to mine for coal or plough a furrow, and to love it for the demands it makes on their endurance. When one has toiled to make or obtain something, one is not disposed lightly to give it up, and a deep respect for the rewards so hardly won becomes ingrained in Lowland Scots. There is very little to spare for redundant decoration of buildings or the beautification of an environment that thwarts one's efforts so consistently and indifferently. 'It is a curious reflection,' said Edwin Muir, 'that in an industrial country without traditions the desire for pleasure can create towns as sordid in a different way as Motherwell or Airdrie.' He was referring to the creation of Prestwick, the site of an international airport now apparently in decline since the beginning of the 1980s. Prestwick is a seaside resort, near to Ayr, on the south-west coast. It is a little town of villas, built originally as a convenient resort for the bourgeoisie of Glasgow who kept seaside houses there and sailed or paddled in the Firth of Clyde. It is a trim, tight little town, more or less a dormitory for commuters who work in Glasgow or the surrounding area, and it prides itself on being cleaner and less depressing than Mother-well or Airdrie which are towns firmly in the middle of the industrial belt between Glasgow and Edinburgh. It is not, however, gay. On a summer's day, the Firth of Clyde may sparkle and shine blue, the sky may be azure, the beaches may glitter yellow as gold, but Prestwick has none of the festive gaiety of Brighton or Bognor. It straggles along the coastline towards Troon, smug and pious.

There is little life in Prestwick compared with the coarse vitality of Motherwell or Airdrie or, for that matter, Kilmarnock which has not changed in character so very much since Muir described it in the 1930s as 'a grimy, tumble-down place with an air of general slatterliness, but full of character . . . Poverty which does not hide itself in closes and alleys, but walks about the street openly, as it does in Kilmarnock, is more human than the specialised poverty which is produced by large cities . . .' Apart from some large, well-maintained and prosperous houses and households, Kilmarnock is not a booming town. Neither is Prestwick, but it seems more shameful to parade an unalterable poverty there in defiance of the town's earlier tradition of being a bourgeois enclave. However, Kilmarnock and Prestwick have at least one tradition in common. According to the Scottish novelist William McIlvanney, who was brought up in Kilmarnock and listened, as a child and young man, to the stories that old men there had to tell about it, 'the mental climate in the West of Scotland is not conducive to the more delicate aesthetic pretensions, and Kilmarnock is typical of the West of Scotland.' There is a certain vital life in a town such as Kilmarnock, and a dead hand of self-satisfaction in Prestwick, neither of which contributes to the development of the fine or applied arts.

This is not to say that the Lowland Scots are not intellectual, but their interest is directed more towards the vexed questions of politics, philosophy and religion. They are mentally agile, but not visually imaginative. Though they are passionate in defence of a principle, they do not fly to speech until they have thought it through. This gives the Lowland Scot the largely unjustified reputation of being slow. More truthfully, his only reluctance is to commit himself precipitately to a word or course of action that may turn out not to be in his interest.

If the Lowland Scot is introverted, the blame may partly be laid upon the weather which, for a good eight months of the year, closes in upon him and hangs heavy, damp, cold, and threatening round his head. Darkness is as regular and as long as day, so that it is little wonder he is conditioned to expect and endure the worst that nature and men can throw at him. If he appears to be sour, dour, taciturn, graceless, and ungenerous, not to say rude and sometimes violent, he has much to contend with. Moray McLaren declares the sons of drear Lowland soil to be 'severe in aspect, restrained in manner, serious in thought, and slow and measured in their expression of thought'. But they are redeemed by 'deep feeling which is sometimes shown in a passionate and silent concentration of their energies, their spirit, and their intellects upon some task, some endeavour great or small, or upon some intellectual exercise, philosophy, or religion.' The Lowlander also possesses a laconic sense of humour which must be discussed at length in another chapter, a humour as grim and unsparing as his analysis of any matter he is asked to consider and pronounce upon.

But, nevertheless, thrifty and thrawn though the Lowlander may be, he is liable to go to extremes, to exaggerate his own importance and that of his country. His pride may lead him to excess. And drink will certainly lead him to excess. His exaggerated nationalism and rationalism only point up his provincialism; his teetotalism or intemperance (both opposite poles of his thoroughness) points up his inability to be joyful. His constant claim that a man's a man for a' that, and his refusal to call anyone, but God or the Prince of Wales 'Sir', point up his appalling social insecurity and fear of being underestimated by his supposed 'betters'. He is an inverted snob of the most dedicated kind. All this, and more, can be thrown with justice at the head of the Lowlander as he bows it over his ledgers, his Bible, his plough, his pickaxe, or his dram. Yet all this is worthwhile, in a peculiar way, because his grim faults and stern virtues have enabled him to survive. The softer manners of the Highlanders and the English have not corrupted him. He has not become degenerate in his habits, customs or character: they survive more or less intact, despite repeated assaults by the more frivolous on his tenacious conservatism. He sees nothing wrong in being (selfish is too perjorative and inaccurate a word) dedicatedly self-interested. He is not small-minded – his ideas and opinions have gone forth and increased in every country of the world, and his sober virtues are the cornerstones of the capitalist culture of the West. The Lowlander has been warlike, certainly, but really there was little necessity to fight physically – he has triumphed in the pulpit, in the press (there is a whole book to be written about Scottish journalists, editors and newspaper proprietors), in literature, in law, and in his accounts books. He has survived – and, more than survived, prospered. The Lowlands are not in themselves prosperous, but the harvest and the ore that have been gathered and amassed are of men and their iron wills. The Lowland Scot is not, like his Highland countryman, picturesque. But since there has been too little profit in picturesqueness, the Lowlander reckons he has had the better of the bargain. Like any accountant, he weighs the profit and loss and is well satisfied that he has a solid balance in his favour to be prudently tucked away and increased. Not a lot can effectively threaten the man stout in his principles, his belly, and his Building Society account.

4

*

Caledonia, stern and wild: the invention of romance

S COTLAND, for long enough, was *terra incognita* to the English. One intrepid eighteenth-century traveller, relieved to find himself safely south of Carlisle, mopped his brow and wrote, 'I passed to English ground, and hope I may never go to such a country again.' To penetrate even so far as Dumfries was an experience as shocking as an expedition to darkest Africa, an anthropological sortie among near neighbours who, in all the strangeness of their customs and dialects, might just as well have been Hottentots. This is scarcely to exaggerate the tremendousness of a journey north of the border even after the Union of 1707. Travel was certainly difficult, even after General Wade, who liked better to level the heights and make rough places smooth, had laid down roads and thrown bridges across rivers. The new roads did not please the old men accustomed to trekking up ben and down glen. They thought the new roads would only bring Lowlanders and redcoats, and there was not much to choose in iniquity between either species of intruder into the Highlands.

The Scots regularly forayed into England as reivers of cattle and raiders of gear. Where exactly the border might be found was often a matter of serious dispute – not for nothing was the Border country known as the Debatable Lands. A romantic, spirited, prideful and chauvinistic picture of the men and lords of the Border country was promulgated by Walter Scott, with the active connivance of James Hogg, 'the Ettrick Shepherd', in *The Minstrelsy of the Scottish Border*, published in 1802. It was an immediate success. 'To a man like Scott,' remarked Robert Louis Stevenson, 'the different appearances of nature seemed each to contain its own legend ready-made, which it was his to call forth.' Edwin Muir found it exasperating that the ubiquity of Scott's presence, particularly in the Borders, compelled one to see things, even those that pre-dated him, as clothed in his mark and set with his seal. It can, indeed, often seem as though Scott has taken a brush and not so much highlighted the history and character of the Scots, as painted the past with a coat of aspic to preserve and enhance a galantine of tradition. But Scott was not merely a literary romancer: he was a political idealist. It was his responsibility to stage-manage the reception of George IV on his royal visit to Edinburgh in 1822. As the first reigning monarch to set foot on Scottish soil since Charles I and to redeem the memory of James VI and I's ill-tempered tour of 1617 (the Scots have long and unforgiving memories), George was entitled to some significant expression of loyalty and national enthusiasm for the Hanoverians. If popular sentiment could be rallied, thought Scott, if the old monarchical feeling could be stirred and Scotland's pride gratified by the gracious visit of her sovereign, much might be done for the cause of Scottish nationalism and national unity. To that end, Scott envisaged and organized a national pageant. He enrolled the Highland chieftains, the Lowland lairds, and the Edinburgh baillies in the venture, and George himself co-operated beautifully. To Scott, who wore Campbell tartan trews, the King presented himself, gorgeous in a kilt of Royal Stewart tartan provided by the Laird of Garth. In the train of the King, also suitably accoutred for the occasion, was a certain London alderman, Sir William Curtis, who all but outshone his monarch by being bigger, fatter, gaudier and more ostentatious in the finery of his adopted Highland dress. He certainly outshone the genuine Highland chiefs. It was very magnificent, and it was meant to be.

It was a matter of some perplexity to Scott that King George was hugely unpopular with most of the Scots: there remained an element of Jacobitism in the national character, and the depredations of the brutal Hanoverians, particularly the Duke of Cumberland, were still sorely remembered by the Highlanders. However, there were levées at Holyrood Palace, lengthy and splendid dinners, a solemn service at St Giles, a command performance at the theatre, speeches and expressions of loyal gratitude, and a state procession to Edinburgh Castle, the whole accompanied and garnished by music, dancing, poetry, song, and all that was considered to be peculiarly Scottish in character. The entire state occasion had one lasting result – it gave Highland habits, washed and brushed up and given a genteel gloss to gratify the sophisticated royal taste, a national character which they have ever since retained in the popular imagination. As John Buchan remarked, it ushered in a golden age for haberdashers. The kilt, once proscribed by George's own Hanoverian predecessor, George II, assumed the status of Scottish national dress. No matter that it had once been a convenient, adaptable, all-purpose length of cloth coloured with natural dyes, it was now an amply tailored garment in the form of a pleated skirt and complemented by an article of clothing the Highlander had never worn – a formally cut jacket. A bogus Celticism became the rage, and Scottish Lowland households, whose ancestors would as readily have worn woad as the dress of their bitterest secular foes, were provided, says Buchan, with family tartans by imaginative tradesmen.

Scott had merely, and masterfully, codified an already burgeoning sensibility; but he succeeded in arresting anachronisms, setting them like flies in amber as a preventative against further decay, and ornamenting them to suit the spirit of the age which he himself had been largely instrumental in creating. Robert Louis Stevenson once described his medieval romance, *The Black Arrow*, as 'tushery' – an imaginative invention of a particular period, smacking of ancient oaths and redolent of

modern morality. It is not too much to describe Scott's achievement as tartanry and tushery. *The Lady of the Lake*, Scott's most
famous poem and the one that most immediately and directly
caught the popular imagination, had been published in May
1810. In 1809 he had renewed an old acquaintance with Cam-
busmore, which lies a few miles south-east of Callander. A week
later he mounted a horse and rode from Loch Venachar to
Stirling in five hours, to verify that it could be done. He then
proceeded west to inspect the landscape surrounding Loch
Lomond. Fired by the sublimity of the wild, natural beauty he had
explored, he began to write the romantic narrative poem that was
to be *The Lady of the Lake*.

By the summer of 1810, two months or so after the poem had
been published and avidly read, the rush was on. 'The whole
country rang with the praises of the poet – crowds set off to view
the scenery of Loch Katrine, till then comparatively unknown.'
The flood of tourists and trippers, only some of the twenty
thousand who had bought copies of the poem, astounded the
natives, the indigenous peasantry of the area, who lived on
everyday terms with the scenery they were now obliged to look
upon as suddenly picturesque and romantic. They expressed the
greatest astonishment that visitors should take such gratification
in water, trees, hills, and the flora and fauna they themselves took
so much for granted. Visitors still descend in their thousands
upon the Trossachs which is an area sometimes described as
'Scotland's Lake District' – the association being perhaps due, in
part, to the enthusiastic tour of the Trossachs made in 1803 by
Dorothy and William Wordsworth. At the eastern end of Loch
Katrine, facing cloud-capped Ben Venue, they disembarked from
a rowboat and met their friend Samuel Taylor Coleridge, who
welcomed them with a cry, 'exulting in the glory of Scotland'.
They looked about them in wonder, Coleridge gabbling in their
ears. Dorothy later noted:

About and below us, to the right and to the left, were rocks,
knolls, and hills, which, wherever anything could grow – and

that was everywhere between the rocks – were covered with trees and heather; the trees did not in any place grow as thick as an ordinary wood; yet I think there was never a bare space of twenty yards: it was more like a natural forest, where the trees grow in groups or singly, not hiding the surface of the ground, which, instead of being green and mossy, was of the richest purple. The heather was indeed the most luxuriant I ever saw; it was so tall that a child of ten struggling through it would have been buried head and shoulders.

In 1853, John Ruskin and his wife Effie, with John Everett Millais, visited Glenfinlas, a little way from the village of Brig o'Turk. Millais' portrait of Ruskin striking a pose beside a rushing stream is a precise, detailed picture of a Trossachs scene – the crags and crevices, the tumbling, foaming, secret little burn, and all the bright colour of a summer's day. Here, Ruskin noted 'the skies all turquoise and violet, melted in dew: and heavenly bars of delicate cloud behind Ben Venue in evening.' As he watched the sunset, enraptured, his wife and Millais were busy becoming enraptured with one another, falling in love behind his back while Ruskin enjoyed his spiritual, aesthetic pleasures.

Romanticism had been preceded by Celticism, more or less invented by James Macpherson. 'We spoke of Fingal,' records James Boswell in his *Journal of a Tour to the Hebrides*. Indeed, who was not speaking of Fingal, Ossian and, by implication, of James Macpherson? Dr Johnson delivered his magisterial, disbelieving dicta on this burning literary issue, but there were others who, vociferous and convinced, spoke out as partisans of a poetry that could be adduced to confound critics of the supposedly barbarous Scots who, it was now evident, had cultivated a Caledonian Homer long before England had risen out of savagedom.

In 1759, on the bowling green at Moffat, then a fashionable Scottish spa, Alexander Carlyle and the dramatist John Home had met a young giant, six feet three inches in height, standing substantially on thick-set legs encased in old-fashioned jack-boots. They had discoursed pleasantly on many topics, including

Gaelic poetry, customs and superstitions. The young man had casually mentioned that he had some pieces of Celtic poetry in his possession. Home begged to be shown specimens, but there was an obstacle to his full appreciation: he knew no Gaelic. 'How then can I show them to you?' inquired James Macpherson. 'Very easily,' suggested the celebrated author of that affecting tragedy, *Douglas*; 'translate some of the poems which you think are good, and I imagine I shall be able to form an opinion of the genius and character of Gaelic poetry.' No sooner said than done.

Forthwith, Macpherson delivered to Home a fragment called *The Death of Oscar*. The translation was taken to Dr Hugh Blair, the literary arbiter of Edinburgh. Home and Blair concurred in their judgement: here was a literary revelation of transcendent importance, poetry of vast antiquity and rare genius. Macpherson was urged to continue his translation, but the twenty-two-year-old repented his promise to 'send as many fragments as would be contained in a shilling pamphlet'. He was persuaded to continue the task of delivering a forgotten heritage to literary Scotland, and copies of Macpherson's manuscripts were sent to Walpole and Shenstone who, gratifyingly, much admired them. In 1760, a slim volume entitled *Fragments of Ancient Poetry collected in the Highlands of Scotland, and Translated from the Gaelic or Erse Language*, graced with a preface by Dr Blair, was published. Blair explained that the work contained Gaelic verse of tremendous antiquity, anterior to the clan system, and bore no trace of Christian influence. A claque of critical acclaim arose and was heaped upon the hapless Macpherson.

'Hume and Home, Ferguson and Blair, Lord Elibank, Lord Kames, Lord Hailes – in fact everyone – joined in the chorus of acclaim,' states Henry Gray Graham in *Scottish Men of Letters in the Eighteenth Century*, 'and were fierce at any who dared to impugn their genuineness, or to slight their beauty. Had not these verses been handed down from remote ages? Did not chiefs keep their own hereditary family bards whose themes were the feats of their clan and the wars of Fingal? Had not Adam Smith heard a piper of Argyllshire repeat some of these very poems? Did not distinguished chieftains – Mackays, Macleods, Macfarlanes – assert that they knew them well? Furthermore, were not the very names of the heroes, Fingal, Ossian, Oscar, Diarmid, still given in the Highlands to large mastiffs, as the English gave the name of Pompey and Hector, and the French gave the name of Marlborough to their dogs? So wrote, so argued David Hume, full of his usual extravagant patriotism and wild defiance of Southron suspicion.'

Macpherson's hints that he had given but a fragment of a great poetical epic inflamed his admirers to urge funds upon him to facilitate a search of the Highlands in a bid to rescue the magnificent but, as yet, incomplete tradition from oblivion. Macpherson initially parried attempts to dispatch him northwards, but his refusal became a hesitance and his hesitance a reluctant consent. In September 1760, he rode off in search of an epic he alone knew had existed. His spirits improved when letters of introduction gained him the hospitality and help of lairds and ministers from Perth to Benbecula. His knowledge of Gaelic was imperfect, but his self-confidence was complete. To quote Henry Gray Graham, 'Chiefs in their houses showed him dusty manuscripts hard to decipher; ministers helped him to translate Gaelic, . . . venerable blacksmiths, sons of bards, recited long screeds of Fingalian verse in high nasal accents with the prospective reward of a gill of whisky or a roll of tobacco. Onwards he travelled . . . over island and mainland. Schoolhouse, croft and manse welcomed him, and chieftains gave him the loan of treasured manuscripts, containing household receipts, genealogical notes and old verse in chaotic confusion and distressful cacography – some were lent and never seen again.'

Macpherson returned four months later to report that the great Ossianic epic had been retrieved. A Celtic Homer had been brought to light after thirteen hundred years. In 1761, with a humble dedication to the court favourite, Lord Bute, an edition of *Fingal, an ancient Epic Poem, in six books, together with several other poems composed by Ossian, the son of Fingal, translated from the Gaelic language by James Macpherson*, was published to almost universal approbation. Churchill and Wilkes might jeer in London, but no dissentient voice came out of Scotland. Blair, 'with the pride of a discoverer and the pomposity of a critic, descanted in his familiar burr on the age, the style, and marvellous beauties of the blind [*another remarkable coincidence to link Ossian with Homer*] son of Fingal. When the lectures were published in 1763, his *Critical Dissertation* was hailed as a masterly and convincing performance. It was, indeed, as learned a disquisition as could be written by a man who knew nothing of his subject,' says H. G. Graham.

Publication of *Temora, an ancient Epic in eight books, composed by Ossian, the son of Fingal*, completed the immortal work. Macpherson's tenuous hold on reality was relinquished: he became a celebrity, a swaggering, vainglorious, aggressive translator who resented being unable to claim himself as an original poet. David Hume retracted his faith in Ossian and in Macpherson, describing the proud and capricious fellow as 'a mortal than whom I have never known more perverse and unamiable'. The more suspicion grew, the more Macpherson blustered. He cast aside critics, and he assumed ever grander airs of a man of the world. But criticism continued and the public taste for the melancholy monotony of the poems – moaning winds, sounding shores, misty hills and halls of shells – began to decline. To confound critics and excite public interest, Macpherson placed certain Gaelic manuscripts on show at a bookseller's in London. Since nobody could read Gaelic, they remained uninspected and were withdrawn. But Macpherson was able to claim, subtly, that he had given proof which no one had bothered to confirm.

Macpherson went to Florida as surveyor-general and secretary to Commodore Johnson, with whom he quarrelled furiously and lost his appointment. He returned to London and composed a translation of the *Iliad* in three months flat. It was a considerable failure, and the fuss about Ossian died down with the reputation of the translator. It was revived in 1775 by Samuel Johnson who took an opportunity to give his opinion of the Ossianic *oeuvre* in his account of *A Journey to the Western Isles of Scotland*. Johnson's views on the subject were already known, but now he took care to damn not only Macpherson but the mendacity of the Scots in general: 'I asked a very learned Minister in Sky, who had used all the arts to make me believe the genuineness of the book, whether at last he believed it himself? But he would not answer. He wished me to be deceived, for the honour of his country; but would not directly and formally deceive me.' Johnson goes on to confute the arguments originally given by David Hume in defence of the genuineness of the epic and takes another swipe at the Scots to conclude the matter to his entire satisfaction: 'The Scots have something to plead for their easy reception of an improbable fiction: they are seduced by their fondness for their supposed ancestors. A Scotchman must be a very sturdy moralist, who does not love Scotland better than truth: he will always love it better than inquiry; and if falsehood flatters his vanity, will not be very diligent to detect it.' Working up to his crescendo, Johnson piles Pelion on Ossa, or Fingal on Ossian: 'But this is an age in which those who could not read, have been supposed to write; in which the giants of antiquated romance have been exhibited as realities. If we know little of the ancient Highlanders, let us not fill the vacuity with Ossian. If we have not searched the Magellanick regions, let us however forbear to people them with Patagons.'

Macpherson was ruffled by Johnson's unpleasant passages, offensive charges and injurious statements. He strutted and fretted for a while before writing a letter to Johnson informing him that 'his age and his infirmities alone protected him from the treatment due to an infamous liar and traducer'. Neither Johnson's age nor his infirmities stopped him from replying in ripest style: 'I have received your foolish and impudent note . . . I will not desist from detecting what I think a cheat from any fear of the menaces of a Ruffian. I thought your book an imposture. I think it an imposture still . . . Your rage I defy, your abilities since your Homer, are not so formidable, and what I hear of your morals inclines me to pay regard not to what you say, but to what you shall prove.' Worried that Macpherson was quite capable of proving a point with a bang on Johnson's head, the honest but trepid Doctor equipped himself with a cudgel six feet long, tipped with a knob three inches in diameter. Macpherson spluttered for a while, and Johnson jeered, but no blows were struck.

For a *History of Great Britain*, the bookseller Strahan paid James Macpherson £3,000, a considerable sum. It was condemned by Hume as 'the most wretched production that ever came from his press', but it enabled Macpherson to live in a house in Putney, and maintain another in town, drive to the City in impressive carriages, and become Member of Parliament for Camelford in the Tory interest. In 1785 an enthusiastic subscription was raised by a number of Highland gentlemen who wished to have the original Ossianic Gaelic manuscripts published. To these respectful but provoking pleadings, Macpherson turned a deaf ear. His own proposal was that the Gaelic should be published in Greek characters, the better to convey the Erse sounds. There was some precedent for this enterprise, he suggested, since it was well known that the Druids had written in Greek. When Macpherson's chests were opened after his death, no Ossianic documents were found. A report issued in 1805, nine years after 'Ossian' Macpherson had ceased to be, discredited him still further – the poems were declared to be hopeless in their chronology, confused in topography, wrong in their nationality (the Irish laid claim to the Gaelic heroes), spoke of customs the ancient Celts had never observed, were written in poetic styles they never used, gave names to heroes that they had never borne, and described armour they never wore.

Though the authenticity of Macpherson's discoveries are still a matter for dispute, credit is due to a remarkable imagination that wrought an epic – indeed several epics – which cast a glamour over the whole of Europe and its literature. The works of 'Ossian' Macpherson opened magic casements on a Celtic world forlorn, an antique world that, though it never existed but in Macpherson's song and fable, captured the romantic spirit of 'Young Werther' and the imagination of Napoleon Bonaparte. Ossian, Fingal, Oscar, the Border lords and lairds, the Bruce and the Wallace (both demi-mythical heroes in the legends they accreted), are passionate characters of a misty past that, though warlike, appears to have been based on honour, pride, fine feeling, and nationality.

The Scots heroes struggled against a plain, mortal enemy that strove to subdue them. These were men fighting other men. It is more difficult to sing of heroic battle waged against sheep, or machines, or money, or relatively blameless tourists. The sword and the fire and satirical flytings will not much impede their relentless advance. When passion fails to overcome oppressors, and merely inflames a spirit which cannot nowadays be subdued by drenching it with blood, sentimentality is a consolation that calms the savage impulse in the Scottish breast. 'The unfortunate thing for Scotland,' wrote Edwin Muir in *Scottish Journey*, 'is that it is not an obviously oppressed nation, as Ireland was, but only a visibly depressed one searching for the source of its depression.' In the early 1930s, the period about which Muir was writing, the Scots were depressed superficially, like everyone else, by the Depression. But the source of their depression was rooted in immemorial grievances against the English, by the failure of the 1745 rebellion, by the wholesale clearances of crofters and their cattle from the Highlands, and by a general sense of despair that the Scots were no longer their own masters.

Edwin Muir, in this context, refers to 'the strange popularity of "Annie Laurie",' a song which, he felt, is 'a symbol of modern Scotland. The melody itself has an obvious fascination which might make one sing it twice or thrice, until one discovers that it is mechanical in its rise and fall. As for the poem, it is an almost unique anthology of hackneyed symbols.' Muir considered the enduring popularity of 'Annie Laurie' to be 'a sign that true folk sentiment in Scotland has for a long time been degenerating, so that a sham substitute is more pleasing to Scottish ears than the real thing.' The song was a milestone on the road to the Kailyard, a literary school of literature rooted in the cabbage patch and which blossomed in the rural sentimentality of works by J. M. Barrie, Ian Maclaren and S. R. Crockett. Trevor Royle, in *The*

Macmillan Companion to Scottish Literature, describes the essential ingredients of the Kailyard as

> characters who represent solid virtues: the minister or the village worthies who voice pastoral morality, the industrious son who rises by dint of hard work and his own endeavour, the honest tenant farmers who give of their best for their families' improvement. Behind them are the stock rapacious landlords, self-satisfied incomers and the ever-present and awesome figures of death and disease. These characters inhabit a well-defined arcadia of village life, far removed from the ills of nineteenth-century Scotland, its industrial development, poverty and high mortality rate. The city appears only as a distant drum; instead, the virtues of village life are emphasized. The world created by the Kailyard novelists is little more than a projection of eighteenth-century Romantic views about nature and its beneficial effects on humankind.

The Kailyard pleased and comforted not only the native Scots but a worldwide market which took Barrie's, Crockett's and Ian Maclaren's sentimental fictions to heart as the real, dear thing. Expatriates, looking back on Scotland through a mist of tears and rosy memory, were confirmed in their view that they had left behind the kindest, the couthiest, the dearest and the best in the land of lost content. It was a bathetic picture that can be accounted for, says Edwin Muir, by

> the breakdown of Calvinism, a process salutary in itself, but throwing off as a by-product an obliterating debris of sentimentality, and the rise of an industrial system so sordid and disfiguring that people were eager to escape from it by any road, however strange. The flight to the Kailyard was a flight to Scotland's past, to a country which had existed before Industrialism; but by the time the flight took place Industrialism had sucked that tradition dry of its old vigour; it was no longer of importance except as a refuge from the hard facts of Scottish

town life. The Kailyard school of literature was thus really a by-product of Scotland's economic history. All the songs and stories of Scottish country life after the Industrial Revolution got into its stride were for a long time dreams of comfort or escape. To anyone living in Glasgow or Dundee even the Kailyard must have seemed heaven.

In *The Scot Abroad*, Robert Louis Stevenson gives a prime example of the passionate longing of the Scot for the Scotland behind the mist of his tearful sentiment:

> There is no special loveliness in that grey country, with its rainy, sea-beat archipelago; its fields of dark mountains; its unsightly places, black with coal; its treeless, sour, unfriendly-looking cornlands; its quaint, grey, castled city, where the bells clash of a Sunday, and the wind squalls, and the salt showers fly and beat. I do not even know if I desire to live there; but let me hear, in some far land, a kindred voice sing out, 'O why left I my hame?' and it seems at once as if no beauty under the kind heavens, and no society of the wise and good, can repay me for my absence from my country ... When I forget thee, Auld Reekie, may my right hand forget its cunning.

Stevenson admitted every drawback of life in Scotland, a life which almost killed him in childhood, but did not deny that he had had every advantage: 'The happiest lot on earth is to be born a Scotsman. You must pay for it in many ways, as for all other advantages on earth. You have to learn the Paraphrases and the Shorter Catechism; you generally take to drink; your youth, as far as I can find out, is a time of louder war against society, of more outcry and tears and turmoil, than if you had been born, for instance, in England. But somehow life is warmer and closer; the hearth burns more redly; the lights of home shine softer on the rainy street; the very names, endeared in verse and music, cling nearer round our hearts.'

That last sentence might almost be a few lines of advertising copy, under an atmospheric photograph, for a brand of whisky to be advertised full-page in *The New Yorker*. Stevenson is adept at having it both ways: yes, life in Scotland can be difficult, tedious, repressive, cold, wet, introverted, and all the rest – but what a man Scotland makes of her son!

The Scot, raised in these testing conditions, turns out thrawn, hardy, self-sufficient, perceptive, imaginative, and virtuous. He is a man to be reckoned with at home or abroad; his heart is as big as Ben Nevis, his feelings as profound as Loch Ness, his kindliness warmer than a peat fire, and his courage as enduring as the Cairngorms. He has reason to be thankful for having been brought up in a hard school – it has tempered his character as firm as a sword, but his spirit can be broken by sentimental memory. The Scot is a lion in the world, but a lamb by his own hearth. The land, if not the Scot, has been sentimentalized. In *Return to Scotland*, written in 1930, more or less at the same time as Muir's *Scottish Journey*, Moray McLaren comments:

> Now of all Great Mountains which the Victorians (in their somewhat tardy acceptance of Wordsworth) chose to admire, those which they treated most shabbily and rendered most ridiculous, were the Highlands of Scotland ... I think the reason was partly snobbish; for the Highlands were supposed to be the playgrounds of the aristocracy and the Court. Also, there was a picturesque romance about them – Prince Charlie, the faithful Highlanders, and all the rest of it; that business being now sufficiently remote to be slopped over without treasonable suspicion attaching to one. The sentimental orgy set in, accompanied by that invariable friend or opposite side of the penny to sentimentality – brutality. The Highland crofters, those who in an anachronistic spirit of independence had clung on to their own bits of land for centuries, were evicted and sent off to America so that London brewers might have good shooting. The brutality side of the question is luckily somewhat, though not entirely, mended now, but there still remain in most seaside lodgings those innumerable pictures entitled:

'Evening on Loch Lomond,' 'The Monarch of the Glen,' and so on, as dreadful relics of the sentimentalization of the Highlands.

By the 1850s, the Highlands and the quaint customs of that land were firmly in vogue. In 1845, McIan published a sumptuous volume, fully illustrated, describing *The Costumes of the Clans*, dedicated to Queen Victoria and subscribed to by the gentry. The Queen invented her own tartan and covered Balmoral with it. 'The heather grew in his heart,' said one contemporary of McIan, 'and there was no music he loved so well as the bagpipe on the wild hill-side.' McIan was but one imaginative historian of Highland dress: the eccentric and mysterious Scotto-Polish brothers Sobieski-Stuart, on finding themselves in Scotland, claimed to be grandsons of Bonnie Prince Charlie and passed their time agreeably in inventing and painting and working up provenances for their interpretations of tartans ascribed with apparent authority to the individual clans of Scotland. Tartan and tartanry is nowadays a thriving business: visitors to Edinburgh religiously stop to consult a table of tartans and clan names outside a Princes Street haberdashers, where they are usually gratified to discover that their own improbable surnames can be connected with an Ur-clan name, thus entitling them to adopt a particular design of tartan. Since some clan chiefs are now American citizens, and clan gatherings are attended even by Japanese tourists (who have a passion for whisky and golf, in addition to tartan), it is not improbable that the tartan should have become an international status symbol and badge of pedigree. There is still a good deal of nonsense talked about who is entitled to wear what tartan among those who have become more Scottish than the Scots. Tartan, like many another Scottish fetish, has taken on a wider, almost global significance.

There are those who come to the Highlands and Islands looking for 'Mary Rose' and 'Brigadoon'. They will not have far to look for guides eager to confirm them in their romanticism and Celticism. A particular band of tourists of this type was waspishly described in *Hunting the Fairies* by Compton Mackenzie who, as an honorary Scot and patriot, constructed his own fantasy Scotland in novels such as *Whisky Galore, The Monarch of the Glen*, and *Rockets Galore*. He was an early member and supporter of the Scottish Nationalist Party, with Robert Bontine Cunninghame Graham and others, and was a friend of the nationalist poet Hugh MacDiarmid. His Mrs Urquhart-Unwin is an American matron, 'all gooey on Gaelic and fairies and all that sort of thing,' who travels with her own clarsach, a Scottish instrument resembling a harp but which, since Mrs Urquhart-Unwin 'found that your smaller instrument was not resonant enough for our audiences in the States', has been 'specially made for us in Boston'. Mrs Urquhart-Unwin is overwhelmed by her first dinner with Kilwhillie and Ben Nevis, two Anglo-Scottish grandees:

> The dining-room at Kilwhillie was not such a stately affair as the great dining-room in Glenbogle Castle, but when the guests were gathered round the big mahogany table installed there by Kilwhillie's grandfather, Mrs Urquhart-Unwin found the scene completely satisfying to her prevision of Highland life. She looked soulfully at her host in his doublet of mulberry velvet buttoned up to the neck with silver dogs. She looked soulfully at the Chieftain of Ben Nevis entirely in tartan buttoned up to the neck with eagles' heads of silver. She looked soulfully at their lace jabots. She looked soulfully at Neil Mackillop's rifle-green dinner doublet and black tie. She looked soulfully at the black dinner doublet of Dr Macgregor above the red and black chequers of his clan's tartan. She looked soulfully at Angus MacQuat in the full dress of a piper slowly marching round the table to the strains of 'Over the Sea to Skye'. She even looked soulfully at white-haired Mr Fletcher and sandy-haired Mr Mackenzie in trim, sober clerical attire. She was grateful that the piping made speech for the while impossible because, as she said to Kilwhillie after the piper had retired for a while to give himself and the assembled company a rest, her heart was too full for words.

'I can hardly believe I'm any longer in this old world of ours at all,' she leaned across the table to tell Mrs MacDonald.

'We all enjoy these occasions,' said the Lady of Ben Nevis. 'Even I who am English love them just as much as my husband.'

'Oh, are you English, Mrs MacDonald?' the visitor from over the Atlantic asked sympathetically. 'Haven't you any Highland blood at all?'

'None,' Mrs MacDonald boomed without a sign of a crack in her bell-like tones.

'Oh, well, we can't all be Highland, can we?' Mrs Urquhart-Unwin sighed.

This extract from *Hunting the Fairies* is not only a cheerful swipe at the soggy, sentimental mysticism of Scotto-Americans, but equally a mild dig at the pretensions of the landed gentry of Scotland and at novels of the romantic kind which luxuriate in the keeping up of antique practices. The novel knocks on the head any number of anachronisms which are still ceremonially observed in Scotland among all types and conditions of Scots at the drop of a cockade or a tweed bonnet. 'The normal development of a nation is a development founded solidly on its past,' said Edwin Muir rather piously in *Scottish Journey*. 'The development of Scotland during the last three centuries has been a development bought at the expense of shedding one bit of its past after another, until almost the only thing that remains now is a sentimental legend.' The sentimental legend is now up for sale. One of the least attractive motifs of Scottish culture is the sight of a pre-pubescent girl, her little velvet jacket clinking with medals, her mini-kilt bobbing round her thighs, her arms arched above her head, her feet pounding out the steps of a sword dance. She is the star of the Highland Games, and perhaps a more appealing figure, in a chocolate-box style, than the kilted, caber-tosser peching away on the sports field, and somewhat more aesthetic than a canny-eyed Highland cow peering through wads of shaggy red hair. They are all acts in Scottish national show-business, fairground figures, stereotypes in a music-hall variety bill. They are what the paying customer wants and they are what Scotland provides, taking the money at the door.

Tom Scott, glossing MacDiarmid's *Lament for the Great Music*, declares pithily: 'The Scotland of today is no longer Scotland, but a philistine travesty of itself. It is Scotshire, a county in the north of England, an ex-country, an Esau land that has sold its birthright for a mess of English pottage.' So lost are the Scots, that they no longer recognize their own heritage, only the debased symbols that now represent it.

5

*

The Scot on the make:
the pursuit of success

THE split in the Scottish character is nobly and notably characterized by the fact that, no matter how squalid the conditions of life may have been in Scotland, the national perception is that the Scots and their country were really, in resources and men, rich and successful. This is partly accountable to projection – pride in national heroes and Scottish heroism in military, commercial and political enterprise – but also to the constant care the Scots took to be personally respectable. There remains, deeply embedded in the Scottish character, a profound satisfaction in the conventional respectability of the sober-minded working and middle classes, and a deep distrust of fecklessness, particularly as exemplified by the poor who are mostly regarded as having brought their miseries upon themselves. Strict adherence to duty is highly regarded – to think of, or describe, hard work in trying conditions (whether as a bread-winner in the mines, on the land, on a production line, or as a domestic drudge) as being near to slavery or bondage, is close to heretical doubt about the virtue of honest toil, family life, and the justice of the Almighty. Careless attitudes towards moral obligations are sternly reprobated.

'The division between the respectable and the unrespectable,' remarks T. C. Smout in *A Century of the Scottish People 1830–*

1950, published in 1986, 'might be construed as moral: the division between the skilled and the unskilled [*worker*] was institutional . . . Up to the 1950s, it was still a major split, and even today a craft apprentice relaxing in a pub might give his opinion of labourers in language that he would not, even in the company of his colleagues, apply to the boss.' The respectable kept themselves, their families and accommodation clean, they associated with their 'betters' – it was a great thing (respectability and solidity by association) to be on friendly terms with a solicitor, a doctor, or a partner in a commercial firm: identification with merit conferred merit. The respectable Scot did not bet or drink except on socially approved occasions such as an outing to a race meeting or at a conventional celebration. A skilled workman or a clerk kept his nose and his collar clean, making good in a godly manner. 'The tendency,' says Smout, 'was systematically to avoid drunkenness, gambling, swearing, and fighting, as far as possible to pay debts on time, and to present a clean and decent home to the neighbours. Such behaviour demanded self-discipline and had a pay-off in material terms: "respectable" workers could better withstand spells of unemployment and had a better chance of slight upward mobility for their children.'

The poor remained poor because, of course, they were morally inferior – virtue was its own reward; lack of money leading to a disreputable appearance implied a clear lack of moral fibre. Among the poor, the canons of respectability were often piously observed: if they could not be rich, they could at least be decent and achieve the form, if not the substance, of respectability. They could aspire to godliness through cleanliness. Here again virtue was its own reward – though it might be rather cold compensation. The mote cast out of one's own eye, one could comfortably take a superior attitude towards those who failed to achieve standards of life that one had, with difficulty, attained, and struggled to maintain, for oneself and family. Where material possessions were not readily available as evidence of moral and material status, moral rectitude was a substitute more enduring and procurable. Better, moral superiority might bridge the deepest class barriers. Many a man might make a fortune, but to do so he might imperil his eternal soul: heaven was the final reckoning in which, if the Magnificat were to be believed, the mighty would be humbled and the deserving poor elevated to their proper rank which the base world had unaccountably failed to recognize. Poverty, well-manneredly and stoically endured, was a passport to good standing in eternity.

Class division and hatred probably arose, according to Smout, among the Scottish miners who detested 'the employers and landowners who lived on the profits and royalties of their industry'. At the turn of the nineteenth century into the early twentieth century, there was a strong feeling in Scotland that each man was allotted to his estate. It was regarded as hubristic to aspire to change it by elevating oneself. Those who successfully did so were not regarded with much enthusiasm by employers and landowners and were objects of envy by those they had surpassed. Despite the desperate struggle to rise out of the slums and intolerable working conditions, few enough succeeded: passion and motive were not enough – the considerable hurdle of the distrust of the middle and upper classes had to be overcome. They were not likely to budge easily, to move over in order to make room for aspirants from a class they had been taught to despise, and sometimes fear. Fear was, however, a lesser emotion: the Scottish working classes were, despite some activities mildly revolutionary in character that had sent frissons of apprehension through the upper and middle classes during the period of Chartism, docile. They did not have the true revolutionary spirit. They were fiery but not inflammable. They had been repressed so systematically, and so long, that they had no real, solid base from which to proceed against their oppressors.

Unfortunately, [says Smout] by upbringing and increasingly by education, the employing class had been taught to regard the working class as irresponsible, inferior, different, another species, whom a manager must learn to 'handle'. So by the 1940s and 1950s Scotland was lumbered with an industrial stalemate: socialists had not convinced their fellow workers of the need to struggle with the bosses for actual control of the economy in the name of industrial democracy, and capitalists had not convinced their work force of the benefits to themselves of working hard for the firm, benefits that would lead to the flexibility of attitudes and high wages of, for example, postwar Germany and Scandinavia. What was left was ca' canny, restrictive practices, suspicion, separate canteens for worker and management, and a general belief that if one side proposed a change the other side should resist it. It is hard to think of a more depressing industrial ethos, or one more likely to guarantee a snail's pace of economic growth.

Outside Scotland, the Scot discovered that he was more likely to be accepted on his own terms, and that work was more liberally rewarded. Outside Scotland, poor and working-class emigrants were less fettered by conditions that conspired to keep them at the bottom of society. They were inspired by an example that achieved mythical status: the successful Scot nonpareil surely is the Admirable Crichtoun, otherwise known as *Scotus admirabilis*, reverenced by his prosy biographer Sir Thomas Urquhart, the Knight of Cromarty, a writer no less admirable than his subject for learning and energy. The short, meteoric career of Crichtoun is described in *The Discovery of a most Exquisite Jewel*, published in 1625, some seventy years after Crichtoun's death by misadventure – murder, in fact – in Mantua. Crichtoun's exploits have a Munchausen flavour, save that he never rendered himself ridiculous. Crichtoun was a paragon, the most perfect flower, the most accomplished representative of his race . . . but Sir Thomas's style is catching, and it will be best to go to the ripe original wherein Crichtoun is described as one who:

> . . . for his learning, judgement, valour, eloquence, beauty, and good-fellowship, was the perfectest result of the joynt labour of the perfect number of those six dieties, Pallas, Apollo, Mars, Mercury, Venus, and Bacchus, that hath been seen since the

days of Alcibiades: for he was reported to have been inriched with a memory so prodigious, that any sermon, speech, harangue, or other manner of discourse of an hour's continuance, he was able to recite, without hesitation after the same manner of gesture and pronounciation, in all points, wherewith it was delivered at first: and of so stupendious a judgement and conception, that almost naturally he understood quiddities of philosophy: and as for the abstrusest and most researched mysteries of other disciplines, arts, and faculties, the intentional species of them were as readily obvious to the interiour view and perspicacity of his mind, as those of the common visible collours, to the external sight of him that will open his eyes to look upon them: of which accomplishment and Encyclopaedia of knowledge, he gave on a time so marvellous a testimony at Paris, that the words of admirabilis Scotus, the wonderful Scot, in all the several tongues, and idiomes of Europe, were (for a great while together) by the most of the eccho's, resounded to the piercing of the very clouds.

Crichtoun could discourse fluently, and at length, with perfect confidence and 'seraphick wit', on any given subject in any one of twelve languages, in prose or in verse. He was proficient in Hebrew, Syriac, Arabic, Greek, Latin, Spanish, French, Italian, English, Dutch, Flemish, and Sclavonian. But he was no dull man of thought and words, merely: Crichtoun was an accomplished athlete, excelling equally in 'hawking, hunting, tilting, vaulting, riding of well-managed horses, tossing of the pike, handling of the musket, flourishing of colours, dancing, fencing, swimming, jumping, throwing of the barr, playing at the tennis, baloon, or long-catch'. Indoor games were child's play for the wonderful Scot: chess, billiards, cards, and dice. He would come fresh from intellectual dispute or the sport, ready to meet the softer but no less stimulating challenges of the chamber: 'singing, playing on the lute, and other musical instruments, masking, balling, reveling . . . and plying closer the courting of handsome ladyes, and a jovial cup in the company of Bacchanalian blades.' These last diversions, says Sir Thomas sternly, 'did most of all divert, or rather distract him from his speculations and serious employments.'

In appreciation of 'the rare and most singular gifts, wherewith God and nature had endowed him', Crichtoun accepted the glittering prizes bestowed upon him by universities and mighty patrons throughout Europe – diamond rings and purses of gold. His last employment was in the service of the Duke of Mantua, whose eldest son impetuously ran a blade through the body of the Admirable Crichtoun, whereupon the entire Mantuan court went into mourning for nine months to show the memory of Crichtoun the proper respect befitting his wonderful talents.

There is, in this story, something of the fabulous and it is notable that Crichtoun's career was conducted mostly outside Scotland. The reason for this may be that the Scots 'kent his faither'. There is no possibility, in Scotland, of a Scot being better or worse than the old man. If a Scot outstrips his father in achievement, there are envious Scots ready on all sides to give him a bumping reminder of his origins. Hubris is not permitted to a Scot by his fellow countrymen. If he merely equals his father, that comes as no surprise to the Scots: there is no reason to suppose that the son of such a father should outdo him. If a Scot fails significantly to match his father's achievements, then that too is unsurprising – for who could have hoped much of the son of such a father? These attitudes work equally for the son of a tycoon or a tinker. Generally, when the old men shake their heads or wave their sticks, muttering, 'I kent his faither,' they intend to be disparaging of success or philosophical about failure. The thing is to keep a man firmly in his place in Scotland: not to do him down, particularly, or to establish him in high esteem, especially – but to maintain the balance, to give credit or blame to the degree, strictly, that it has been merited, considering a man's background.

Generally, however, despite one's parentage, the ideal in Scotland is to 'get on', which often enough means to get out. In all classes in Glasgow, wrote Edwin Muir, the main ideal was respectability or rising in the world.

In such people the wish to get on was not merely a natural desire, but the chief article in an exalted mystical faith, an orthodoxy which it would have been mere vicious perversity or worse not to subscribe to. Inherited Calvinism was at the bottom of their contemptuous reprobation of anyone who, out of weakness or amiability or scruple, refrained from striving to his utmost to make money; for their attitude to such people was indistinguishable from that of the elect to the damned a century before [*in the early to mid-nineteenth century*] . . . I have referred back this worship of success to Calvin, and I think he was largely responsible for it; but it was sanctified also by an orthodox economic theory which taught that competition was equally necessary to increase the general wealth and strengthen the individual character . . . A rise in salary was a moral rise; a business promotion, a promotion in spiritual grace.

The individual ideal held up to Scottish schoolchildren is that of David Livingstone who got his education where he could while working in the mills of Blantyre as a child. He toiled by day to earn a living, and burned the oil by night to get as much knowledge as he could from books. Then, confirmed in his religious faith, he went forth to give himself selflessly to the Africans, to the greater glory of God and his country, and to be held up as an inspiration to generations of Scottish schoolchildren. At some point, it might have been mentioned that his early life had been – to say the least – demanding. The thing was, he had been disadvantaged poor, and by dint of effort he succeeded in becoming a great man. Nothing could stop him on his upward progress. That Livingstone never made money, or at least never made it in respectable quantities, was neither here nor there. He was a man of ideals translated into action. There had been no shame in gracefully endured poverty, when there were few who were rich. And there was no shame in continuing to be poor, so long as making money was not the principal aim. Success in Scotland is not exclusively counted in material terms, though money is not to be discounted. Many useful things can be done with money, and a little put by is a great comfort.

Edwin Muir saw this clearly in the 1930s: '. . . what raised this religion of getting-on to a really intense faith was the squalor of the surroundings amid which the go-getter lived. The immediate goal that he set before him was not great wealth, but rather respectability, and all his environment reminded him of its opposite. In no place can respectability be a more intense passion than in a town which at every step one takes suggests the very thing it fights against: open filth, disorder and degradation. The pushing young Glasgow man felt that he was directly fighting all that this filth, disorder and degradation finally meant: that is, the slums.' Slums, in the 1980s, are still with us. The high-rise blocks, built in the post-war years in Glasgow, are like most of the high-rise blocks in other cities in Britain – decaying, degrading, and dispiriting. But life in Scotland in the 1980s is, it must be said, less dirty and less degrading than it was fifty years ago – though levels of unemployment remain disgracefully high and wages are generally low.

Calvinism, and the urge to 'get on', have prompted the myth of Scottish tight-fistedness which is neither meanness nor a dis- inclination to spend money so much as the reluctance to see money 'wasted' or, money having been acquired by adherence to Calvinist moral precepts, to see it spent idly or immorally. Since money is hard to get, it is disgraceful to spend it frivolously, for less than its full value. Environment is an inadequate explanation on its own, for the Scottish genius for exploiting individual natural ability and harnessing it to the spirit of the age. It must indeed have been an urgent aim to get out of the squalor of the Glasgow Gorbals; but many people remember the Gorbals as a warm-hearted place, and sharing poverty with one's own kind, without shame, provides a sense of communal security. Perhaps what prompted the move towards success was equally the Scottish sense of pride.

The Scot has an eye for the main chance, which is not always viewed as a vehicle for amassing money first and foremost. The

Scot has a proper sense of his own worth and demands that it be recognized by others. Appreciation in financial terms is only one aspect of this *amour propre*. The Scottish word for respectability is 'bein', which comes directly from the French 'bien', which in turn derives from the Latin 'bene'. Another derivation, a little more disparaging, is from the expression, 'aw frae the bein' (all from the bone), which implies that something or someone is proud, elevated or highly pleased – in allusion, says Jamieson's *Dictionary of the Scottish Language*, 'to the fleshy parts rising from the bone when the body is swollen'. Bein certainly contains a prideful element, but bein generally means respectability – possession of a fur coat or hat for going to church on a Sunday, or a well-kept house, or a good job. It means that a certain degree of wealth may be discreetly and appropriately displayed without exciting envious or derogatory comment. Bein may be taken to imply a solid, bourgeois, prosperous appearance. The matrons of Princes Street are bein women. It does not mean showy excess, or affectation. Such will be very quickly reprobated, and serve only to diminish the respect one wishes to gain and hold.

'Getting on' means making the most of the talents God has given a Scot; but success is judged to be a matter of degree, by an understanding common to all classes that to do one's best is sufficient. A student at a University is still thought to have been given a prime chance in the race of life. He will be expected to take his degree and make fullest use of it after graduation. There is no understanding or sympathy for any student who takes his education less than seriously or opts to drop out for some vague, philosophical reason. A Scot is expected to keep a grip on himself and his business – to go bankrupt is still regarded as partly a moral failure rather than a mere matter of bad luck or fecklessness. A miser is despised, and ostentatious grandness is not respected. The golden mean of respectability rules.

Having heard the Scots praised for their inexorable, irrepressible urge to better themselves, non-Scots may find it strange that Scotland is not a thriving, prosperous little country, right and tight, and smugly secure in its rectitude and riches. It is beginning, in the second half of the twentieth century, to secure a home base for its energies and inventiveness, but still the foreign countries call and more and more educated Scots continue to drain out of Scotland, attracted by facilities' and money more readily available elsewhere in the world. Defoe, in the eighteenth century, had the measure of it: 'The Scots are as diligent, as industrious, as apt for Labour and Business, and as capable of it, when they are abroad, as any People in the World; and why should they not be so at Home? and, if they had Encouragement, no doubt they would.' Scottish Nationalists damn the British government (of whatever hue, red or blue) for failing to provide incentives for Scots in Scotland; the Scots themselves are envious of success in Scotland and jealously guard their supposed classlessness, nurture their moral superiority, and nurse the grievances of their history; and the dull meteorological and intellectual and artistic climate of Scotland depresses and represses initiative. The Scots invent, but fail to exploit. There is, too, the question of inappropriate enthusiasm. As has been remarked, the Scots are liable to be carried away by an idea that, taken to logical conclusions, leads to disaster. George Douglas Brown, author of *The House With Green Shutters*, remarks:

So flushed and riotous can the Scottish mind become over a commercial prospect that it sometimes sends native caution by the board, and a man's really fine idea becomes an empty balloon to carry him off to the limbo of vanities. There is a megalomaniac in every parish in Scotland . . . in every district, almost, you may find a poor creature who for thirty years has cherished a great scheme by which means to revolutionize the world's commerce, and amass a fortune in monstrous degree. He is generally to be seen shivering at the Cross, and (if you are a nippy man) you shout carelessly in going by, 'Good morning, Tamson; how's the scheme?' And he would be very willing to tell you if only you would listen. 'Man,' he will cry eagerly behind you, 'if I only had anither wee wheel in my invention – she would do, the besom! I'll sune have her ready noo.' Poor Tamson.

A Scot, the Revd Charles Rogers, declared that, 'Scotsmen proceed everywhere; and wherever they are found, they are esteemed for their probity and honour, and are characterized by an energy which knows not how to yield, and a determination which is invincible.' T. W. H. Crosland, an English critic, in carping vein, says that this is a view put about by the Scots themselves for their own advertisement and profit. 'The Scotch themselves spare no effort to have it believed that if you want men of true probity, you must go to Scotland for them. Employers have taken them at their word and continue to take them at their word, and other things being equal, if there are two applicants for a position in the average commercial house, and one of them is English and the other Scotch, the Scotchman gets the preference, simply because he is Scotch.' It may not be wholly true to say that the Scot is more honest than any other man, but that self-interest comes first is certainly true of the Scot. It is normally more profitable to be honest, and more respectable. To this extent, J. M. Barrie's epigram that 'the grandest moral attribute of a Scotsman ... that he'll do nothing which might damage his career' is certainly justified. It is a principle of self-interest rather than strictly one of morals. 'Thrift and punctuality ... clothe him with virtues like a garment,' says T. W. H. Crosland.

To be successful in the eyes of fellow Scots, a Scot must maintain his Scottishness. Once out of Scotland, the elements of Scotland that made him must not be discarded in favour of foreign *mores*. The hard man must not become soft, however tempting the seductions that the Scot abroad and on the make may encounter. They will surely corrupt him, and bring about his moral or material downfall. My great aunt, hearing that I was intending to go to London after graduating from Edinburgh University, earnestly advised me to speak only to policemen and, if possible, exclusively to Scottish policemen. In her view, the sole aim of all other people was to do me down and rob me of money, job, reputation, and life. These valuable possessions could only be preserved among my own kind, and then only among those Scots paid to be dedicated to law and order. She herself had lived in

London most of her life and could speak with authority about the perfidy of foreigners now that she had, in old age, come home safely to Ayrshire.

Ian Maclaren, the Kailyard novelist, describes the academic Scot, a son of the village of Drumtochty, who has become a professor. He is a good son to his aged parents, writing home once a week, and has redounded amply to the credit of his family and friends who are constantly eager for news of his continued success. His character is blameless, his situation prodigious. His earnings are high, his learning deep, his character spotless, and his gratitude to the folks at home who enjoy, vicariously, his success, is gratifying. But this is sentimental, since recognition of success is given only to the respectable sons of Scotland – bankers, lawyers, academics, captains of commerce, doctors and directors of great enterprises. Jack McLean, the controversial and vernacular columnist of the *Glasgow Herald*, in 1985 applied his mind to the more notorious Scots whose success is less conventional:

> I suppose that the very moment that the Scots contrive to insert a champion into the UK consciousness they feel an immediate sense of loss. As soon as Billy Connolly, for instance, hit the big time and developed a taste for his own independence, the nation had the clubs out. Some of it though, was justified. Connolly took to being pals with unctuous idjits like chat show hosts: he took to Southern living, and Oxbridge-educated bints: he went a bit soft. Sure, it *is* a softer life down in the Home Counties and Connolly doubtless wanted to get out of the cold, damp, bitter, climes of our national affection: he had talent enough for exile.
>
> It is hard to take all the same: Billy Connolly at the horseriding, uttering demure wee words like 'lovely', and 'super', going vegetarian. You can't help feeling let down a bit, and Billy would be daft to care about that.

Connolly, who made his name as a stand-up comedian in Scotland, found his act exportable and almost immediately took it and himself the hell out. But his image is exactly that of the hard man, the Glasgow keelie, the Sauchiehall Street Saturday-nighter throwing out jokes and throwing up a mixture of chips and Tennent's Special Export beer. Connolly is big, bearded, doesn't give a bugger for anything, and says so brutally. As an image-maker for the Scots, confirming Southern prejudices, he is as contemporary as Harry Lauder is dated. The Scots adored him and he played up to them. He roared against every Scottish solecism, and the Scots, recognizing one of themselves putting the Scots in their place and colluding with them in their national taste for satirical self-derision, reinforcing the Scottish stereotypes, shrieked with pleasure. They liked his wickedness and his wit. Now that Connolly is a success in the South, they are not so pleased. Now he appears to the Scots to have become corrupted by easy living and seduced by his own success. He has cast aside some of his Scottishness, and he will not easily be forgiven. He still trades on, but is thought to have rejected, his roots. He has skidded on his own banana boots.

'Going soft' is the thing most Scots fear for themselves and their successful exports. It is as though being Scottish, or maintaining that Scottishness, is a constant struggle, a continuously conscious effort. Jack McLean, having wagged the finger at Billy Connolly, shakes a fist at another folk-hero, Jimmy Reid:

> The former spokesman for the UCS [Upper Clyde Shipyards] work-in was not only a Scottish hero, he was a working-class hero to boot. He was something of a hero to myself as well, back in the days when he was the Scottish Secretary of the Communist Party. He was a different political animal altogether then. Far from being an articulate, liberal, soft-line Communist, Reid was once regarded as an articulate, Stalinist, hard-line Communist Party apparatchik. It was a style of course, and Jimmy was ever a man of style. He was criticized for it within the party of course. I never criticized him: it was his best quality; it is what made him fit into journalism as easily as he did.

Here comes the criticism now, however. I am joining in with the other critics. I join most of the Labour Movement in it. No doubt Jimmy Reid was sincere in his strictures to the miners in his columns to the ordinary readers: Reid was ever a sincere man. And it is hardly my place to reprove a fellow columnist for his opinions, no matter how wrongheaded I think them to be . . . [*But, nevertheless, and notwithstanding, Jack McLean lays into a Reid who has seemingly sold his radical birthright for a mess of liberal mush.*] One of his blatts described Jimmy as 'powerful, provocative, punchy', when anyone can see that his views are bland and obvious in the main, and would pass for punditry in a golf club lounge bar. Jimmy Reid, failed radical, has turned into a joke columnist: the sort of *Daily Beast* columnist who is invariably 'The Man Who Says What He Thinks!' Reid is reputed to get given fifty thou a year for his weekly vapourings.

Jimmy is doubtless due his fifty grand. He is doubtless due his changed opinions. I am not sure that he is due the both of them together, though I can see how the one leads to the other. What he is due as well however, is an archetypal, even stereotypal, statement of our land. He is due a goodly dose of criticism, for ah kent his fayther. Is not the child the father of the man? And what would the Orator of the Yards have made of the journalist of today, now grown wealthy and flushed with success?

This, in Scotland, is powerful stuff. The man who betrays, apparently, his early convictions, his principles, his origins, and himself, is generally held to be odious and opportunistic. Had he held odious opinions and used them for his own advancement without compromise or fear, he would have been held up as a model Scot, a radical *sans peur et sans reproche*: for we are a nation of radicals (at whatever pole) and we like our radicalism *pur sang*. But the man who goes soft, who moderates his opinions and shuffles his feet when they should be still in a stance, is a dangerous fellow in Scotland: he has learned subtle Southern ways that have always been the doom of the guileless and noble Scot – that, at least, is the Scottish view. Stand still, and stand firm, and stand till the last Scot drops, is still the popular tactic. It takes little account of the Scottish aptitude for quick, intellectual, lateral thinking and capacity for self-preservation under fire.

Honourable failure, if a Scot has been true to principle and faith, is not derided in Scotland. Failure, after all, is a constant. Failure, with time, sometimes becomes glamorized and romantic: thus, Robert Bontine Cunninghame Graham can gild the wilted lily when he writes, at the beginning of *Success*, 'The unlucky Stuarts, from the first poet king slain at the ball play, to the poor mildewed Cardinal of York, with all their faults, they leave the stolid Georges millions of miles behind, sunk in their pudding and prosperity. The prosperous Elizabeth, after a life of honours, unwillingly surrendering her cosmetics up to death in a state bed, and Mary laying her head upon the block at Fotheringay after the nine and forty years of failure of her life (failure except of love), how many million miles, unfathomable seas, and sierras upon sierras separate them?' Their failure was noble, and reflected the national devastations Scotland has continually endured. Scotland's heroes are paradigms of a larger consciousness, and her successes are examples of revenge taken cold for constant humiliations. Every failure is a nail in the Cross of Scotland; every success is a triumph for the Saltire.

Success, naturally, is preferred, however much it may be necessary to reduce the successful Scot to regular Scottish size. Admiration for the Scot who has got a good job – 'a very good position' – is very like the admiration given to one who holds off a siege single-handed. Success may be due to a fairly unique combination of wild imagination in large things and careful attention to small detail. The Scot is often regarded as a plodder, calculating and cautious, picking his way between pitfalls. There is that element in the Scottish character, of course, a discrimination in details that will appear pernickety to others. But, more often than not, the Scot will have a larger vision of the common good or his own benefit. His lively mind will see beyond the pedestrian, everyday grind to far horizons where success ineluctably beckons. His imagination, in daydreams, knows no bounds. If he can get the design of his wings right, he will be a high flyer such as to make eagles envious.

It's all or nothing, in Scotland: the Scot is either a peasant or a princely plutocrat. The middle class, except in the cities and large towns, hardly exists in the sense of England's encompassing bourgeoisie. The great divide in Scotland is between the rich employers and landowners and the poor country or inner-city dwellers. Standards of living have risen since the 1930s, but they are not high, and though many demand assistance from national and local government, there is not much expectation that they will get it. The key to advancement is still seen to be education, and education means a thorough drilling in the three Rs. Lord Cockburn, in his *Memorials*, propounded the view still held by most parents in Scotland: '. . . all the modern substitutes of what is called *useful knowledge*, breed little beyond conceit, vulgarity, and general ignorance.' Putting forward ideas not directly useful in fitting a man for a good job and salary is worse than useless – ideas and, worse, philosophy can only corrupt and distract the eager mind. The mind is a thing to be disciplined. 'Schools and colleges', wrote Robert Louis Stevenson, 'for one great man whom they complete, perhaps unmake a dozen; the strong spirit can do well upon more scanty fare.' He was talking about Robert Burns, who received little formal education but who is generally recognized to have become a great poet despite, or because of, his disadvantages. He is the exception, and Livingstone is the better exemplar: the Scots regard learning much as Dr Johnson regarded Greek – every man should get as much of it as he can.

Scottish schoolmasters from the time of Knox to the days of Nelson, says Charles McAra in 'Scottish Schoolmasters', an essay contributed to *Memoirs of a Modern Scotland*, were accountable to the Kirk Session or the Presbytery. Schools were open to all classes on payment of a small fee, and the schoolmaster was liable to dismissal if he was not satisfactory. Satisfaction was judged not only on teaching ability but also upon sobriety, adherence to the Kirk's strict interpretation of scripture, and subscription to the Westminster Confession of Faith. 'These conditions no longer apply,' notes McAra, 'but two lingering effects can be observed. One is that some Scottish schoolmasters are occupationally prone to turn into auld wives, prissy, precise, prim-mouthed wee men always keeking over one shoulder in case "they" are watching. The other effect has been the direct opposite. Just as Burns was irked by the censure of the Holy Willies, so some Scottish schoolmasters have chafed against the yoke of obligatory rectitude and in a predominantly hodden grey profession have chosen to go figuratively clad in crammasy – much to the delight of pupils, who always welcome the kenspeckle, provided it is worn as a panache for proficiency and not a cloak for incompetence.'

There still survives, too, the bully. He is not only a modern figure: the Scottish schoolmaster, perhaps fearful of not coming up to scratch by softer means, too often ruled with a rod. Cockburn remembers sorely Alexander Christison, head of the Edinburgh High School, later elected in 1806 to the Chair of Humanity in Edinburgh University, who, 'though a good man, an intense student, and filled, but rather in the memory than in the head, with knowledge, was as bad a schoolmaster as it is possible to fancy. Unacquainted with the nature of youth, ignorant even of the character of his own boys, and with not a conception of the art or of the duty of alluring them, he had nothing for it but to drive them; and this he did by constant and indiscriminate harshness.'

Education, until lately, took little account of Scottish culture. It was geared to passing exams; Henrysoun was abandoned in favour of Chaucer, Fergusson for Keats, the Stuarts for the Georges. McAra states that 'in Edinburgh in the late Thirties it was possible for a boy to arrive at the university eager to study literature, but woefully ill-prepared, appallingly ignorant of contemporary literature in general and in particular unaware of what was going on in his own country. Undergraduates of my acquaintance were more likely to have heard of Annie S. Swan [*a Scottish romantic, sentimental novelist*] than of Neil Gunn.' It was not much better in the 'fifties. Most literate Scots with some feeling of nationalism or nationality and an experience of the wider world, will regret that they were taught very little about Scottish history, literature, and culture in Scottish schools. Hugh MacDiarmid's own experience of education in the Borders was that 'Standard English' was the rule and that deviations from it were punished. The vernacular, even now, is for everyday; Standard English is the speech of the classroom.

Standard English was, and is, the language used by those who wish to get on. And getting on is the *ne plus ultra* of Scottish education: a lad of parts with talent, however humble his circumstances, is actively drilled to enter a university where he will take law, medicine, engineering, or a course of instruction that will lead him to a profession. There is no sense among the Scots that a working-class man who has taken a degree has got above himself – there is no upper limit to Scottish aspirations. Now, as ever, education is perceived to be the best hope of avoiding unemployment, which in the mid-1980s can reach as high as forty per cent in some areas of Scotland. An education calls for financial sacrifice among families, a sacrifice of youth in some cases when a student applies himself rigorously to his books; but such sacrifices are gladly made for the advancement of the individual and his family, for the advancement even of Scotland as a whole.

Stevenson's dictum that Scottish schools and colleges make one man for every dozen they unmake gives the lie to the myth of the superiority of a Scottish education. The efforts made in Scotland to educate the mass of the population in the eighteenth and first half of the nineteenth century were remarkable and, to a very large extent, successful in what they set out to do – which was to provide basic literacy and a basic moral education. Scottish education has rested on these laurels too long: it has been, in the latter part of the nineteenth century and for most of the twentieth century, a comparative failure. It did not, for many years after World War II, adapt to the altered needs of individuals or society as a whole. Like industry, it was deeply conservative, restrictive, canny, and unimaginative. At no point did it much involve those it purported to educate, or respond to their needs. In the early years of this century, the radical educationalist A. S. Neill, a Scot, wearily reflected on his achievement as a young teacher obliged to respect the regulations of the Scottish Education Department: 'Tonight after my bairns had gone away, I sat down on a desk and thought, What does it all mean? What am I trying to do? These boys are going out to the fields to plough; these girls are going to farms as servants . . . I can teach them to read, and they will read serials in the drivelling weeklies, I can teach them to write, and they will write pathetic notes to me by and by; I can teach them to count, and they will never count more than the miserable sum they receive as a weekly wage . . . My work is hopeless, for education should aim at bringing up a new generation that will be better than the old. The present system is to produce the same kind of man as we see today.' The system was profoundly reactionary and class-based.

Scottish education never took much heed of the English view that education of the working class would surely lead to its undoing: the Scots did not believe that education corrupted morals or promoted dissatisfaction. On the contrary, a sound – albeit most basic – education could only lead to improvement of the individual in a civilized society. Two powerful figures in the eighteenth century promoted this enlightened view – Adam Smith, who taught at Glasgow University, and his disciple Dugald Stewart, Professor of Moral Philosophy at Edinburgh University. Malthus looked upon Scottish working-class education and was satisfied that the 'knowledge circulated among the common people . . . has yet the effect of making them bear with patience the evils which they suffer from, being aware of the folly and inefficacy of turbulence. The quiet and peaceable habits of the instructed Scotch peasant compared with the turbulent disposition of the ignorant Irishman ought not to be without effect upon every impartial reasoner.' Where education, and thus enlightenment, was given to every man, there would be found benefits to the state of sweet reason and consequent happiness or, at least, quiet acceptance of the human condition.

Scottish education was, points out Smout, democratic to an extent but, basically, meritocratic in that a small élite, from the mass who had gained basic literacy, was selected as worthy or able to proceed to higher education. In the schools under control of the Church in Scotland, all pupils received their elementary education together – but only a few proceeded further. There was substantial pressure on a working-class child to go out to work as soon as possible and thus contribute to the family purse. Those who remained at school, and who went on to university tended to be the children of middle-class parents. It was usually up to a working-class child to continue educating himself in his few leisure hours and, by a supreme effort, to maintain himself at a university. Many who entered the Arts or Divinity faculties failed, since there was no entrance examination and they were either not intelligent enough, or were educationally unprepared, to succeed in gaining a degree.

'The presence of working-class undergraduates [*in Scottish universities in the closing years of the nineteenth century*] however,' says Smout, 'enabled national spokesmen, in a self-congratulatory mood, to maintain the delusion that any Scotsman could, through the tradition of national education, raise himself to any height he cared to aim for, if he had brains and was capable of effort and sacrifice.' Education, involving effort and sacrifice, was therefore regarded not only as a means of escape from the rut but as a badge of moral worth. And it is no coincidence that among the most popular degrees were those of Divinity and Master of Arts – graduates, the morally superior, could be trusted to reinforce their own experience as ministers and teachers of Scottish children. It could be claimed that the opportunity was there for a Scottish child and that it could be lost only through fecklessness or moral incapacity. The system, largely class based, was therefore self-perpetuating.

The significant achievement of Scottish education was that within thirty years, from the passing of Young's Act in 1872 to the beginning of the twentieth century, illiteracy in Scotland had been more or less eliminated. Basically, the three Rs were taught, and children able or wishing to proceed further were either taught at burgh schools ('Higher Class Schools') or, if the means were available to pay for an expensive education, at the new Merchant Company school and those of the Heriot Trust in Edinburgh.

These fee-paying schools were exclusively for the education of middle, upper-middle, and upper class children who were consciously prepared for superior employment. From these schools, and from fee-paying schools in Glasgow, came advocates, solicitors, judges, captains of commerce, landowners and employers. Now and again, even these expensive fee-paying Scottish schools were not considered grand enough, and Anglo-Scots or Scots wishing to anglicize their children, boarded out their offspring at English public schools in the reasonable expectation that they would either remain in England on equal terms with their class-mates or return to Scotland better equipped to take over the responsibilities of the established professions or serve the state as mandarins in the Civil Service. These schools naturally reinforced the sharp class divisions in Scotland and inculcated attitudes and values derived as much from English upper-class canons of behaviour as from Scottish capitalist virtues.

'It is difficult to tell what the Scottish population thought of their education,' says Smout. With considerable acuity, he remarks that the Scots 'had long been conditioned, in a spirit of "here's tae us, wha's like us," into accepting it as the best in the world.' They had been told that education was important, that it was freely available to all, that it offered opportunity – but it had not much advanced from its early reliance on the three Rs: 'formalism reigned supreme: the theories of Continental and European reformers were treated with a smug indifference, and the ideas of the Scottish educational dissidents A. S. Neill and R. F. Mackenzie, though accorded wide respect abroad, were regarded at home either as fads or as subversion.' The Scots are deeply distrustful of anything that smacks of the dangerous development of the psychology of the individual if it threatens to detract from immediate usefulness. The child was regarded for too long as an adult in miniature, and his imagination, if it appeared lively, was beaten back into the straight and narrow. Education was, until the 1950s at least, regarded as an academic discipline, and the principal means of enforcing discipline, attention, and – it was probably thought – intelligence, was regular application of the tawse, a thick leather strap applied with some force across the palm of the hand. The Scottish mind, often subtle, is sadly rigorous and unimaginative when applied to the problems of education. Improvements in the system have occurred, slowly, and often grudgingly, over the past thirty years, and it may be that the Scots may be able to boast again that a Scottish education is treasure laid up in the bank or in heaven – but for the time being, and to the considerable confusion of many pupils, it remains a blunt instrument with which the Scots attempt to knock some brains and sense into their children who are expected to make a success of themselves and be a credit to the country that has constantly ill-rewarded their efforts.

If life is a constant struggle, it is expected that a child should learn its lessons young. If he learns early to knuckle down, to strive and take the knocks, he will be better prepared for later vicissitudes. The Scottish child is bred equally for success or failure – often he is led to expect both. It is not in the Scottish nature to give a child false expectations of an easy path in life: if he learns bitter lessons early, he will not be disappointed later. This is a mark of a poor country.

Prosperity tends to breed complacence, whereas hardship is thought to inspire rugged self-reliance. In fact, poverty can more readily result in energy, that might be constructively directed, merely being absorbed in a straightforward struggle for existence. It is not necessarily the case that daunting conditions inspire one to overcome them – it may be difficult enough merely to cope. The Scot, it has been said, is fierce in attack but becomes quickly demoralized in defeat. It is the exceptional Scot who, with a herring and a pound of oatmeal in his bag, goes out to become a billionaire. The heroic struggle for most Scots is the battle to maintain a good position once it has been achieved. Since the daily, continual effort is so intense, it may seem as though life in Scotland is static. Edwin Muir got it slightly wrong, perhaps, when he perceived the Scots as apathetic: 'The Scots have always been an unhappy people; their history is a varying record of heroism, treachery, persistent bloodshed, perpetual feuds, and long-winded and sanguine arguments ending in such ludicrous sackends as Bothwell Brig. But they were once discontentedly unhappy, and they are now, at least the better off of them, almost contentedly so. And this acceptance of the sordid third or fourth best, imported from every side, is what oppresses one so much as one walks down their streets.'

Though the Scots long for better days, all their history speaks against the possibility of achieving them. This is inevitably depressing, and the Scottish tendency to look back, not so much in anger as despair, is no incentive to do better for the future. The future, if a Scot looks forward, appears problematical. Best, then, to hang on to what one has, or to leave it all behind and start afresh furth of Scotland. The Scots, at least, are conservationists and preservationists: 'what cannot be cured must be endured' is a common apophthegm. There is a deep core of fatalism in the Scots that either excites, or more often dampens, efforts towards improvement. If the ideal state cannot be achieved in this world, no doubt it will be granted to the Scot in the next. Then all things will be balanced; afflictions will be remedied and the prideful shall be humbled. Meantime, the Scot does his best to get through this vale of tears, without shedding too many of his own or being dampened by those of others. He is a great believer in chance and has a lurking respect for luck: in the end, he is more optimistic than not. Scotland may be a depressed country, but – curiously – the Scots are not depressives.

6

———— * ————

A nation epidemical: the migrant Scots

ROBERT LOUIS STEVENSON, describing the sudden collapse of an Edinburgh tenement building (a 'land') in the second half of the nineteenth century, conjured a fantasy of expatriates: 'all over the world, in London, in Canada, in New Zealand, fancy what a multitude of people could exclaim with truth: "The house that I was born in fell last night!"' Scotland's inability, sometimes for good reasons, to retain its homegrown talent is not always a matter for regret. Karl Miller, discussing the schoolteacher Hector MacIver in *Memoirs of a Modern Scotland*, declares that MacIver

> did not blame writers for leaving Scotland or for not writing in Scots or about 'Scottish' subjects: the patriotism which ignored or disparaged them was rejected entirely. The Scotland he cared about included its diaspora. I think he would have accepted that Lord Reith is as much a phenomenon of Scottish Culture as Hugh MacDiarmid, whom in some respects he resembles; that John Buchan, whose romanticism led him to Oxfordshire, Westminster and Canada, is as Scottish as Compton Mackenzie, whose romanticism led him to settle in the Hebrides and finally in Edinburgh's New Town; that no account of nineteenth-century Scottish cultural history can

afford to neglect such expatriates as Carlyle, or even such expatriate stock as the Mills.

On Friday 19 November 1762, the twenty-two-year-old James Boswell paid his official respects to the prospect of London then at his neatly shod feet. He clambered from the chaise that had brought him from Edinburgh in four days, and stood 'upon Highgate hill and had a view of London. I was all life and joy . . . and my soul bounded forth to a certain prospect of happy futurity.' On 20 November he sat down to report fully to a school friend, John Johnson: 'At last I am got to this great Metropolis the object of my wishes for so long; the Place where I consider felicity to dwell and age to be a stranger to. I am all in a flutter of joy. I am full of fine wild romantic feeling to find myself really in LONDON.'

Even towards the end of a life more than usually filled with vivacity and vexations Boswell was writing still, much in the same vein, 'O London! London! there let me be; there let me see my friends; there a fair chance is given for pleasing and being pleased.' He had been neither pleased nor pleasing in Edinburgh, and even London had tested him severely. He had failed in all but his greatest achievement – the *Life of Johnson*, published in 1791 – and only four years remained to him of fame and the pursuit of it. In himself, Boswell probably best exemplified Johnson's dictum that 'the noblest prospect which a Scotchman ever sees is the high road that leads him to England.' It is a quotation that still deeply irritates and animates Scotsmen. They no longer approach London by way of Highgate Hill and do not stop to take stock of the city or futurity at their feet. The train draws in from Glasgow Central to Euston, and out the Scots pour into North London to be dispersed by bus, tube or cab to support a football team, to make a fortune, a name, or merely a noise.

Exodus is a permanent feature of Scotland, and London is but one of many alternatives, often as actively hostile to the Scot as any territory on which he has made his mark over the centuries. Whether to bolster his self-confidence, or to distinguish himself from the ruck of other expatriates in a foreign land, or simply to capitalize on his sole asset, his nationality, the Scot remains Scottish even in his adaptability. He never forgets, like Stevenson, that 'the old land is still the true love, the others are but pleasant infidelities.' Infidelity implies no lack of fascination for the new mother/mistress, the Circe that is the United States of America, the Laïs of Australia, the Amaranth of Africa, the Calypso that is Canada. The siren of success irresistibly lures the Scot to hurry in pursuit. It is a matter of national pride (Scottish pride, that is) that among the signatories to the American Declaration of Independence there were at least four men of Scottish origin – Ross, Morris, McKean, and the Revd Dr John Witherspoon who was indeed born in Scotland, at Gifford, in 1723. He went to America in August 1768, and the last twenty-six years of his life were employed in the service of Princeton University, of which he was President. He was naturally succeeded in office by another Scot. Among American politicians, Aaron Burr and Alexander Hamilton were of Scots descent. Paul Jones, something of a scapegrace in his own country, founded the American navy, and the millionaire philanthropist Andrew Carnegie made his fortune in the United States having arrived there, more or less penniless, from Scotland.

It is invidious to single out the United States as the repository of Scottish genius – Russia, no less, was indebted to Scots emigrants who rose to positions of high state importance militarily, administratively, in many professions, and were absorbed into the Russian aristocracy. The portraits of eminent Scotsmen who made their names and fame in the British colonies, in Africa, in India, in Australasia, adorn enough foreign postage stamps to fill a decent-sized album. The significant exodus of native talent and energy which still goes forth from Scotland diminished the resources available to the mother country, but proportionately – some might say disproportionately – enriched the countries of exile.

The story of the Scottish emigrations, prompted by poverty, famine, political principle, boredom, and victimization, is – to some – a richly romantic story, based in tragedy and historical inevitability or opportunism. From approximately 1715 to the latter years of the nineteenth century, significant numbers of Highland and Lowland Scots were diffused throughout the world. Being a Scot became more often a state of mind than a geographical location. There are millions throughout the world who reckon themselves to be, literally, blood brothers and sisters to the Scots who remain at home. There is no difficulty whatsoever in assembling a room full of sentimental Australians, Canadians, North and South Americans, or Africans for a Burns Supper or a St Andrew's Day dinner. Their hearts are, for that moment, in the Highlands though their physical presence is in Sydney, Toronto, Boston, Rio, or Nairobi. Their emotions, rallied by haggis, whisky, sherry trifle, and a piper in full ceremonials, conjure the cry of the whaup in the heather and sunsets over Arran and the Western Isles. In *The Laroch*, R. B. Cunninghame Graham wrote movingly, and as purplishly as the heather, about the land they, in imagination, looked at darkly through the bottom of their whisky glasses: 'Desolation reigned where once was life, and where along the loch smoke had ascended, curling to heaven humbly from the sheilings thatched with reeds, with heather, and with whins, the thatch kept down with birchen poles fastened with stones, and on whose roofs the corydalis and the house-leek sprang from the flauchter feals.' (They might pause here, for a moment, to reach for Jamieson's *Dictionary of the Scottish Language*, to remind themselves that 'flauchter feals' are long pieces of turf cut with a long two-handled instrument known logically as a 'flauchter-spade'. Of course, of course; how could they have forgotten?) But there are none now to cut the turf: 'no acrid peat reek made the eyes water, or pervaded heart and soul, with the nostalgia of the North – that North ungrateful, hard, and whimsical, but lovable and leal [*loyal, honest* – Jamieson], where man grows like the sapucaya nut, hard rinded, rough, and angular, but tender at the core.'

Cunninghame Graham was a patriot with a command of phrase to twist the heart as he lamented the tragedy of the Clearances, of Scotland dispossessed of men, women, children, tradition, and soul: 'All, all were gone – gone to far Canada, or to the swamps and the pine-barrens of the Carolinas, to Georgia, to New Zealand . . .' and he keenly regrets the failure of the '45 and the defeat at Culloden: 'Land, sky and loch spoke of the vanished people and their last enterprise – their first and last, when far Lochaber almost imposed a king on England . . .' His melancholy anthropomorphism imbues the Scottish landscape with tinges and hues of regret that find a bleak echo in every expatriate heart tuned into the sad music of an old song.

But not all was lost: there was a world to gain. The epidemical Scots are said to have a proverb, quoted by Cunninghame Graham in *A Traveller:* 'the gangin' foot aye picks up something, if it is but a thorn.' This sounds suspiciously off the cuff, like something Cunninghame Graham made up in a burst of happy inspiration. If so, the Scot will say, with grudging respect for a felicity, it's 'nae sae bad'. It expresses perfectly the cautious opportunism of the Scot on the road towards something – God alone knows what – that is either perdition or prosperity. There is, in any event, no sense sitting idly at home. Just as likely as a thorn in the foot is a bag of gold by the roadside, even if it means digging up the road to earn it. That a man with skills will not, generally, starve unless he chooses to be idle, seems to be the principle on which Scottish survival is founded. Hazlitt remarked: 'The Scotch are proverbially poor and proud; we know they can remedy their poverty when they set about it. No one is sorry for them.' The Scots have gone forth and multiplied not only themselves but their fortunes as doctors, clergymen, scholars, mathematicians, astronomers, soldiers, authors, artists and statesmen. As technicians, they are greatly in demand; as merchants, they are treated with respect; as financiers, they have been regarded with awe. Though it must be said, to deflate this encomium (a Scot will always feel suspicious and uneasy when praised too highly), that there have been some notable Scottish scapegraces larded among the credits to Scotland. But these are not dwelt upon.

The experience of a Scottish accountant in British Columbia in the late 1970s is instructive as an example of current attitudes to Scotland and the Scots in Canada and, presumably, in the United States and Australia: he experienced genuine rudeness and resentment when, after completing a two-year contract with a firm of accountants in British Columbia, he announced his intention to return to Scotland. Friends encouraged him to stay, dilating on the glittering triumphs ahead of him in Canada, but perhaps – he now thinks – these friends were envious that he could choose to take his family 'home', as one of the élite who could afford to do so, and make a not wholly commercial decision. He found resentment from Canadians when he was given a rise in salary; they promptly complained about his success, perhaps semi-humorously and without guile: 'You Scotsmen, you always get on.' The Scot who returns, a successful man, to Scotland is greeted with envy on all fronts – from fellow expatriates, from the natives of the adopted land he is leaving, and not least from those he comes home to. These last will mutter among themselves, none too kindly, speculating on his motives for return, commenting on any differences in him they may observe, and closing ranks against any foreign notions he may innocently have imported. His status, however much it may have improved abroad, will immediately, on return to Scotland, diminish to the level it had reached before he left and he will inevitably have to prove himself again in Scotland.

The Lowland Scots are not clannish abroad, as has been said. In Canada, they can be encountered in numbers only at the local Presbyterian church to which the Scot adheres. The Scots abroad do not form support groups like the English who, in foreign parts, will instantly organize a social or a cricket club. Stevenson in Samoa happened to hear of another Scottish expatriate in the islands. They met once, as a matter of form, merely to shake hands and acknowledge their common national identity. The Presbyterian Church, both within Scotland and outside it, has been a considerable force in the lives of Scottish emigrants. In order to deliver subtle sermons that would be understood, the Church found it expedient to educate the Scottish people. The

Scots were drilled to read, at least – it was more difficult to make
them understand the complexities of the disputatious theology
propounded from the pulpit; but literacy, not independence of
mind that might lead to dissension, was the main objective.
Argument could be confounded easily enough once basic understanding was established. The Lowland Scots who emigrated
were, therefore, literate. That they were also browbeaten and
obedient, dour and industrious, thirled to piety and industry by
religion and education, was a considerable advantage in the short
term to their employers and, in the long term, to the Scots
themselves. In *Westering Man*, by Bil Gilbert, a biography of
frontiersman Joseph Walker, the chapter entitled 'The Disposable People' provides a concise, lively history of the Scotch-Irish
in America after 1745. The English and the lowland Germans
had settled more or less comfortably into new lives around the
coast of the Eastern seaboard. What was needed was some
initiative to explore the wild interior of America, and, the English
and Pennsylvania Dutch being disinclined to stir themselves,
'colonial planners turned their attention to the lowland Scots –
the Scotch-Irish, as they came to be known in North America.'
They were something of a second choice, better than nothing,
since 'they were not as skilled, industrious or orderly as the
Germans; but were thought to be very hardy, and they were then
perhaps the most disposable people in all of Christendom.'

They were known as the Scotch-Irish because Lowland Scots,
about 20,000 of them, were transplanted from Scotland to
Ireland from about 1605 to 1620 in order to relieve James VI and I
of his militant countrymen by setting the Scots and the Irish at one
another's throats: a neat solution to the Scottish problem and the
Irish problem. The Presbyterians and the Catholics could fight to
their heart's content among themselves and, thus occupied, be
less troublesome to England. The Scots made a thorough meal of
the Irish, prospered, and established military and economic
power-bases from which they could consider their grievances
against England, and act to redress them. The English moved to
slap down the Scots in Ireland by taxation, religious pressures,

and import controls, so that by the beginning of the eighteenth century the Scotch-Irish were reduced once again to a condition of poverty and impotence. At this point, recruiting agents from the North American colonies moved in with insidious promises of free land and golden opportunities in the New World.

The demoralized Scotch-Irish, seeing little profit in staying put in Ireland, fell for these expansive promises which were in fact directed more towards the comfort of settled Americans than the emigrants, who were privately thought to be a suitable first line of defence against the Red Indians who caused terror and alarm among English and Dutch settlers. Thinking that the Scotch-Irish 'if kindly used will be orderly . . . and easily dealt with', and were likely to be grovellingly grateful for their rescue from poverty, the Americans were astonished to find that they had imported foxes into their hen-coops: the Scotch-Irish settled where they landed and refused to budge. They certainly refused to march in orderly procession far into the interior to take up penny-an-acre properties in the wilderness and pave the way as troubleshooters for grandees like land-owning Philadelphians eager for easy, profitable, trouble-free development to the West. The Americans had wanted colonists, and they not only had got them, they were stuck with them. There was no reason to move inland when the coast was self-evidently underdeveloped. The audacity, the ingratitude, the self-interest and bloody-mindedness of the Scotch-Irish appalled the American potentates who had brought this swarm of 'bold and indigent strangers' upon themselves.

They settled, mostly, in the Appalachians where, for seventy-five years, from the 1720s, says Bil Gilbert, they 'starved, froze, drowned, were burned out; were stung, poisoned and mauled by beasts; scalped, ravaged, tortured by Indians; went mad, became suicides and drunks, chopped each other up in bloody intramural feuds and brawls.' When they had learned to survive, they squared their shoulders, kicked the rocks that had taught them such grim lessons, let off a few parting shots to echo as a reminder that they had been there, and lit out at last for the frontier. They battered their way across America to the Pacific, secure in their capacity to meet any difficulty with brute force. They were not subtle: they were as refined as a pile-driver. Gilbert sums up the qualities that enabled them to succeed:

> They had become an exceptionally physical people who admired prowess more than cleverness, were inclined to confront their problems, express themselves, and take their pleasure through action. When stimulated, they were capable of extraordinary feats of energy, violence and bravery, but they were impatient, easily bored, made indolent and slovenly by routine, repetitious work. With all individual exceptions granted, they were, because their survival had often depended upon their being so, pragmatic, avaricious and pugnacious. They were not over-burdened with abstract principles or conventional ethics, but they were mortally stubborn about expressing and protecting their interests. ('Lord, grant that I may always be right, for Thou knowest I am hard to turn,' ran a Scotch-Irish prayer.) They had become a very hard or, as some of their critics claimed, even brutal people. But the North American frontier was a hard, brutal place. On it many of the Scotch-Irish traits which gentler Europeans regarded as weaknesses and vices turned out to be strengths and virtues.

As has been remarked already, the Scot's determination, Calvinism, devotion to achieving his purpose (which came, like grub, before ethics), and his training in various hard schools run by his mortal enemies – Nature and the English – fitted him for survival. If he could not, or would not, adapt to the land or circumstances, then the land and circumstances must be adapted to suit the Scot. He gave his new environment little that was soft in the way of art, learning, or the gentler things of civilization – he took his learning from his situation and, gauging its weaknesses, used it mercilessly for his own profit – where profit was possible. He might merely have got a thorn in his gangin' foot, but he'd cut a branch from a tree, lodge it firmly under his armpit, and hobble on. Gilbert properly says that, 'It is at least arguable that more than any other single happening, their [*the Scotch-Irish*] response (tempered by their European history) to the Appalachian frontier created our [*American*] cultural and behavioral norms. Others were to contribute to, alter and decorate it, but the Scotch-Irish laid down the base, to which everyone else adjusted.'

Apart from the Scotch-Irish from Ulster, Scots from the Highlands had been sent as prisoners after the 1715 rebellion to the plantations in Virginia, Maryland and South Carolina where, as bond-servants, they generally made the best of a not-too-bad job. They were thought superior to the black slaves and often set in authority over them. Transportation was, more often than not, the beginning of a new song rather than the end of an old one. Once established, the Scots busily, efficiently and officiously set about consolidating their position. The first Governor of North Carolina, William Drummond, was a Lowland Scot, and James Blair became Governor of Virginia. He was resentfully accused, probably with perfect justice, of showing partiality to other Scots. Successful settlement encouraged the emigration of other Scots, Highlanders in particular, and land grants of not less than one hundred acres were registered to them with increasing frequency during the eighteenth century.

The Indians of the East Coast liked these Scots: 'When the Highlanders landed they were caressed by all ranks and orders of men, but more particularly by the Indians . . . [*who*] flocked from all quarters to see the strangers, who, they believed, were of the same extraction as themselves, and therefore received them as brothers.' This welcome had something to do with the particular form of dress of the Highlanders who, fresh off the boats, still wore their plaids and tartans and feathers in their bonnets. But as they established themselves they showed their true colours to the white Americans, who discovered them to be ubiquitous, ambitious, and capable. Soon the Scots infiltrated the professions, the army, the political administration, medicine, religion and commerce. They were everywhere, knocking out niches for themselves and generally behaving like energetic ants among idle grasshoppers. English and Dutch settlers who had preceded the Scots had grown soft and indolent; they were easily upstaged and undermined. No sooner had one group of Scots established themselves than there was another boatload on the way, just as canny-eyed and covetous. They were much disliked by the Americans. At the date of the signing of the Declaration of Independence there were eleven Congressmen of Scottish origin, and George Washington numbered nine Brigadier-Generals of Scottish descent among his staff. After the War of Independence the Scots became fully assimilated into the American way of life and culture to which they contributed so profoundly. They gave up their kilts, their Gaelic, and their clannish traditions and became patriotic Americans first, sentimental Scots last.

What was left in Scotland? Not much, according to Edwin Muir whose main impression, in the early 1930s, was that:

> Scotland is gradually being emptied of its population, its spirit, its wealth, industry, art, intellect, and innate character. This is a sad conclusion; but it has some support on historical grounds. If a country exports its most enterprising spirits and best minds year after year, for fifty or a hundred or two hundred years, some result will inevitably follow. England gives some scope for its best; Scotland gives none; and by now its large towns are composed of astute capitalists and angry proletarians, with nothing that matters much in between. Edinburgh is a partial exception to this; but Edinburgh is a handsome, empty capital of the past. And no civilization that is composed merely of exploiters and exploited can endure for long. Glasgow, Dundee, Aberdeen and Greenock are now following Edinburgh. They are monuments of Scotland's industrial past, historical landmarks in a country that is becoming lost to history.

That the history of Scotland is becoming a sentimental legend to its former nationals is pointed up by the necessity, in 1985, to teach the descendants of Scotto-Americans about their heritage. Or, at least, as a piece of neat, chauvinistic opportunism in the best tradition of Scottish enterprise, that is the view of one Hamish Tear who, after two years in Colorado, is reported in a Scottish newspaper as having said that most Americans know very little about Scotland. There is very little reason why American Poles, Chinese, Japanese, Italians, Jews, Lithuanians, Czechoslovaks, Greeks, or any other representative group of the huddled masses that America has attracted should know anything about Scotland, which they generally believe to be an outpost of England. Thanks to Mr Tear, however, they may now learn that it is a country with a distinct identity, possesses a quantity of trees and mountains, several golf-courses, some accessible islands of cold beauty, and that most Scots speak English, or a variety of local dialects more or less comprehensible to English-speakers. The claymores have been broken up. The Scots are safe to visit.

Canadians, by contrast, have not forgotten their Scottish traditions. Many Scots, as United Empire Loyalists, moved to Canada from the Carolinas after the War of Independence; other Scots moved to Nova Scotia from New York, New Jersey, Maine and Pennsylvania and formed a Scottish enclave. Regular emigrations, even into the 1980s, continue. Fresh Scottish blood invigorates the old. The result is that many Canadians are more Scottish than the Scots – small boys can be seen parading in Canadian back gardens, puffing at the bagpipes, a sight not common in Scotland. Interviewed in the *Scotsman* on 2 March 1985, the Canadian short-story writer Alistair Macleod stated:

My parents were both from a place in Canada called Inverness County – named that for the obvious reason. When people from Scotland went over there [*in the late eighteenth century*], they went to a large extent in family groups from individual islands, like Eigg, and intermarried and carried with them the whole body of whatever it is that people carry with them – folk-lore, emotional weight. Because it was all open to them, they settled pretty much where they wanted to. Cape Breton Island and Nova Scotia remained rural for a long time, and fairly isolated. And because there was no-one else to integrate with, they stayed very much to themselves almost for six generations.

So that if you look at my ancestry and my wife's ancestry, there's no-one who's not from the Highlands and Islands of Scotland. All of our ancestors bear those names: Macleod, Maclellan, Macdonald, Rankin, Beaton, Walker, MacIsaac, Gillis, MacDonnell, Campbell, Macpherson, Maclennan. In 1985, this is still who we are. And that is why there is this affinity on the part of those who emigrated for those who remain. When you think that this is good you say that people were stable for several generations: when you think of it in negative terms, you could say that they were static. Although my wife has adequate Gaelic, we are really the first generation where the breakdown of that culture is beginning to occur.

The Scots do not readily abandon their own heritage: they are not eager to be assimilated into another culture if their own can be imposed upon it. Alistair Macleod does not think of himself 'as anything like an "instant" North American, not sure of his mother's maiden name. The idea of the melting pot, much encouraged in America, has not been encouraged in Canada; you know, the idea that people come from Scotland or Norway or wherever, and that once they've dipped in North American waters, they forget all their history and become instant American. The cliché is that you think of America as the melting pot and of Canada as a mosaic composed of individual areas – here are the Scots, and here the Ukrainians, the Icelanders, and they're spread out like that across the country. I think of it as inhabiting a single room within a larger house; inhabiting both.'

This carefully cultivated and preserved feeling for the mother country is a difficult emotion for the indigenous Scots to deal with. In 1985 it was alleged by the *Toronto Star* that Glasgow was supposed to be playing host to the third International Gathering of the Clans and had failed to respond appropriately. The lack of organization and facilities for participants and spectators was said to be scandalous. 'Eight bands led the way through the rain-sodden city centre and the celebrants followed in buggies and rented cars. But they found that their Scottish hosts were far from ready to receive them,' said the newspaper. 'Glasgow simply forgot they were coming and the city has been able to offer its overseas visitors nothing more than a civic reception and the free use of a local gallery for the festivities.' Three thousand Americans, Canadians and Australians mooned bemusedly through Glasgow looking for local colour – a touch of tartan through the rain, perhaps; but an Australian, Mr Bruce McPhee of Melbourne, was Scottishly stoical: 'Scots just do their own thing and I know a lot of Scots think the Gathering is a joke. It is Canada, America, and a few Australians who take the most interest.' The *Toronto Star* found and quoted a Glasgow grand-mother who didn't know 'what all the fuss is about. It's not a long time since I've seen a man in the kilt.' Commenting in the *Glasgow Herald* on 24 May 1985, Rennie McOwan and Douglas Lowe pointed out that sensitivity to class had entered the clans. In a passage to warm the heart of Edwin Muir, they wrote:

The clan societies in the United States and Canada are often moving and touching affairs in their heart-warming enthusi-asm. What makes one uneasy is the bid to hob-nob with British aristocracy, so it starts to become a modern class thing, a question of social standing, and although latterly, in Highland history, clan chiefs did become Highland landlords with an Anglicised background and feudal ideas dominated the auth-oritative but close and familiar relationship between clansmen and chief, it is far removed from the idea of mutual bond. A modern clan society that has a society 'social' standing is false.

It can also be an anaesthetic between a person and Scot-land's needs, a tartan mist across the eyes which clouds such unpalatable facts as multiple urban deprivation, growing un-employment, increasing migration, the unacceptable face of feudalism (never mind capitalism) in some Highland areas, the absentee or foreign owner of the former, great clan lands, and the emptying of glens of native people.

The Scot abroad tends, generally, to be upwardly mobile, anxious to 'improve' himself materially and socially, so that it is hardly surprising he remembers his country's past only in so far as it reflects and benefits himself and his status. The problem appears, to McOwan and Lowe, to be that a Gathering of the Clans is a fabricated event, sponsored or at least encouraged by the Scottish Tourist Board and local authorities in hopes of some material gain, but that the Scots themselves are not glamorized by such an affair and tend to ignore it. 'They do not regard it, in the main, as something for them but for others who are more eccentric or exhibitionist. They simply see no connection between them and some clan chiefs of the droopy kilt, the Mayfair accent and London homes, and who can blame them? . . . the weakness of the clan gathering in Scotland is that the heart-and-emotion overseas formula is being unthinkingly operated over here and the climate and the atmosphere does not suit it.' Unless some realism and modern thinking about how best to enrich Scotland is adopted by the clan chiefs and their cohorts, argue McOwan and Lowe, gatherings of the clans in Scotland 'will be a colourful affair of some minor tourism interest but largely irrelevant to the territories once held by one of the world's great races.' Much the same may be (and is) said about the Edinburgh Festival.

In the late twentieth century, expatriates and their descendants come to Scotland to recover or play out their heritage, to discover or, perhaps, re-invent it. There has been a subtle change in the Scots themselves: Dr Anne Smith, as Scottish a dame as you could wish to meet, is thirled to travel for various good reasons, prime among them the fact that Scotland reinforces the Scottishness of its children. Dr Smith considers that the single strongest advantage of travelling furth of Scotland (and beyond England) is that in Italy, or Greece, or anywhere in the globe, she is no longer obliged to think about her Scottishness. She cannot entirely cast it aside, but it is a relief not to have it constantly in her mind as the sole, unassailable *modus vivendi*. That there are other races, other cultures, other traditions, other heritages, perhaps just as good in their perverse ways, is a modern revelation to the gangin' Scot formerly so encased in his Caledonian rectitude. He no longer goes forth as a proselytizing missionary of his own culture, religious creed, or his own undoubted superiority of character.

Yet it was precisely that missionary spirit that has been the greatest success, many believe, of the Scots. More or less as a direct result of the Scottish emigration, prompted by poverty and failure in Scotland, the modern world as we know it has come into being. The Scots may be said to have invented the modern world. Professor Norman Stone, a Scot, has recently written: 'If you measure the richness, in terms of content and future, of countries of the world that contributed towards the civilization that we now know, Scotland would be way ahead of anywhere else except maybe Jerusalem.' If the Jews have given the world the moral precepts of the Mosaic Law, the Scots have given the no less influential tenets of Calvinism that, transformed into Presbyterian Puritanism, have superseded the supposed fecklessness of Catholicism. Irish Catholicism in particular was much denigrated and despised by moral Scottish Presbyterians who, when they gained a toehold in any potentially antipathetic culture, imposed the harsher values of Protestantism and all that it implied for the moral good of the community they infiltrated and infected.

To continue to quote the pithy Professor Stone: 'In Catholic countries, a great part of the GNP went into groaning, baroque buildings, on Vatican lines, while entrepreneurs were chased out and the poor were eventually fobbed off with soup-kitchens and pawn-shops . . . In Scotland, and other Calvinist countries, you had a small box marked "church", a small box marked "school", and a small box next to them marked "work-house"; you were lucky, in fact, if there was not a gallows next door, destined for the poor vagrant. The result? Protestant countries were literate by 1600, and by the nineteenth century led the world in technology and enterprise.' No doubt this is a grand over-simplification of a long and complex process, but it is instructive to wonder what the Scots might not have made of, say, Mexico had they landed and colonized there rather than in North America. Calvinism enabled the Scots to pull themselves up by their boot-straps, to attend immediately, even under the most testing conditions, to the pressing priority of establishing settlements that within a very short time boasted a school (and quickly, more often than not, a university), a church, a law court and – soon enough – a constitution. The Scots, like most Protestants, were aware of power and set about single-mindedly to get it and keep it in order to establish themselves and their precepts.

Success is the spur for the Scots, and to win it they transcend the self in order to establish the collective within which the individual can function in his own, and the collective, interest. That conditions were not favourable for success in Scotland itself is Scotland's tragedy – that conditions were established elsewhere for success is Scotland's glory and, for better or for worse (there is some continuing dispute), the Scots have had a profound and significant influence on the Western world as we experience it today. That that influence combines faults with virtues is inevitable – the Scots, as a race, may be idealists but it was not within their capacity to found the ideal state in Scotland or elsewhere. The Scots had ideas derived from ideals which they propounded and practised – it is to their intellect, as much as to their technological genius and their industriousness, that we bow the head in wonder if not always in approval.

7

_____ * _____

Clans and chiefs:
communality among the Scots

O NE of the most enduring myths about Scotland is that
Scottish society remains somewhat Ruritanian, composed
of princes and peasants. There is no doubt that the grandest
Scottish titles are very grand indeed and are, in most cases, much
superior in lineage to many English titles which, if they have not
been bought outright, have at least shady origins. Not many now
are pre-Norman: not a few are *arriviste*. The longest-established
Scottish titles derive from lands immemorially held by chiefs and
their clans, and there is very little dispute about origin – however
much doubt there may have been, on occasions, as to the fitness of
the possessor of a title to hold it. English lords probably had more
money, but the Scottish lords and lairds had more style and class.
As late as 1826, when Glengarry died in the wreck of a steamer off
the coast near Fort William, the pomp of a horse-drawn hearse
was denied him by clansmen furious at the offence that would be
given to the ancient proprieties. In keeping with tradition, the clan
chief was borne to his grave, carried shoulder high, by the hands
of his own people. Full ceremonials were accorded Glengarry's
corpse, and the occasion of his burial was ornamented by an
appropriate flash of lightning and peal of thunder that counter-
pointed the wailing of 'Ochone, ochone' by his loyal kinsmen.
This remarkable potentate died with debts of £80,000. To meet

them, his estates had to be sold. This was not uncommon, since clan chiefs had begun to develop a taste for the good life enjoyed by their English peers.

The Scottish aristocracy are considered to be romantic. When they had polished up their manners, they set about acquiring enough money to maintain them. Either they sold their estates, or they married English and American heiresses, wooing them with talk of great tracts of land and castles. What they omitted to say was that the cattle lived on the ground floor, the castle had no roof, and the piper who paraded round the breakfast table, blowing his bagpipes, considered himself no whit inferior to his supposed master. 'Everyone in Scotland,' claim Ann Barr and Peter York, authors of *The Sloane Ranger Handbook*, confidently, 'lives in the big hoose, built, crenellated and turreted either in 1450, 1760, 1870 or 1911. One cannot live in a modest "gentleman's house" in the country in Scotland – there aren't any. There are no modest gentlemen. The land is poor so everyone has thousands of acres.' The 'big hoose' is generally dispiriting. 'Decor and good taste die up there in the thin air. Outsiders are shocked and fascinated by the brown, orange and yellow lampshade circa 1953 in their hideously uncomfortable bedroom in the unheated part of the castle. When you run a bath the water's brown and the ornamental fountain on the front lawn empties. Dew settles on the bedclothes before dawn.'

Small wonder the owner or heir of the 'big hoose' prefers a small service flat in Knightsbridge, close to Harrods and only a taxi ride away from his club in Pall Mall. Restoration and gentrification of big and horrendously money-devouring houses can only nowadays be undertaken by rich Americans, Europeans, or oil-rich sheikhs who will generally turn their Scottish properties over to a charitable foundation (reserving some rights of residence for themselves) for tax purposes and, at a fraction of the cost a Scot would have to shell out, rehabilitate the property in a suitably ethnic fashion. Despite the attraction of Georgian, Victorian, and pre-Adamite castles, mansions, and shooting lodges in Scotland, many are falling irreversibly into terminal disrepair and must soon be demolished unless they can be retrieved for use as hotels, adventure centres for burnt-out executives, charitable foundations and time-sharing holiday homes, or rebuilt and refurbished as tourist attractions.

Partly owing to marriage, partly owing to the reluctance of Scottish chiefs and their families to reside on (or even keep) their Scottish estates, partly owing to the need to earn money in commerce, finance, or the professions, that puzzling hybrid known as the Anglo-Scot has evolved. The Anglo-Scot is as likely to be upper-middle class as aristocratic, since the bourgeois Scots who made money in the late eighteenth and nineteenth centuries turned to English schools and Scottish imitations of English public schools as appropriate for the education of their children. The Scottish *nouveaux riches*, who had prospered as landowners or employers in the tobacco trade, in shipbuilding and in the ownership of coal mines, looked to the established English upper and upper-middle classes for their social cues. They may not have adopted all the conventions of the English social order, being cautious Scots who reprobated all but the sternest values, but they recognized a certain social polish that was useful in business and they knew the value of a sound education that was, as has already been noted in a previous chapter, conducted in circumstances that offered possibilities for social and commercial advantage and advancement.

In Glasgow and Edinburgh, fee-paying schools were set up for the sons and daughters of the grand bourgeois. *The Prime of Miss Jean Brodie* by Muriel Spark gives an accurate picture of one of these Edinburgh schools, for girls, as it existed in the middle years of the twentieth century.

The Anglo-Scot is raised in a different tradition – a tradition that sets him apart from Scottish egalitarianism and reinforces class distinctions that are basically foreign to the Scots. It is undeniable that the Scots are snobbish – but they are snobbish about being Scots, not about their place in a social hierarchy. The English hierarchical class structure is, at best, shaky in Scotland. It is an import that has been partially imposed upon the Scots who are, for all their pride of lineage, closer to Americans in their view of social class distinctions. Americans who have made successes (in conventional terms) of their lives do not, as a general rule, attempt to disguise or minimize humble origins. Neither, as a general rule, do the Scots. It is no disgrace in Scotland to have 'made good', and in America it redounds to a man's honour to have done so. What does exist in Scotland, more strongly than pride of class or allegiance to a social norm, is pride of family and pride in self.

The Anglo-Scot is undeniably split: it is a matter of some social benefit to claim Scots ancestry, but it is thought rather provincial to live there full-time. The Anglo-Scot who lives in London, or in the Home Counties, will rattle on endlessly about his Scottishness and his longing to be back in Scotland during the Scottish social season; whereas the Anglo-Scot in Scotland will ceaselessly attempt to affect a social superiority by accentuating his English education and interests so as to distinguish himself from the Scottish rank and file. He will be more and more gentrified in a country of natural gentlemen. He will hardly endear himself to the Scots who have very little patience with such affectation. The Anglo-Scot has an identity crisis (of the most chronic rather than the acute variety) which is his alone. He may think better of himself by maintaining his affectations, but his pretensions cut no ice with the generality of the Scots.

The most ineradicable thing about a Scot is his accent. Most Scots see no reason to change their accent when they leave Scotland, but those who do are probably on the make and recognize that a broad Glaswegian or a sing-song Aberdonian accent is, to most foreigners, impenetrable. The Scottish comedian Stanley Baxter has even published a translation of some of the more puzzling Glasgow idioms. It would have been useful to a Portuguese shopkeeper confronted a few years ago by an Ayrshire schoolboy who thought he had been shortchanged. Indignant at the attempt to swindle a money-conscious Scot, the boy held out one hand and, with the other, pointed a finger at his eyes, saying, 'C'moan, c'moan, d'ye see ony green in my e'en?' Broad Scots is as much a foreign language in Tunbridge Wells as in Lisbon, and it is almost inevitable that an expatriate Scot or an Anglo-Scot will wish to dissociate himself from the basic crudity of much Scottish speech. A Scot who returns to Scotland with his accent changed is thought to have changed everything else – he is regarded with deep suspicion. Because, of course, language is basic to a distinctive culture, and it is influenced by regional or local accents. Edwin Muir thought that the Scots regarded the 'possession of an accent approximately English . . . as a mark of social and intellectual superiority'. That was certainly true in the mid-eighteenth century when a large number of Edinburghers turned out (Boswell among them) to attend the Irish actor Thomas Sheridan's lectures on correct English usage. Muir reinforced his statement about possession of an English accent by pointing out that, 'English is the language of the schools, the universities, the pulpits, the business world, the Press, and finally of the Bible itself, which, though it is not read now as widely as in the past, has had a deep influence on Scottish ways of thought, even about the English, and has, through centuries of usage, engendered a reverence for that tongue.' The recent success of the translation of the Bible into Broad Scots, and the decline in influence of standard Oxford English in the media (regional accents, though not regional dialects, are now acceptable on radio and television), perhaps have undermined the reverence for standard English in Scotland over the past few years, and the upsurge of nationalism – though SNP politicians still address constituents and the Commons in standard English – gave the Scots a more conscious awareness of their own speech.

'We have a great tradition in Scotland of linguistic ability,' wrote Hugh MacDiarmid complacently. 'It's a facet of our internationalism as compared with English insularity.' And Edwin Muir admitted that the Scottish 'ability to speak English is an accomplishment, however, and little more; and though it may bring with it a slight contempt for colloquial Scots, as a language suitable only for humble needs, it does not involve any wish or any intention of becoming English or denying the Scottish tradition.

And besides, English as it is spoken in Scotland is very different from English, and certainly very full of Scottish character.' A proficient Scots speaker of standard Queen's English in Scotland is quite liable to lapse suddenly into a turn of phrase or a word that would be perfectly incomprehensible to an Oxford don or a lady from Leamington Spa. And it is a fact that a Scotsman, however Anglicized, travelling by train from Euston to Glasgow, or from King's Cross to Waverley Station, will imperceptibly change his accent on crossing the border. The Scots, adept mimics of modes of speech, perhaps do not confine their natural impressionism to language – the Scots are 'sedulous apes' of manners that they adopt superficially for a particular purpose but which do not profoundly alter their basic Scottishness.

T. C. Smout points out, in *A History of the Scottish People 1560–1830*, that the middle class of the eighteenth and early nineteenth centuries consisted mainly of self-made men. Many of the industrial pioneers were sons of farmers or small lairds in the West of Scotland, and inventive tradesmen. The aristocracy and the landed gentry played very little part in building up Glasgow's business class. 'None of the pioneers were the sons of a noble-man, a baronet or a knight: the aristocracy and the upper echelons of the landed gentry put their children elsewhere. Though they did play their part in industrialisation in other parts of Scotland, it was usually as mine-owners, as investors in transport improvements and as sympathetic landlords rather than as entrepreneurs. The children of professional men, too, were surprisingly rare among Glasgow pioneers.' And 'little was seen of men from the humblest walks of life, the landless agricultural worker, the unskilled labourer, the poor Highlander, and so forth. They found a career in commerce above their reach. The other missing groups presumably disdained it, and looked to a career in Edin-burgh, or in the army or the church, if they could not immediately fulfil their ambition of becoming landowners themselves.' The aristocracy and landed gentry confined themselves to landown-ing, investment and the professions and thereby effectively re-moved themselves from the day-to-day life of provincial society, except when they wished to agitate for a candidate's election to Parliament or be elected themselves.

Up to the mid-nineteenth century, communality gave the Scots their name for rich originality. The Scots were never exclusive in their interests or their recognition of genius. They lacked, certainly, an ability fully to exploit it at home in their own interest, but their major contributions to the wider world have derived from a willingness to harness together the best from all sections of the Scottish society without sacrifice of individuality. The Scottish middle-class, which originated with industrialism, was too widely based to become self-interested as a class and to attempt to set itself apart as a separate section of society – it was inclusive, by and large, rather than exclusive, and took opportunities where they presented themselves. As the century advanced, and gave way to the twentieth century, the Scottish middle class of the larger towns and the cities became more self-conscious and attempted to restrict membership: but until it had identified itself as middle class, on a hierarchical basis, it derived its superiority from morality rather than money, from propriety rather than property.

As often as not, the members of the middle class had very little in common with one another and this, too, prevented the formation of a strong class-based front. Snobbery did exist, of course, but more as a distaste for those who did not observe social conventions rather than as lack of respect for a man's social origins. It has been pointed out that poverty is no great shame in Scotland, and is not considered disgraceful so long – vitally – as it is gracefully endured. The gulf between the Highlander and Lowlander persisted for generations less as a social thing than as a disagreement about moral values. Social rivalry exists less as a matter of material detail than as a matter of moral principle. But the Scots are an envious lot, and the McJoneses have nevertheless a good deal to answer for in their dedication to material one-upmanship.

There is enough competition among foreigners to claim Scottish blood to make the Scots conscious of their Scottishness and, therefore, of their uniqueness and superiority as a race. There really is no need to gild the lily by raking up the past to discover an aristocratic connection. In any case, one never knows what one might find in the best-connected circles – better a cupboard full of good china and silver than the rattling skeleton of some ancestral scapegrace. A good reputation is better than any number of quarterings on a hopelessly blotted escutcheon. Unaccountably, the English and others appear to derive a perverse satisfaction from ancient or far-off family ne'er-do-wells and black sheep who add unfortunate colour to the ancestral history. In Scotland, it is necessary that family members should add to the dignity of the family rather than detract from it, and pride forbids the admission of failure, however spectacular or – to others – amusing. It is not class that counts in Scotland, it is personal dignity in a country where the opportunities offered by egalitarianism imply a responsibility to society rather than an unbridled licence or freedom to exploit that tradition to assume a superiority for oneself or to degrade others.

Awareness of social difference is still, to some extent, dictated by religious and ethnic differences. Irish immigrants to Scotland were particularly abused: they were employed as cheap labour and their allegedly drunken, spendthrift ways, supposedly attributable in part to the pernicious influence of Rome, were found distasteful by staunch, rectitudinous Protestants. Irish immigrants, and – by inference – all Catholics were presumed to be dirty, impious, improvident, and culpable because they did not recognize their moral decline and act to alter the conditions of their degradation. The Highlanders were considered little better in their indolence and, worse, arrogant dignity. The comical Highlander 'Sandy' was as much a figure of fun and ridicule in Lowland Scotland as the Irish 'Paddy': neither could be relied upon for intelligence or industry. The social conditions in the Highlands, as much as in Ireland, were known to be squalid, poverty-stricken, and the natives sunk in listlessness. And who was to blame for these conditions? Not, of course, the sanctimonious Lowlander who had raised himself and his family, therefore his part of the country, from the sin of poverty and the awful consequences of apathy. That there were differences of attitudes between Highlander, Irish Catholic, and Protestant Lowlander is to put it mildly: it would have taken an unthinkable leap of imagination for either side to recognize even a tithe of the other's perception, and neither was capable of sympathy, far less empathy.

This was all quite different from the genuine egalitarianism that flourished in Edinburgh and Glasgow in the eighteenth century. The social clubs of both cities were open, more or less indiscriminately, to all, and a free exchange of views on all subjects was encouraged. From this receptivity and openness flowed the Scottish Enlightenment that produced major and world-shaking ideas and inventions. T. C. Smout, in *A History of the Scottish People 1560–1830*, comments that several of the social, convivial and intellectual clubs were 'the meeting place of the town and University. Adam Smith was also a member of the Literary Society of Glasgow College, founded in 1752; it included most of the professors and many distinguished citizens, and the minutes of the Chamber of Commerce from 1783 onwards testify to the respect in which Smith, in turn, was held by the leading citizens when they came to formulate policy.' Glasgow and Edinburgh were not like London – they were small enough so that everyone knew everyone else and they were continuously in contact with one another. The American city of this period that comes to mind as most resembling Edinburgh or Glasgow is Boston in the eighteenth century. 'It was also to the Literary Society,' Smout says, 'that Joseph Black, when a lecturer at the college, communicated his discovery of latent heat. Black's greatest work, however, was surely his patronage and encouragement of the young James Watt which led to the discovery by the latter of the principle of the separate condenser. There is something altogether symbolic of the intellectual atmosphere of eighteenth-century Scotland that one of the most epoch-making inventions of the industrial revolution should have come about through the meeting of an instrument-maker from Greenock with a chemistry lecturer from Belfast over a collection of astronomical instruments given to the college by a Glasgow merchant who had made his fortune in the West Indies. It was in such an atmosphere at once intimate and intellectual, but in no sense exclusive, that the seed of eighteenth-century genius was most readily able to take root and to grow.' It was this collegiate, collusive effort that took no heed of social differences, that marked the inquiring Scot and his ability to profit from apparently improbable acquaintance with all manner of men and their particular knowledge.

Outside the urban centres, however, in the villages and small towns, there was no (and there still is no) middle class to speak of. Those who, through improved wages and social conditions, might regard themselves as having moved up from working class to lower-middle or middle class are curiously reluctant to identify themselves with a class they still regard as oppressors and snobs. They do not want, in their turn, to be regarded as tarred with the same brush. The middle class, in the mid-twentieth century in country districts, was represented solely by the dominie, the minister, and the doctor. They were the lynch-pins of community life, always reliable as organizers of local meetings, conscripted automatically as elders of the kirk, and immediately available as sources of a reference or advice on matters that, in urban areas, might now be handled by the Citizens Advice Bureau. They were educated men who lived among, and understood, the country people. Very often, mutual respect existed between them, and there was very little feeling of social superiority or inferiority in their relations one with another. As late as the mid-twentieth century, this state of affairs existed in small mining and fishing communities in Scotland. The middle class considered itself an exportable commodity, and perhaps one reason for the lack of class consciousness in Scotland was that the middle class left it regularly and in large numbers to exercise its professional and commercial talents elsewhere. Emigrants tended to return, however, after making their pile, informing the Scots and infecting them with the benefits of their wide experience. Scottish bourgeois society, says Smout, 'might have been provincial, but it was never merely parochial'. And what the bourgeois knew, the working class quickly picked up through observation and education, probably discarding whatever was not immediately useful.

It is perhaps pious to say that clan chiefs and their clansmen were comrades in arms and brothers under the skin. Respect for a nominal superior has never been given lightly by the generality of the Scots. Before the Industrial Revolution, and before the Clearances, master and man, chief and clansman, laird and liege, shared the same sort of life – its pleasures and its vicissitudes – fairly equally. They worked in concert towards common ends, and were united at least in purpose. Each had his own dignity and would not take kindly to depreciation of that dignity from any source. The Scot always knew how to puncture pomposity, prick pride, and pin down pretension. Steadily, nevertheless, the Scottish middle class has become gentrified, and in the process has lost its sense of humour about itself. Moray McLaren refers to 'that lack of courage in pleasure, that fear of being laughed at which is the curse of the Scottish middle class.' In *Return to Scotland* he comments on the difference between London refinement and the Edinburgh variety which 'is . . . always betraying itself by ridiculously coarse lapses, which the native savageness is responsible for'. In McLaren's view, the bogus refinement of the Scottish urban middle class is partly due to internationalism – 'or Americanization, if you prefer that word – [*which*] has invaded the Scots middle class as much as any other middle class.' But behind the glitter and the conscious attempt to seek pleasure lie 'the remains of a puritanism embedded in the minds of these people by four hundred years' subjection . . . their fathers from out that past peered through their eyes and compressed their mouths into involuntary shapes of disapproval.'

The 'refinement' of the Scottish middle classes is a conscious effort. 'Nice' becomes the most depressing word in the language, since it means something has been sufficiently sterilized to make it acceptable to the taste of a modern middle-class Scot who has no wish to be disturbed, or excited, or in any way engaged, with what is presented for his attention. 'Niceness' keeps the savage at bay, and clothes him in propriety. Since the Scots middle class is such an amorphous concept, members or aspiring members of it strive to establish their credentials by aping aristocratic manners (in so far as they understand them) and acquiring the necessary material props. Since the models they adopt are usually English or American, they tend to combine a pseudo-English accent with the glitz of the American consumer society which demands a degree of conspicuous consumption that is, basically, contrary to the thrifty Scottish character. This can only lead to profound mental conflict. The attitudes of the modern Scottish middle class are very little different from those that held sway a century ago: thrift is held in high esteem, dirt is reprobated. Drunkenness and gambling are still regarded with a severe eye. Promiscuity is not encouraged. To be fair, the rigours of morality are being relaxed: in the late twentieth century, allowance is at last being made that misfortune may befall him who is not necessarily blameworthy. This is a significant step forward in liberal-Puritanism, and may lead (one hopes) to the recognition that values other than those found in one's own kailyard are at least worthy of some consideration – though God knows, once a dangerously liberal idea has been allowed to take root, to what manner of excess it may lead.

In dealing with the Scottish aristocracy and upper-middle class, we are obliged to refer again to the Anglo-Scots. Since the Highland Clearances, the Scottish aristocracy has had very little to do with the day-to-day life of Scotland. A few representative hereditary Scottish peers are entitled to seats in the House of Lords, and some have made their mark on politics – notably, in modern times, Sir Alec Douglas Home who renounced his earldom to become Prime Minister (but was given a life peerage on retirement), and the Earl of Ancram who took a degree in Scots law at Edinburgh University in the mid-1960s. From an Oxford-Edinburgh academic base he moved to the Scottish Bar and thence into Parliament to become, in due course, a Minister at the

Scottish Office. There are others who have shone bright, according to their lights, in politics, commerce, and the professions in
Scotland, but generally the Scottish aristocracy takes very little
part in community or local activities. They are no longer expected
to do so, and the days have long gone when they were accorded
loyal deference by the lieges. They have no power, no real status
(except a residual iconic value) because they have effectively
effaced and removed themselves from the arena of local and
national affairs, and their passing from the scene occasions no
real regret. The Scots persist in harbouring some resentment
over what is still perceived by some as their selling up and selling
out their country for a mess of English pottage. That is to put it
colourfully and a mite simplistically, but the generalization feels
true enough to many Scots.

The Highlands, to continue to generalize, have become a vast
game reserve for Sloanes, American or German plutocrats, and
Japanese mandarins of industry who dress themselves up in
plus-fours, their hip-flasks filled with Suntory (more likely,
though, brimming with single malt whisky produced by a
Japanese-owned Highland distillery). Here they are, and here
they will stay from 12 August to the end of September, until
everything that flies, runs or swims has been shot, gralloched or
hooked. The Anglo-Scots all know one another – through careful
intermarriage, they are all related, however distantly, and form a
distinct group united by blood, financial interests, a common
interest in preserving their class superiority (which, unlike Scottish middle-class superiority, is not based on moral grounds but
rather on blood ties in the English style), and a keen sense of
self-preservation. The Anglo-Scot delights in dressing up when
the occasion presents itself. At the drop of a skean-dhu he will dig
out his seasoned kilt, tough old brogues, well-worn tweed jacket,
and stick a bonnet with a feather on his head. Thus accoutred, he
will ramble a local Highland Games or attend an agricultural
show, giving the encouragement of his splendid presence to the
local community who are always glad to see the laird and his lady,
and their house party, enjoying themselves in the open air, hailing

everyone affably. The Anglo-Scot is a colourful type of regular tourist, who will disappear, like the grouse he is in Scotland to shoot, at the end of the season.

In October, the Anglo-Scots of Perthshire, Aberdeenshire, Angus, and the Border country (these being the areas that have the best grouse moors) return to London and the Home Counties to prepare for the round of autumn charity balls, the political conferences, the resumption of Parliament, the beagling season, and the new school and university terms. There is not much to detain them in Scotland: as Geoffrey Madan remarked of the great Argyllshire estate of Ardkinglas – 'The amount there is *of* it; the little there is *to* it.' The land is for grouse and deer – hardly for humans.

There is a particular snobbery about the Scottish social season: it is, without doubt, 'the real thing'. Nobody can buy tickets to it; admission is by invitation only. By Sloane reckoning, Scotland is an aristocratic society. Those social chroniclers, Ann Barr and Peter York, calculate that Scotland possessed some 10,000 noble families in 1800. 'Reckoning on at least four members each, this is 40,000 aristocrats. Three generations later it is probably 120,000.' Few aristocratic Scottish heads have fallen under the axe. Tumbrils rolled to the scaffold or the executioner's block in Scotland only now and again in exceptional circumstances, so that Scotland, a small country, can boast a higher ratio of nominal chiefs to Indians than any other since Tsarist Russia or pre-Revolutionary France. The land could not support so many in idleness or comfort, and thus the sons of noblemen or lairds were put into the professions and the military in order to earn money enough to be able to acquire capital and land. Mrs Elizabeth Grant of Rothiemurchus, born in 1797, wrote of her great-grandfather who 'felt some difficulty in maintaining his sons; the result in the generation to which my grandfather Dr William Grant belonged was that he with a younger brother and a set of half-uncles much about their own age were all shoved off about the world to scramble through it as best they could.' The result is, of course, that every now and again application is received by the

Lord Lyon King of Arms in Scotland from a Canadian, Australian or American descendant of some noble Scottish family for a grant of arms, or a petition is made for the revival of some Scottish title that has fallen into abeyance.

Scottish titles are ancient, remark Barr and York, 'and outsiders don't understand them. A young Australian, after meeting Cameron of Lochiel, thought that Boat of Garten and Mull of Kintyre must be clan chiefs too. There aren't many surnames, so the *smart* McSloanes are followed by their estates and preceded by The.' The smart McSloanes have contrived to keep at least a foothold on their ancestral estates, and the more ingenious have never lost the ancestral castles or shooting lodges. It suits the smart McSloanes very well to rent out a few days' shooting every season to rich *hoi-polloi* in order to pay for the rest of the season's shooting to be enjoyed privately and in gentlemanly manner by the owner and his friends.

The Scottish season itself is kicked off with the Oban Ball in the last week of August. It follows the Argyllshire Gathering at Oban, held on the same day. 'During the day,' say Barr and York, 'men strut about in kilts and plaids carrying cromachs, and sometimes get drawn into a tug-of-war. Women congregate in the Members' Enclosure in point-to-point kit, from which drab disguise they emerge in the evening, full-skirted, tartan-sashed [*the tartan sash is* de rigueur *for Scots, but the English need not affect it – indeed, it is thought rather uppity of them to do so*] and often astonishingly jewelled. Parties come over from Mull. The Princess of Wales's mother [*Mrs Shand-Kydd*] goes, and the names of people in house-parties used to be published in the local press. Rowdiness is out.' In full cry after the games of the season, Nicholas Coleridge reported in *Harpers & Queen*, in November 1983 how he 'reeled through the Oban to Lochaber ball zone.' He drove, but the romantic or nostalgic cram into the Euston to Inverness sleeper, and at an ungodly hour of the morning lurch into the Station Hotel at Inverness for baths (tubs you can lie in at full stretch, endless hot water, wonderfully fluffy towels) and breakfast (toast, marmalade, porridge – with salt, not with sugar and cream – and finnan-haddock with poached eggs) while waiting for the cars.

The *ceilidhs* (Anglo-Scots like to use the ancient, ethnic Gaelic words whenever possible) are held, Coleridge notes, 'in damp village halls hung with tartan rugs, clan banners and antlers appliqued with clumps of heather'. He found it easy to identify someone doing the Highland circuit. They are driving as fast as their hatchback can carry them, ricocheting over cattle-grids, swerving round hairpin bends, ears popping on the Pass of Drumtochter. 'Rushing around madly is great fun. There is no time to stop, not even for a dram, so the glove compartment rattles with hip-flasks of Famous Grouse and bottles of Sweetheart Stout. The Highland circuit is a social assault course played against the clock. A month in the Highlands feels like a year in the Urals. Every ball is exactly one hundred miles further than you'd expected.'

There are eight balls every season, and applicants for tickets are positive-vetted: it is less difficult to join the SAS than to pass muster under the censorious eye of the stewards who approve the guests far in advance of the actual events which include balls at Oban (25 and 26 August), Inverurie (29 August), Aboyne (2 September), Portree (7 and 8 September), Spean Bridge (9 September), Inverness (16 September), Forfar (19 September), and Perth (23 September), which concludes the dance pro-gramme. Women are obliged to wear floor-length dresses, and men must wear Highland dress or white tie. Dinner jackets are only just acceptable, though anyone daring to dress down in such a manner is likely to feel like a character in a Bateman cartoon – the man who wore a dinner jacket to the Perth Hunt Ball. On the first night of the Skye Balls, white dresses and tartan sashes are obligatory for women. Coleridge quotes Roddy Martine, whom Ann Barr describes as 'the only Scottish Sloane Ranger', editor of the *Scottish Field* and co-author of that indispensable vade-mecum, *The Swinging Sporran*, a step-by-step guide to Scottish country dances: 'The same reel frequently has several names. The Duke of Perth, for instance, is called Brown's Reel or

Brownie's Reel in Angus and East Fife, while to the south-west of Lanarkshire, Ayrshire and Galloway it is known as Clean Pea Strae or Pease Strae. Similarly, you often find the Inverness Country Dance called Speed the Plough. Contrary to popular belief, reeling isn't a static tradition. The Reel of the 51st Division, one of the most popular, was thought up in Colditz.' Scottish country dancing is punishing exercise, more akin to a rugger scrum than a polite dip and turn and kick of a pair of flatties. It is more like a national sport than a decorous diversion. Roddy Martine, on a visit to America, 'once went to Grandfather Mountain in North Carolina . . . and hundreds of American Scots were dancing politely round on the mountainside in 90 degrees. They had no idea reeling should be wild and reckless and violent.'

Scottish wildness, recklessness and violence these days is mostly channelled into sport – hunting, shooting, fishing, and football. Golf, though it rouses the competitive spirit, is a decorous game, though a certain satisfaction may be gained from giving a small ball a good thump with a club. Golf is a social, rather individualistic pastime, whereas football is a mass spectator sport. Rugby is still, by and large, for the nobs – football is for the plain man. At one time, in the late nineteenth century, it was so popular that the Church and employers inveighed mightily against it, on the ground that it diverted the working man from work and duty (mostly the same thing). The game takes on a religious element (including the idolization of individual footballers) in that regular games between Glasgow Celtic and Glasgow Rangers are considered spiritual as much as religious contests – Celtic being supported mainly by Catholics and Irish, Rangers being cheered on by Protestants. Neither side is inter-denominational: it would be difficult for a Catholic football player to sign for Rangers, and Celtic takes some care not to antagonize its Catholic fans. Paul Fussell, an idiosyncratic American critic of manners, considers that football is a displacement activity for the Scots, enabling them to identify with winners to compensate for the fact that most football supporters are losers in the game of life. International matches are perceived as tests of Scottish pluck and skill against

English or other alien teams: a sporting victory becomes, naturally, a moral victory – though it is not unusual for Scots to expect to lose even a symbolic test of strength. Fussell also notes that football becomes a suitable subject for conversation in pubs and at work when arcane knowledge of the sport enables a working man to trot out 'dogmatism, record-keeping, wise secret knowledge and pseudo-scholarship of the sort usually associated with the "decision-making" or "executive" or "opinion-moulding" classes."'

Football violence is not new: it was noted in the 1880s, and in 1909 the Rangers–Celtic Cup Final match at Hampden Park was the scene of serious disturbance: bottles and metal objects were thrown on the pitch, spectators swarmed over the turf, the goal posts were torn up and thrown down, fires broke out, gaslights were broken, and stones were thrown at the police and firemen. They promptly threw them back, and the result was serious injury to thirty people and minor injury to a hundred more. Sectarian feeling was perhaps behind this sort of riot, but religious division between spectators was more overt in the 1920s and 1930s when, on one notable occasion during a Celtic–Rangers match, the flag of the Irish Free State was hoisted in competition with the Union Jack, and there was plain hate between Orangemen and Catholics. Few middle-class Scots were involved: few attended the match, because football is almost entirely working-class in its support.

Football unites the Scottish working men, giving them a common interest – it sometimes seems like an exclusive interest, to judge by the conversation in bar-rooms over the weekends and on the factory floor on Monday mornings. The violence of the Scots at football matches, though sporadic and mostly confined to sectarian religious or nationalistic fervour, strikes fear into the hearts of the middle-class English. London streets, on the afternoon of an international match between Scotland and England, are cleared around the ground, shopkeepers board up their windows, pubs close their doors, and the police draft in reinforcements. Drink is banned on supporters' trains, no drink is on sale in the ground or allowed to be carried into the ground, and officials piously plead for peace on the terraces. Bill Murray, author of *The Old Firm: Sectarianism, Sport and Society in Scotland*, published in 1984, comments that sectarian violence earlier this century was possibly encouraged rather than determinedly damped by football club officials as a crowd-puller, so that sectarian violence became institutionalized as part of Glasgow male recreation.

Nowadays, the clubs need all the publicity and support they can get – violence has helped to diminish attendance at football games, and perhaps the fact that the important games are televised has kept the punters away on a Saturday afternoon. In any case, the working man is no longer exclusively dependent on football as an outlet for his energies and enthusiasms, now that he has discovered middle-class interests and can, in most cases, afford to enjoy them. It is at the lowest end of society, among the dispossessed and the disenchanted, that violence flares on and off the pitch. Football is no longer the powerful opiate it once was among the generality of working-class Scots. There are other battles to be fought beyond the gates of the football club. Football has lost its grip as the great adhesive medium that united the working man in a common interest and pride in the spirit of his team.

Rugby has been notably free of spectator violence: the nobs knew how to behave themselves, it must be supposed, though perhaps their outlets for passion were different in kind. No mother worried about her son or daughter attending an international rugby match at Murrayfield in Edinburgh, or a Border country game. Sheepskin coats, tweed jackets and flat caps, camel hair duffel-coats, and hip flasks were the order of the day rather than the motley-coloured bomber jackets, denims, and tackety boots to be found at Ibrox or Hampden Park. Rugby was played at fee-paying schools and academies of higher education, and at the universities in Scotland. Rugby was a sport for middle-class and aspiring upper-class players and spectators. Since it was confined largely to these classes, it was not a large crowd-puller and only attracted mass attention when national teams played teams from Wales, Ireland, France, England, and the Commonwealth. Here, as much as in football, a national victory in rugby equated with a moral victory over another country.

Sport, in Scotland, divides as much as unites the Scots. They are as sectarian in sport as in religion or pride of being a native of a particular place within Scotland: Borderers, Glaswegians, Edinburghers, Highlanders, Islanders, are all, variously, chauvinists. They are all united, nevertheless, in distrust of the aristocratic or Anglo-Scot who keeps his distance from ordinary life in Scotland. Dukes still reside comfortably in their castles, earls still eke out an existence in family seats, but the Scots know little of their diurnal lives. It would be invidious to name names, but there is a core of opinion that the Scottish aristocracy are utterly futile, that their role in modern Scotland is non-existent, and that they have degenerated into wimps and drunks who, even if they were capable of shaking themselves out of their torpor, would be incapable of making any real contribution to the welfare of the country. One might hesitate to endorse this view by giving examples of the degeneracy alleged against the present body of Scottish nobility, and one would be obliged to do so only if the nobility of Scotland seemed likely to arrogate to themselves any form of influence in public affairs. But they keep, wisely, quiet and continue to seek consolation in management of their private affairs, in more or less exclusive contact with their English peers and with one another. They trouble Scotland very little, and are not much missed.

For all the snobbery associated with a Scottish title and a connection with it, the Scottish nobility and the Anglo-Scots do not partake of the Scottish ideals – they have identified themselves, in morals, education, class, politics, language, family ties, financial interests, and residence, with England and the English. They maintain vestigial, nostalgic, somewhat ceremonial links with Scotland but their hearts and minds, except for a few weeks in August and September, are elsewhere. Though the great names of the Scottish nobility resound like clashing metal throughout the history of Scotland, their descendants can make little financial or political capital from the residual nostalgia or respect that such names arouse among the Scots. Since they have no power, and no prospect of any, they have wisely moved on or obligingly died out, their purpose and ambitions at an end in a country that has no need and little love for them.

8

---- ＊ ----

Formerly of better account:
Scotland's Golden Agers

ONLY a Scot, perhaps, could look fondly and optimistically
on Scotland, that land, according to Byron, 'of meanness,
sophistry and lust'. But Scotland was ever worth fighting for.
Scotland has had her heroes – Robert the Bruce, the demi-
mythical Wallace, the Young Chevalier; and her tragic dramas –
Flodden Field, the death of Mary Queen of Scots, Culloden, the
Massacre of Glencoe, the Covenanting period and its allegedly
spotless martyrs. It has had its Camelot – the court of James IV,
who, according to Lindsay of Pitscottie, 'brocht the realm to greit
manheid and honouris', ruled an age of 'guid peace and rest', and
in himself personified all the noblest virtues of his people.
Foreign visitors had been, in some respects, impressed. In 1498
Don Pedro de Ayala, a Spanish diplomat, reported favourably on
Scottish hospitality, on the handsome appearance of the Scots
(though 'they are vain and ostentatious by nature') and on the
kingdom as being 'very old and very noble'. The Scots themselves
he characterized as 'courageous, strong, quick, and agile', but
added, 'they are envious to excess'. Even Dr Johnson, no partisan
of Scotland or apologist for the Scots, softened his views after a
trip to the Highlands and Islands, and conceded that Scotland
and the Scots had their points which, though not necessarily
wholly admirable, were at least different. Scottish victories over

so many vicissitudes, natural and of their own or other people's making, earn regular – though often grudging – respect from would-be critics.

This is perhaps a convenient point at which to describe a few of Scotland's heroes from what have been supposed to be Scotland's Golden Ages. It should be pointed out, before anyone proceeds in expectation of an encomium or an *éloge*, that the Scots have an infinite capacity for absorbing failure, for valuing and honouring a noble but doomed stance. If tragedy, or failure to capitalize on success, is their constant condition, they are apt to memorialize and remember both as grand in inception, at least.

Like the visionary Martin Luther King, Lord Belhaven had a dream – a dream of Scotland in the days of its majesty and innocence before threat of oppression by the Union with England. In his speech to the Estates in Edinburgh in 1707, bewailing the end of 'ane auld sang', reported by Daniel Defoe in his *History of the Union*, Belhaven – like any fearful seer of Scotland – saw his country diminished in every way. In hindsight, his most apt and prophetic utterance was, 'None can Destroy Scotland, save Scotland's self.' To put itself under what Belhaven saw as vassalage would be tantamount to treachery and treason against Scotland and the Scots by Scotland and the Scots.

Belhaven saw the fading away of a 'Free and Independent Kingdom' with the loss of 'A Power to Manage their own Affairs by themselves, without the Assistance and Counsel of any other'; the levelling of a 'National Church . . . voluntarily descending into a Plain, upon an equal level with Jews, Papists, Socinians, Armenians, Anabaptists, and other Sectaries'; the Peerage of Scotland reduced so as to be 'put upon such an Equal Foot with their Vassals, that I think I see a petty English Excise-man receive more Homage and Respect, than what was paid formerly to their *quondam* Maccallanmores'. The law of Scotland would be cast down: 'I think I see our Learned Judges laying aside their Practiques and Decisions, studying the Common Law of England'; and the Military would be humbled: 'I think I see the Valiant and Gallant Soldiery either sent to learn the Plantation

Trade Abroad; or at Home Petitioning, for a small Subsistance as the Reward of their honourable exploits . . .' The 'Honest Industrious Tradesman' would be loaded with new taxes, and the 'Laborious Plew-Man' left with his corn spoiling on his hands for want of a market. 'But above all . . . I think I see our Ancient Mother CALEDONIA, like Caesar sitting in the midst of our Senate, Rufully looking round about her, Covering her self with her Royal Garment, attending the Fatal Blow, and breathing out her last with a *Et tu quoque mi fili* . . . Are not these very afflicting Thoughts?'

The Scots, in Belhaven's opinion, were to be put to an extremity that only the providence of God could ameliorate. To make such a speech required a man with a Janus face, looking back to Golden Ages and, despite present inconvenient but surely temporary conditions, looking forward to an Ideal State which the Scots, left to themselves, should be sure to achieve. The Lord Chancellor, replying to Belhaven's pleas, remarked that, 'He had heard a long speech and a very terrible one, but he was of the Opinion, it required a short answer . . . Behold he Dream'd, but, lo! when he awoke, he found it was a Dream.' Lord Marchmont's sour and superior little reply is certainly witty, but it was a cynical answer to a heroic, deeply felt oration. Belhaven the dreamer was pricked and deflated by one of those salty barbs the Scots themselves use to bring down to earth any Scottish idealist.

Belhaven was an emotional patriot or chauvinist – he was as much a realist who knew, to its profoundest depths, the character of conqueror and defeated. He spared himself, and Scotland, the illusion that the Scots would get the better of a deal with England. Historically the English were as avaricious as the Scots, and they were better equipped politically to exploit their cupidity. The Scots, for all their vaunted cunning, could not hope to triumph as a stronger or more Machiavellian partner in any alliance that, referred to as a Union, was not visibly a marriage of equals. The Scots, if not immediately wounded by English self-interest and commercial ambition, were quite likely to shoot themselves in the foot by expecting fair treatment from the master to whom they had put themselves, possibly irrevocably, in harness. England would wax stronger as a result of the Union, Scotland would wane in influence and be weak in self-defence. The hostility between the two countries would not be diminished – if anything, it might be exacerbated – by their uneasy joining together. This perception was hardly original – it derived from immemorial fears of subjection. Belhaven's idealism resided in the belief that Scotland, left to its own devices, could thrive as a politically independent state – if only her sons and daughters put heart and mind into the effort to raise the country from its despair. There had been in the past no shortage of courageous leaders ready and willing to give the lead, by the sword or by intellect, able to rouse popular enthusiasm in the cause of independence from England, the oppressor.

In *Folk Heroes of Britain*, Charles Kightly points out that 'all the strictly contemporary accounts of Wallace are English, and therefore hostile, while none of the Scottish – and therefore laudatory – accounts of him are contemporary, having been compiled between sixty and a hundred and seventy years after his death.' The gap between reality and record becomes a gap between fact and near-fiction. The result is that William Wallace has become a demi-mythical figure of Scotland's martial past. However, it appears that he was the all too mortal son of a Scottish knight who held lands in Ayrshire and descended from a Normanized Welshman, Richard le Waleys (William Wallace himself spelt his surname as 'Walays'), who settled in Scotland when given a manor which, originally known as 'Richard's Town', became corrupted to Riccarton, by which name it is still known as a suburb of Kilmarnock.

To the English, William Wallace was 'vicious, false, forsworn, a sacrilegious thief and incendiary, a murderer more hard-hearted than Herod, more crazed than Nero'. To the Scots, the Wallace was, remarks Kightly, 'an incomparable paragon, a wise governor and invincible warrior, a heaven-blessed avenger of his nation's wrongs, and a holy martyr welcomed into Paradise amid the miraculous ringing of earthly bells'. Until 1296 there had been peace and a rather uneasy amity between Scotland and England. The Scots and the English had not always been immemorial antagonists as tradition would like to have it. Scotland had been regarded as a refuge from the Normans, and a considerable number of English refugees had settled in the Lowlands. The marriage of the saintly Margaret, sister of the English king Edgar Atheling, to Malcolm Canmore introduced English courtiers, tradesmen and churchmen into Scotland without too much fuss being made about their presence in what had been regarded as the Pictish and Scottish lands of Anglian Lothian, which then spread between the present border and the Forth. But Scotland was in no sense a satellite state of England, whatever claims the English monarchy might make to its overlordship. In 1292 John Balliol was enthroned as king of Scotland, and his inability to deal effectively with King Edward's claims and demands as 'Lord Superior of Scotland' (a nominal title he took more seriously than did the Scots) resulted in a Scottish raid over the border on Carlisle. Edward replied by annexing Berwick-on-Tweed and massacring its citizens. The Scots countered by attacking Northumberland. The English answered by defeating the Scots at Dunbar and pushing into Scotland, where Edinburgh and Stirling fell to Edward's forces. The humiliated Scots surrendered at Berwick in August 1296 and offered unwilling allegiance to their conqueror.

The Scots, oppressed in various ways by the occupying English, were suddenly spurred into revolt in May 1297 when William Wallace slew the Sheriff of Lanark. Nothing is known – no accurate contemporary accounts or portraits exist – of Wallace's age or appearance, but it is clear that he must have had some charismatic appeal that brought the Scots flocking to his side to support him in rebellion. They were bound to fight in any case: rumour had it that Edward was to raise an army of Scotsmen for a foreign war. Most Scots reckoned, perhaps, that they'd rather fight for themselves, and Wallace seemed to be the natural leader in the absence of any greater or more official general. They began by recapturing Galloway and burning the English out of

Ayr. The Clydesdale forces were supported by a rising of rebels in the area of Inverness who burned the English-held Urquhart Castle near Loch Ness, while Wallace and Sir William Douglas ('the Hardy') rushed to attack the Chief Justice of Scone in Perthshire, a place of particularly sacred and historical importance. After this there was a general rising of the Scots, and their leaders were joined by the young Robert Bruce of Carrick (also of Norman descent), later to be Robert the Bruce, King of Scotland. The Scottish rebels were defeated, however, in the south-west at Irvine in July 1297. They capitulated, and Edward congratulated himself on a famous victory easily achieved. So easily, in fact, that he became complacent and Wallace was enabled to regroup his forces. He raised an immense army of about 15,000 horse- and foot-soldiers (the Scots claimed 40,000) and proceeded to Dundee, which he laid under siege. The English forces sent to relieve the seige of Dundee Castle were defeated by brilliant military tactics at Stirling, with great losses on the English side and only minimal casualties on the Scottish. Wallace swept south, more or less unimpeded, halting at the border over which the English fled before him into Northumberland and thence to Newcastle, where they felt reasonably safe.

They were not safe for long: Wallace, having secured the borders and the south-west, and informed friendly European powers that 'the kingdom of Scotland . . . has now been recovered by battle from the power of the English,' proceeded to invade England. The Scots burned their way across largely undefended Northumberland and came to Carlisle, where they encountered some stout resistance that obliged them to withdraw; whereupon they were foiled in their intention to occupy England by terrific snowstorms in the week of 11 November 1297 and returned to Scotland, depleted in numbers, eleven days later. Wallace had termed himself, to the authorities of Carlisle, 'William the Conqueror', and had succeeded at least in thoroughly enraging Edward, otherwise engaged for the moment with a fight in Flanders. Historical fact denies, but legend alleges, that Wallace invaded England again in 1298 and the Scottish poet and chronicler, Blind Hary, will have it that he got as far as St Albans. The English, too, came to believe in a second invasion, and ornamented the first to describe the fictional return of the Wallace who was alleged to have been a beast of an almost unspeakable barbarity. 'Driving together English men and women, the vile Scots torturers tied them back to back and made them dance naked, lashing them with whips and scorpions till they dropped. They even snatched up babes from the cradle or their mothers' breasts and cut them open, and they burned alive many children in schools or churches.' So related Rishanger of St Albans in pious horror at scenes he had never observed. Kightly observes, calmly, 'that almost the selfsame words had been used to describe a Scots incursion of 1174 by earlier chroniclers, who had in turn borrowed them from an account of a still earlier attack in 1138. One Scots invasion, the southerners evidently assumed, must be very like another.'

Wallace himself was certainly no saint, and very probably no ogre, but he would have had difficulty controlling followers avid for booty and inflamed by blood lust. He might issue 'high-sounding proclamations in the name of an exiled king and a fellow-commander who probably lay dying in Scotland,' says Kightly, but 'his only real authority is the undefined "consent of the community". Like a lion-tamer or like the robber-chief the English named him, he must in fact command only by the sheer force of his personality.' In early 1298, William Wallace was officially 'elected' sole guardian or regent of Scotland, having been knighted and confirmed by a council of nobles and church-men as 'Sir William Wallace, Guardian of the Kingdom of Scotland and commander of its forces, in the name of King John [*Balliol*] and by consent of the community . . .'

From this triumph, it was all downhill for William Wallace who lacked, vitally, support from the Scottish aristocracy for his 'common army', his people's militia which fought not for money but for love of their country and for hatred of England. They were not trained, well-armoured, well-armed men, but men of the lower and middle rank who put their trust in Wallace and their main weapon, the twelve-foot-long spear. Wallace was soundly routed in 1298 by Edward at the battle of Falkirk when ten thousand of the Scottish army were killed. Wallace fled the field, reckoning it more prudent to save himself and, denying the English the satisfaction of his death, remain a rallying point for future revolt. In the late summer of 1298, Robert Bruce and John Comyn of Badenoch assumed the Guardianship of Scotland and William Wallace, having been forced to resign his office, took a minor role as a foreign ambassador desperately attempting to raise support abroad: at home, Scottish lords demanded forfeiture of his lands and goods while others supported him as a hero. They fell to furious fighting among themselves. Edward, meantime, consolidated his gains and in 1303 crossed with full force into Scotland and more or less subdued the country. The Scottish leaders were in disarray, divided among themselves, some defecting and most demoralized. A sum of £200 was put on Wallace's head, but he remained at large for a year, protected by the loyalty of the Scots.

When finally betrayed and captured on 3 August 1305, he was sent south to London where, says Kightly, he was conducted by the Lord Mayor and a great concourse of notables, 'like the trophy of some Roman triumph, to Westminster Hall: where in a mocking ceremony which came uncomfortably close to parodying Christ's passion, Wallace was seated on a bench and crowned with the victor's wreath of laurel "because, as it was popularly said, he once declared he would wear a crown in that same hall."' His fate was a foregone conclusion, although technically, as Wallace made an attempt to claim, since he had never been Edward's subject or at any time sworn allegiance to him, he could not be condemned as a traitor. Edward counterclaimed that, since he had conquered Scotland in 1296 and achieved the submission of the Scottish king, nobility, and people, Wallace had committed felonies and seditions against him as king of Scotland.

Wallace was stripped and dragged behind horses through the streets of London, from Westminster to the Tower and thence to

Aldgate. Care was taken that he should be badly bruised but not killed by this degradation, since it was important that he should be partially hanged at Smithfield, cut down alive from the gallows, eviscerated, and finally beheaded. His heart, liver, and lungs, ripped from his living body, were burned. His corpse was quartered and tarred and the four pieces were sent to be displayed on the gibbets of Newcastle, Berwick, Stirling and Perth. His head was stuck up on London Bridge. If his sentence and death were not sensational enough, or pitiful enough, the events required a divine gilding. Blind Hary declared that English monks were granted a salutary vision of Wallace being received with honour into Heaven shortly after his martyr's death.

Kightly makes the important point that Edward and Wallace were no more and no less brutal than one another. The conventions of war were not pretty, and weakness of principle or magnanimity of spirit towards the defeated was not generally considered useful. But Wallace was not hated for his alleged barbarity so much as he was loathed for what he was – a man of the people: 'actions which were excusable, even commendable, in a king and an army of nobles were beyond measure reprehensible when perpetrated by a knight's son at the head of a force of "middle folk" and peasants. The root of Wallace's tragedy, indeed, was that he was born too low in the hierarchy of a society founded on hereditary status. For though a conservative Scotland was at first prepared to let him do the work which her inadequate king [*John Balliol*] and vacillating nobles could not or would not do, the nation was not yet ready to unite for long behind a man who was neither king nor noble.'

Yet the nobles could not resist without the people and the people could not resist without the nobles, says Kightly, and Wallace left that legacy of knowledge to the Scots and to Robert Bruce who, when he seized the crown of Scotland and took up the struggle again for independence six months after the death of Wallace, was supported by the 'poor common folk' who had been inspired by Wallace. And 'king, nobles and commons together eventually won through to victory.' The War of Independence, which ended in 1328 when England recognized the independence of Scotland, was fought for principles enshrined in the 1320 Declaration of Arbroath, an appeal to the Pope which set out the Scottish case for sovereignty and expressed the Scottish determination to gain and retain it. The words are characteristic: 'For so long as one hundred men remain alive, we shall never under any conditions submit to the domination of the English. It is not for glory or riches or honours that we fight, but only for liberty, which no good man will consent to lose but with his life.' That liberty was a precious jewel and that the Scots had always been a distinct people was proven by their history. Reaching back and fumbling for facts in the dim mists of history, the barons of Scotland pulled out a fanciful conceit: 'our Scottish nation has been distinguished by many tributes to their fame. We passed from Greater Scythia across the Tyrrhenian Sea and beyond the Pillars of Hercules, and sojourned for many a year amid the most savage races of Spain; but nowhere could any people, however barbarous, reduce us to subjection. From there, twelve hundred years after the Departure of the Children of Israel, we came to our abode in the West where we now dwell.'

Independence, so dearly bought, was a mystical legacy to future generations for near enough four centuries. Idealists fought the 1707 Union, none more devotedly than Andrew Fletcher of Saltoun, born in 1653 and descended through his mother's family from Robert I of Scotland, Robert the Bruce. The Union was a direct wound to Fletcher's own family heritage – what his ancestor had fought for could not lightly be given up. Fletcher in his youth had had a martial history: first, he was a politician, member for Haddington in the Convention of Estates in June 1678. In 1681, he refused to take the Test Oath and fled to England where, as a result of his involvement in the Rye House Plot, he was exiled to Holland where he joined Monmouth's unsuccessful rebellion of 1685. For his pains, he was judged a traitor in Edinburgh and forfeited his Scottish estates in East Lothian. In the aftermath of the Glorious Rebellion of 1688 he was permitted to return to Scotland and took up politics again as a prominent anti-Unionist in the last Scottish Parliament of 1703. Fletcher was an ardent lover of liberty, with high and extravagant principles. Though his days of physical battle were over and he confined himself to politics, he is in his way as great a hero as Wallace. Certainly, his character may stand as near enough archetypally Scottish. When one thinks of a Scotsman, one might do no better than to think of Andrew Fletcher of Saltoun as representative of all that is best and worst in the psychology of the Scots.

In 1706, he proposed a federal union in which England and Scotland could continue to have separate parliaments. His determined, hot-tempered patriotism, his passionate idealism, his reactionary battles with the spirit of the age in which he found himself, mark him as a dedicated Scot of the deepest dye. The *Biographical Dictionary of Eminent Scotsmen*, edited by Robert Chambers and published in 1853, provides a detailed account of Fletcher's life and describes him in a final passage, generally reverent and complimentary, but with substantial reservations:

'He was,' says the earl of Buchan, 'by far the most nervous and correct speaker in the parliament of Scotland, for he drew his style from the pure models of antiquity, and not from the grosser practical oratory of his contemporaries; so that his speeches will bear a comparison with the best speeches of the reign of Queen Anne, and Augustan age of Great Britain.' Lockhart says, 'he was always an admirer of both ancient and modern republics, but that he showed a sincere and honest inclination towards the honour and interest of his country. The idea of England's domineering over Scotland was what his generous soul could not endure. The indignities and oppression Scotland lay under galled him to the heart, so that, in his learned and elaborate discourses, he exposed them with undaunted courage and pathetic eloquence. He was blessed with a soul that hated and despised whatever was mean and unbecoming a gentleman, and was so steadfast to what he thought right, that no hazard or advantage, – not the universal empire,

nor the gold of America, could tempt him to yield or desert it.
. . . He was in private conversation affable to his friends (but
could not endure to converse with those he thought enemies to
their country,) and free of all manner of vice. He had a
penetrating, clear, and lively apprehension, but so exceedingly
wedded to his own opinions, that there were few, (and these too
must be his beloved friends, and of whom he had a good
opinion,) he could endure to reason against him, and did for the
most part so closely and unalterably adhere to what he advanced, which was frequently very singular, that he'd break
with his party before he'd alter the least jot of his schemes and
maxims; . . . thence it came to pass, that he often in parliament
acted a part by himself, though in the main he stuck close to the
country party, and was their Cicero. He was no doubt an enemy
to all monarchical governments; but I do very well believe, his
aversion to the English and the union was so great, that in
revenge to them he'd have sided with the royal family . . . To
sum up all, he was a learned, gallant, honest, and every other
way well accomplished gentleman; and if ever a man proposes
to serve and merit well of his country, let him place his courage,
zeal, and constancy, as a pattern before him, and think himself
sufficiently applauded and rewarded by obtaining the character
of being like Andrew Fletcher of Saltoun.'

Lockhart's encomium having finished, Chambers adds a
welcome, moderating note of caution.

Of the general truth of these descriptions we have no doubt;
but they are strongly coloured through a national prejudice that
was a principal defect in Fletcher's own character. That he was
an ardent lover of liberty and of his country, his whole life bore
witness; but he was of a temper so fiery and ungovernable, and
besides so excessively dogmatic, that he was of little service as a
coadjutor in carrying on public affairs. His shooting the mayor
of Lynn on a trifling dispute, and his collaring Lord Stair in the
parliament house, for a word which he thought reflected upon

him, showed a mind not sufficiently disciplined for the business of life; and his national partialities clouded his otherwise perspicacious faculties, contracted his views, and rendered his most philosophical speculations, and his most ardent personal exertions of little utility. Upon the whole, he was a man, we think, rather to be admired than imitated; and, like many other popular characters, owes his reputation to the defects, rather than to the excellence of his character.

Thrawn, disputatious, intransigent, independent, idealistic, honourable, clear-headed but fiery-minded, logical but ludicrous, as likely to knock down a man's arguments with words as the man himself with his fist, Fletcher of Saltoun is a man to match Knox in his dedication to principle, his passionate proselytizing, his ferocity of manner, and, in his devotion to patriotism, as lion-like as Knox in his pursuit of Presbyterianism. Fletcher is remembered too little today, but one of his *obiter dicta*, in a letter to the Marquis of Montrose, is enshrined as a light to literature: 'I knew a very wise man that believed that, if a man were permitted to make all the ballads, he need not care who should make the laws of a nation.'

Perhaps Walter Scott had these words in mind when he set about collecting (and sometimes inventing) the Scottish Border Ballads that, more than any other publication, have given the Scots an element of their identity even to the present day. They evoke a Golden Age in which Fletcher of Saltoun might have found his spiritual home. Scott, in a lengthy historical and social introduction, remarks – among other things – that, 'where the feelings are frequently stretched to the highest pitch, by the vicissitudes of a life of danger and military adventure, this predisposition of a savage people, to admire their own rude poetry and music, is heightened, and its tone becomes peculiarly determined . . . . The morality of their compositions is determined by the same circumstances. Those themes are necessarily chosen by the bard, which regard the favourite exploits of the hearers; and he celebrates only those virtues, which from infancy he has been taught to admire . . . the reader must not expect to find, in the border ballads, refined sentiment, and, far less, elegant expression; although the stile of such compositions has, in modern hands, been found highly susceptible of both.' In the *Minstrelsy of the Scottish Border*, Scott celebrates such as Johnie Armstrang, Kinmont Willie, Jock o' the Side, the Gallant Grahams, battles, and bards. Most are frankly anarchic – Scott points out that 'the music and songs of the borders were of a military nature, and celebrated the valour and success of their predatory expeditions. Razing, like Shakespeare's pirate, the eighth commandment from the decalogue, the minstrels praised their chieftains for the very exploits, against which the laws of the country denounced a capital doom.'

By the late eighteenth century, Scotland had become less a rough, free-market, freebooting society than an educated, near-civilized society – in urban Edinburgh, at any rate: though the country had charms, too, for Sydney Smith who arrived in Scotland in 1798. He found considerable contrasts in Edinburgh: 'I like this place extremely and cannot help thinking that for a literary man, by which term I mean a man who is fond of letters, it is the most eligible situation in the island. It unites good libraries liberally managed, learned men without any other system than that of pursuing truth; very good general society; large healthy virgins, with mild pleasing countenances, and white swelling breasts; shores washed by the sea; the romantic grandeur of ancient, and the beautiful regularity of modern buildings, and boundless floods of oxygen.' The philosophers of Scotland rather puzzled him, however: 'they reason upon man as they reason upon X – they pursue truth, without caring if it be useful truth . . . in short a Scotchman is apt to be a practical rogue upon sale, or a visionary philosopher.'

But even in this intellectual Eden there were drawbacks: the Scots were capable of beauty and grace of mind and architecture, but an incautious Englishman could find things slippy underfoot as a result of the Scottish 'total want of all faecal propriety and excremental delicacy . . . No smells were ever equal to Scotch smells. It is the school of physic; walk the streets, and you would imagine that every medical man had been administering cathartics to every man, woman and child in the town. Yet the place is uncommonly beautiful, and I am in a constant balance between admiration and trepidation –

> Taste guides my eye, where'er new beauties spread
> While prudence whispers, "Look before you tread." '

Dogs and other domestic animals are now alone guilty of faecal impropriety on Scottish streets in the twentieth century, but Smith's observation (also made by Dr Johnson a few years earlier) is indicative of a Scottish concern for purity of mind and philosophic principle over purity of domestic detail. Fact and faeces could always be trampled underfoot, without injury to innocence.

Sydney Smith arrived in the middle of Edinburgh's Golden Age, more or less a hundred-year period known as 'The Enlightenment' which occurred after the failure of the 1745 rising. The aristocracy of Scotland, with no real political power in Scotland, tended to find its employment in England, and a rising middle class was not slow to supplant them on the native social and political scene. The fine and applied arts were never to rise to great heights of genius – though here and there might have been found individual talents of a rare kind – but philosophy and literature flourished. Here, at this time, the Edinburgh savant David Hume 'ruined Philosophy and Faith, an undisturbed and well-reputed citizen,' according to Stevenson's view. The city was ornamented by the creation of the New Town, formally laid out and classically conceived: 'It is what Paris ought to be,' remarked Stevenson.

Allan Ramsay, the poet and wigmaker, opened the first circulating library, to the scandal of the godly, in 1728. The flighty, passionate poet Fergusson, who inspired Burns, lived a bohemian and vivacious life in Edinburgh until he became deranged and died in a madhouse. The times bred the poet James Thomson, the novelist Tobias Smollett, the economist Adam Smith, the historian William Robertson, and the tragedian John Home whose reputation in Scotland was incomparable ('Whaur's yer Wullie Shakespeare noo?'). Science was advanced by the chemists William Cullen and Joseph Black, by the geologist James Hutton, and by the physicist James Watt. The Scots of 'The Enlightenment' achieved, according to Neil McCallum in *A Small Country*, a 'vast totality of accomplishment in nearly every aspect of human endeavour. The sciences and the arts held a condominium for a hundred years that has not been seen elsewhere, before or since.'

The poet sat down with the physicist, the philosopher with the painter, the artisan with the academic, so that no art or science was uninformed by any other. The Scots of 'The Enlightenment' were devoted dilettanti in the best sense, catholic in their interests, encompassing in their energies: in this period, the Scots invented the science of sociology, the discipline of statistics, pioneered the first census (published as the *Statistical Account* in 1791), published the first edition of the *Encyclopaedia Britannica*, wrote legal treatises still consulted today as authoritative statements of law, and bred both Burns and Scott.

The life of the Scottish peasant in the eighteenth century hardly, in comparison, bears thinking about – it was not gay, to say the least: even middle-class conditions of life were, by comparison with life in Scotland today, only a little better than primitive. The Scots could not afford the luxurious aristocratic or bourgeois life of, say, the French, and paid a great deal less attention to art, dress, furniture, and other frivolous but undeniably comforting concerns. But the poetry of Burns gives a cheerful, philosophic, romantic, realistic, and generally spirited picture of Scottish life, not neglecting its inconveniences, hardships, hypocrisies and vexations, but neither omitting its gaieties and domestic diversions. At the core of Scottish life lay, and still lies, Protestantism. However much the aspiring middle classes of Scotland are increasingly secular, they rarely look back for inspiration, except in matters martial, and in a feeling for the spiritual roots of Celticism (a romantic impulse), beyond the Reformation. Burns's 'ribaldry, blasphemy, libertinism and sentimentality are all Protestant, and very narrowly so,' said Edwin Muir, and all the intellectual achievements of 'The Enlightenment' and their offshoots depend upon Protestantism – whether directly, or by reaction against it – for their genius. Chambers was perhaps correct in a broader sense when he attributed Fletcher of Saltoun's greatness to the defects rather than to the excellence of his character. The Scots have always been adept at wringing advantage from apparent disadvantage, Jasons sowing dragon's teeth on apparently barren soil, and reaping a dangerous harvest.

Charles McAra, in *Memoirs of a Modern Scotland*, compares James Crichtoun of Eliock, the Admirable Crichtoun, with the more modern radical figure of Robert Bontine Cunninghame Graham, Don Roberto. 'The common factors are guts, moral courage, audacity, a liking for the bold stroke or the *beau geste . . .* from them came the colour, a kind of impudent gaiety which defeats "all the rest, sullen anger, solemn virtue, calculating anxiety, gloomy suspicion, prevaricating hope."' Both Crichtoun and Cunninghame Graham were figures of rich romance, a mixture of Hamlet and Don Quixote, the sceptic and the idealist, according to Cunninghame Graham's biographers, Cedric Watts and Laurence Davies. The heroes of Scotland may be found in many fields – in the counting house, in the laboratory, in the classroom, in battle, and, in the case of Cunninghame Graham, on the pampas and in Parliament. He was born in 1852 in London, the son of a Scottish landowner who, devoted to get-rich-quick (or quicker) schemes, effectively ruined the family fortunes. Cunninghame Graham could trace his line of descent back to King Robert II and had a right, albeit modified throughout the centuries by political and dynastic complications, to be regarded as the true King of Scotland. He was educated at Harrow and Brussels, before lighting out for South America at the age of eighteen. His mother possessed Spanish blood, and it seemed likely to the young Cunninghame Graham, who had no taste for the family tradition of the military, that he might make his fortune in Argentina. A number of English, Irish and Scottish emigrants had succeeded in doing so. But Cunninghame Graham arrived in Argentina in 1870 to find himself in the middle of a civil war. He was soon struck down with typhus. Cunninghame Graham was not discouraged. It is said, by his biographer Tschiffely, that Graham had almost immediately upon arrival thrown himself into the revolution on the side of the rebellious gauchos, and certainly he acquired the language, the clothes, and some of the habits of these men of the plains.

Graham's love for the country and for its people lasted the rest of his life, for sixty-six years during which he wrote a great deal about South America long after his return to Scotland. Cunninghame Graham is said to have been the model for Saranoff in Shaw's *Arms and the Man*. His writings are scarcely read nowadays – his style is idiosyncratic and difficult, though his contemporaries regarded him very highly as a stylist – but he deserves a literary revival as a literary romantic. The man himself deserves to be remembered as a romantic adventurer and as one of the greatest of Scotland's 'men of parts'. He moved gracefully and easily from the pampas to the drawing-room on his return from South America. Tall, red-haired, long-nosed and bearded, he carried himself with a natural air of boldness and breeding. His mother's London salon was a meeting-place for writers, painters and musicians, and Graham himself was a close friend of Edward Garnett, Joseph Conrad, George Bernard Shaw, and W. H. Hudson. Later, he was a good friend of Compton Mackenzie. In Paris in 1878, he met and married Gabriela de la Balmondière, an orphan but supposedly the daughter of a Chilean merchant of French descent. Gabriela was as remarkable a character as her husband: she was an accomplished botanist, watercolourist, and writer. Among her friends and acquaintances, all devoted to her, she numbered Engels, Yeats, Will Rothenstein, Philip Burne-Jones, the Wildes, the Prousts, and Rider Haggard. She chain-smoked and was an early feminist. She spoke at political rallies in Hyde Park and was thoroughly independent at a time when women, though increasingly conscious of their oppression, were generally expected to efface themselves in political matters. They travelled, alone or together, extensively – to Spain, Morocco, Texas, Mexico (where they abortively tried their hands at farming) – before returning to Scotland in 1881, saddled with debts of about £2,000. On the death of Graham's father, he inherited the three estates of Gartmore, Ardoch and Gallangad, all heavily mortgaged and liable for tax, annuities, and maintenance. The houses he inherited were in a state of sorry repair, and the disposable annual income from the estates amounted only to an estimated £660: in the event, considerably less – as little as half that.

In Mexico, and in Texas, Graham had encountered racial prejudice against Mexicans and black people: he vigorously opposed it then and later. His biographers point out that, when Graham looked back on his time in Texas, he did not sentimentalize the border Mexicans: 'As he showed the situation in retrospect, there was a hierarchy of underdogs in the Rio Grande valley. The English-speakers oppressed the Spanish-speakers and the Indians, the Spanish-speakers oppressed the Indians, the Indians terrorized whom they could. The unfortunates Graham depicts may be more sinned against, but they do their share of sinning too. His life in South America had shown him man as a violent animal; moving to the North, he could see man being both violent and oppressive. His sufferers are not saintly . . . he insists on the common badness of persecuted and persecutor, on their shared inhumanity.'

In 1878, Graham had been elected to the Devonshire, a Liberal club in London, and in 1885 he sought adoption as Liberal candidate for the Blackfriars division of Glasgow. His family had a tradition of Leftist politics and Radicalism which Graham shifted even more towards the Left. As a landowner, he might have been expected to endorse political policies in his own interest, but his manifesto spoke against an aggressive foreign policy, against the game laws, against primogeniture and entail, for reform of the land laws, for more local self-government, graduated income tax, free education and local option on the sale of liquor. Though he was a professed Home-Ruler, the Liberal

Party was not committed to Irish autonomy, and Parnell had thrown in his lot with the Conservatives. Graham was defeated on this occasion, but within six months he was in the House of Commons as member for Lanark.

The political correspondent for *Vanity Fair* described Graham as a parliamentarian: 'Scotch Home Rule visionary. Outward aspect: Something between Grosvenor Gallery aesthete and waiter in a Swiss café. Person of "cultchaw", evidently, from tips of taper fingers to loftiest curl of billowy hair, and with sad, soulful voice to match. Drawls out some deuced smart things. Effect of speech heightened by air of chastened melancholy. House kept in continuous roar for more than half-an-hour. Fogeys and fossils eye him askance, and whisper that he ought to be "put down"; but lovers of originality, in all quarters, hail him with satisfaction.' Graham's stance was, on all issues, uncompromisingly Radical and he rallied the Socialist William Morris to his support. Like Morris, Graham believed in all-embracing diagnoses of society's ills and all-embracing cures. It seemed to Graham that Home Rule and Socialism would bring about a new Golden Age. In the House of Commons, he was unpredictable as a respectful observer of the rules of that chamber: his biographers character-ize him as possessing 'some sense of grand political design, of strategy; in moments of detachment, he was also capable of thinking tactically; but often enough he had too much blood in his eyes, as he pressed forward with his red banner, to see exactly where he was going . . . the amusing dilettante that the House thought it had discerned in his early months there was being transformed into a wild man who would not abide by the rules, an embarrassingly loose-tongued fellow who would not play the game.'

Unemployment in Britain was high in 1887, and there had been alarming instances of street violence in London. Two thousand police had been assigned to mob-control duties, and to complicate matters still more, a demonstration had been planned to protest against the imprisonment of William O'Brien, a Mem-ber of Parliament, a militant who had been involved in a protest meeting in County Cork when 8,000 men, rallied to demonstrate against coercion in Ireland, had been fired on by the police. Three men had been killed. On Sunday 13 November 1887, despite a ban on the meeting, Trafalgar Square was the target for a substantial number of protest marchers. Police were set, two to four deep, to cordon off the Square. Foot Guards were stationed behind the National Gallery, and Horse Guards waited on their Parade ground. The march was broken up at Waterloo Place, St Martin's Lane, and Westminster Bridge – but Graham, who had come to protest against the curtailment of free speech, emerged from Charing Cross underground station and, with a couple of friends, slipped past mounted patrols towards Trafalgar Square where, with linked arms, they approached the cordons of police. What then happened is debatable: the police alleged that Graham threw his hat in the air and rushed the cordon. He was beaten down with police truncheons. Some witnesses gave evidence that Graham and his companions had offered no violent provocation, but had merely raised their arms to protect themselves from injury. Streaming with blood, Graham was taken to Bow Street police station. As a result of his activities on 'Bloody Sunday', Graham was charged and, after a trial of immense public interest, was sentenced to six weeks in jail – of which he served four and a half weeks, emerging to a hero's welcome as a popular martyr.

In all, Graham remained a Member of Parliament for six years, but his political conscience continued to be stirred after he retired to private life and later he enthusiastically took up the cause of Scottish Nationalism when it surfaced in the years following the First World War. He had always argued for Irish and Scottish autonomy, and he was one of the original members of the Scottish Home Rule Association when it was founded in 1886. In 1888, he became the President of the Scottish Labour Party, which under his influence supported Scottish Home Rule. The demand for Home Rule in Scotland, in Graham's view, came 'from no sentimental grounds whatever, but from the extreme misery of a certain section of the Scottish population, and they wish to have their own Members under their own hands, in order to extort legislation from them suitable to relieve that misery.' Nationalism, too, in his opinion, made for peace rather than war. 'Nationalism is the first step to the International goal which every thinking man and woman must place before their eyes. But without Nationalism we cannot have any true Internationalism.' This pious hope (an echo of Lord Belhaven's oratorical dream) was also part of Hugh MacDiarmid's creed when he supported Scottish Nationalism as a means to a true Internationalism. Graham was never xenophobic. Indeed, he warned that 'The enemies of Scottish Nationalism are not the English, for they were ever a great and generous folk, quick to respond when justice calls. Our real enemies are among us, born without imagination ...' He became disillusioned, finally, with factional politics, but continued nevertheless to believe in the efficacy and justice of parliamentary democracy – a democracy rejuvenated by the spirit of Nationalism that might lead, at last, to the relief of Scotland's chronic ills.

The Golden Ager is a constant figure in Scottish life: the Scots are passionate and romantic in their idolization of heroic figures who, like Biblical patriarchs, may lead them to better days, to a diet of milk and honey in a promised land of lost content. The road to national pride, peace and prosperity is perceived as leading through nationalism, through the right to self-determination, towards self-reliance and self-respect. If formerly of better account, there is little doubt in the Scottish mind that, left to itself, Scotland may be so once again.

9

✳

Red Clyde and blue blood:
politics and the Scots

THE Scots, generally despairing of seeing a Golden Age in their own country or lifetimes, have set out to look for or work towards a reasonable substitute elsewhere. No country has lost such a large percentage of its population to emigration. Between 1901 and 1961, 1,388,000 Scots emigrated. During the Depression of the early 1930s, 400,000 Scots left the country to make better lives elsewhere. From 1871 to 1921, 483,000 emigrated. During the First World War, Scottish dead – including civilian casualties – amounted to 150,000. This figure accounted for twenty per cent of British dead, and in some communities, notably the Highlands and Islands, the toll more than decimated the local population. The economic and social implications of these figures cannot be overestimated: no country can afford to lose such a significant number of its people without serious injury to its financial and cultural prosperity. Scotland is an old country, and its energies have been sapped – it has lost too much blood, and it has been starved of nourishment. Small wonder that, occasionally, it produces characters on the national stage who are cut out, apparently, as the traditional pantomime devil dressed in revolutionary red.

Scotland is not merely a democratic country, it is also the most truly egalitarian nation in Europe. Its middle class is not more than two hundred years old, though it has long had a bourgeois tradition of upward social mobility, of a meritocracy. For long ages, Scotland's social classes were its aristocracy and its peasantry. Neither class (until the Industrial Revolution sharply altered perceptions on both sides) considered itself at a pole opposite the other, although it was clear enough who was the titular master and who the man. Democracy depends a good deal on education, and until the latter part of the eighteenth century the laird's son was educated at the local parish school with the rest of the local children. The laird's son might expect to inherit an estate, but opportunity in Scotland was never a matter merely of primogeniture: education was the high road out of poverty. In the nineteenth century, education was the royal road out of the slums and the miseries of hard industrial labour. Evening classes for adults were well attended: at Holytown, in Lanarkshire, James Keir Hardie's fellow students included Andrew Fisher who later became Prime Minister of Australia, and Robert Smillie who rose to become a national leader of the coal miners. James MacDonald, a trade-union leader who was elected as a Liberal MP in 1874, got his Latin and Greek at evening classes while working by day at an ironstone mine near Airdrie, and Andrew Carnegie, born in Dunfermline but an emigrant to the United States at the age of thirteen, educated himself in his spare time while working in a Pennsylvania cotton factory. Education was not free, but it was cheap and – to that extent – open to all. Education was a moral instrument, to a large degree, and though it might seek to teach a conventional morality it also taught a man how to think – a process that somewhat mitigated the attempt to teach him *what* to think. Most of those born into poverty turned naturally to the Left in their political thinking, and towards the last years of the nineteenth century were supported by emotional and intellectual Socialists such as the aristocratic Robert Bontine Cunninghame Graham whose family tradition was Radicalism.

In 1955 the Conservatives won thirty-six of the seventy-one Scottish seats in the House of Commons. It was the last time they have held a majority of constituencies in Scotland. It is a constant complaint in Scotland that when the Conservative Party gains a national majority of seats throughout the United Kingdom, a Conservative Secretary of State for Scotland is appointed to the Scottish Office, despite the majority of Scottish seats being held by the Labour Party. In this regard, the Scots are politically demoralized. The Conservatives are also likely to lose the vote to Liberals in some Border and Northern constituencies, or occasionally to Scottish Nationalists. It comes as no surprise to anyone when leaders of national trade unions, interviewed on radio or television, speak with Scottish accents. The trade-union movement in Scotland dates from the mid-nineteenth century, and almost from the beginning was a talking-shop for Socialist ideals. A Scottish Trades Union Congress was formed in 1897, bringing together some fifty-five organizations representing more than forty thousand members. The strong Scottish presence in the trade-union movement in the twentieth century matches the presence of Scots in the national political parties and in government. This century, there have been several Scottish Prime Ministers – Campbell-Bannerman, MacDonald, Douglas-Home, and Macmillan. There are innumerable Scots who will refuse to work within the democratic Parliamentary process as a means of achieving their nationalistic ideals, but many others perceive the advantage of being the worm in the bud by getting themselves returned to Westminster, moving beyond the parochialism of Scottish politics to a wider national and international stage. Polite, affable, well-meaning Scottish politicians such as David Steel, George Younger, Donald Dewar, Malcolm Rifkind, or Jo Grimond (now retired as an MP), are no wild men of politics: they are experienced men who, though they can work up a fine head of steaming outrage over some evident injustice or party political point, are adept at manipulating the subtle machinery of parliamentary government. Occasionally, however, an original appears and the name of the Scots for violence allied with revolutionary activity rings frightfully in the ears of the electorate. 'There was a time,' says Colm Brogan in *The Glasgow Story*, 'when worthy matrons in Bournemouth and Cheltenham shuddered at the lank locks and the staring eyes of James Maxton, and waited for the day when "Red Clydeside" would justify its title in flames and blood.'

To understand Scottish politics, it is necessary to understand the broad outlines of the history of Clyde shipbuilding and the associated Scottish steel industry – a history that is alive but not madly kicking except in the unforgiving memory of almost everyone on the West coast of Scotland. Very nearly every immemorial grievance held by the Scots is represented in the saga of Clydebank. Shipbuilding and Glasgow are inextricably linked. The ineffable McGonagall could not resist apostrophizing thus:

O, wonderful city of Glasgow, with your triple expansion
engines,
At the making of which your workmen got many singeins.

Shipbuilding and engineering contributed principally to Glasgow's nineteenth-century prosperity and, of course, both industries suffered grievously in periods of economic depression. The Clyde shipyards grew rapidly after 1841, as a result of the adoption of steam propulsion and the increasing use of iron rather than wood. Iron was replaced in turn by mild steel from the 1870s, and the Steel Company of Scotland was founded in 1871. Between 1879 and 1889, the tonnage of steel shipping launched on the Clyde rose from 18,000 to 326,136, and the proportion of steel-built ships rose from 10.3 per cent to 97.2 per cent. The entire economy of the West coast of Scotland and the counties of the middle belt of Scotland depended very largely on Glasgow's heavy industry. The development of marine engineering, the introduction first of the triple expansion engine and then the Clydeside quadruple expansion engines, followed by the development of the steam turbine, gave shipbuilding on the Clyde an unrivalled international reputation. In 1913, the volume of Clyde shipbuilding was three quarters of a million tons; 60,000 men were employed; and the total number of jobs dependent on shipbuilding was about 100,000.

During the years of the great Depression in the 1920s and 1930s, the number of men employed in the shipyards had dropped by about one-third by April 1930, and in 1931 work was stopped on the *Queen Mary* which was not launched until 1934. The *Queen Elizabeth* was launched in 1938. By 1936, the output of the Clyde shipyards had fallen to 60,000 tons and at least two-thirds of the workforce was unemployed. In *Glasgow*, David Daiches comments:

> The 'rationalizing' of shipbuilding in an endeavour to combat depression by increasing efficiency and cutting costs was part of a larger pattern in Scottish industry after the First World War that hit Glasgow particularly hard. The merging of firms to eliminate competition and the movement southward of industrial control helped to make Scotland a depressed area. Already by 1922 there were over 80,000 unemployed in Glasgow. The great railway merger of 1923 . . . brought the control of Scotland's railways to London with the resultant moving of associated industries to England, notably the locomotive building and repair work that had been so important in the west of Scotland. Indeed, Glasgow's locomotive engineering works had been second only to shipbuilding among the city's heavy industries, but their functions, as well as those of the engineering works at Kilmarnock, now became greatly restricted and their labour force diminished correspondingly.

These developments, says Daiches, 'helped the growth of left-wing political activism in Glasgow and on Clydeside.' There was widespread support for the shipbuilders of the Clyde among the Scots – after all, the economy of the West coast and the industrial belt depended largely upon heavy industry. When that failed, the entire social structure was threatened in what has become known as the 'knock-on' effect.

Glasgow had had a tradition of voting Liberal during much of the nineteenth century, but in 1922 Glasgow's fifteen seats returned ten members representing the Independent Labour

Party. Among them was James Maxton who, as a matter of principle, had opposed the First World War and had organized pacifist agitation in Glasgow. He had helped lead the Clyde strike of 1915 to increase industrial wages in Glasgow by twopence an hour to bring them into line with wages in other industrial cities in Britain. He had been imprisoned in 1916 after making a speech at an anti-war demonstration on Glasgow Green. In 1918, he led thousands of ILP members in a huge May Day march through Glasgow. Colm Brogan comments in *The Glasgow Story*: 'When the War ended, the Glasgow Socialist bosses were in the highest state of expectation. They had greatly worried the Cabinet, they had forced the hated Churchill to negotiate personally with Davy Kirkwood [*who was returned as ILP member for Clydebank in the General Election of 1922*] and even to offer him black bun [*a heavy fruit cake described by R. L. Stevenson as 'a dense, black substance, inimical to life'*]. They had demonstrated massively in favour of the first Russian Revolution and just as massively in favour of the second. They had made themselves the spearhead of the militant proletariat of Britain, and now the Election [*of 1922*] gave them their opportunity to cash in politically on their industrial achievements.'

The 'wild Clydesiders' were a rum bunch: Brogan characterizes one of them, John McLean, who after the War:

> was let out of jail to contest Gorbals against a Coalition Labour man whose name was a hissing and a swearword because he had joined a capitalist Government and supported a capitalist war. McLean enjoyed something of the popularity that Keir Hardie had enjoyed a generation before, but some of the wiser heads (a strictly relative term) thought he was not the best man for the Gorbals. His candidly confessed atheism was no recommendation in a constituency with such a strong Catholic vote and he suffered from another handicap. Although he was an exceedingly nice man in private dealings, he could not mount a platform without going quietly off his head. He was convinced that his jailers had been slowly and deliberately

poisoning him. He was equally convinced that the capitalist minions of the Returning Officer would pinch his votes and hide them.

He failed to win the seat but among those who were returned in 1922 were Maxton, John Wheatley, George Buchanan, Campbell Stephen, David Kirkwood, Emmanuel Shinwell, and Tom Johnston.

Their effect on the House of Commons and the country at large was tremendous. They had been seen off from Glasgow by an enormous and exuberant crowd. The night train took them in from St Enoch's in Glasgow to London and combat in the Commons.

They made their last speeches [*in Glasgow*] to the light of glaring torches, [*Brogan recalls*] and to the stimulating sound of fervent applause. They looked as if each one of them had his own special Bastille to capture, and they succeeded in making themselves for some years the most talked-of group in Parliament. They had been trained in Glasgow Town Council to make an angry noise on all occasions and to account it for virtue when they succeeded in getting themselves suspended. But their impact on Parliament was much like that of a boxer who hits with the open glove. For a round or two they attracted attention by the noise they made, and then they faded out . . . The Clydesiders failed because they were not outstandingly intelligent and they had nothing whatever to say. Jimmy Maxton, his hair growing longer, lanker and greasier every year, ended as the most popular Member of the Commons, and the most graceful of all speakers in the vein of friendly compliment on honorific occasions. It was rather a queer ending for the apostle of 'Socialism in our time'. The fresh-faced and blunt-spoken George Buchanan worked hard at the Pensions Ministry and then retired to a non-political post which he had well earned. Davy Kirkwood became a Privy Councillor, which, for a back-bencher, is the equivalent of being presented with a marble time-piece in recognition of faithful service to the firm.

He was created a peer, as was Emmanuel Shinwell whose long Parliamentary career and engaging personality made him almost a mascot of the House.

Brogan had little time for the 'wild Clydesiders' who, in retrospect, he regarded as 'mostly a dull lot' – they added 'little to the wit and not much more to the wisdom of the Mother of Parliaments'. Their speeches, he considered, were stodgy, 'infused with a vague secularist humanitarianism, decorated with some painfully obvious quotation from Burns and usually disfigured with some gross or even idiotic misrepresentation of conditions in the Bad Old Days.' But they had succeeded in politicizing Glaswegians or, at least, in channelling and directing a wave of popular political feeling. Says Brogan, 'Glasgow people are highly political. That is to say they hold strong and generally erroneous opinions on all great affairs of State. Their political tradition is fundamentally radical. The workers vote solidly for Socialist candidates who are considered to be the heirs of the old Radicals, although they hold precisely opposite views on most important political matters.' The ILP faded away in the 1920s, and the great Depression drove the Labour Government of 1929 out of office. Glasgow alone kept a number of ILP members in parliamentary office in the general election of 1935. Partly, Glaswegians were loyal to the ILP because David Kirkwood had consistently campaigned for the interests of Clydebank and his efforts were rewarded when, in late 1933, John Brown's shipyard on the Clyde recommenced work on the construction of the *Queen Mary*. The Chancellor of the Exchequer announced that work would commence on the '534' and Kirkwood had a vision of the promised land:

... as I looked at him, juggling with the happiness of thousands, I saw behind him the long Dumbarton Road through Clydebank with four thousand men moving along towards Browns' Yard while the horn sang out the morning welcome. I saw some whose pockets bulged with their 'pieces' [*packets of sandwiches for lunch*] and some who would march out at dinner-time with a new ring in their step. These were the men who, years later, would tell their children: 'I worked on the "534".'

Behind them I saw their homes, now so bare, gradually brighten with furniture and carpet and waxcloth, and children setting out for school, well fed and well clad. And I saw the wrinkles of care and anxiety smooth out from the faces of the mothers. And I saw the boys and youths eagerly awaiting the word 'Go!' to rush forward to begin the life that had so far been denied to them.

In 1937, work commenced on the *Queen Elizabeth*, and soon enough rearmament and the demands of war production ensured continued work in the Clyde shipyards until the mid-1940s when the order books began to fill with commissions to replace naval and merchant shipping losses. Coal, steel and ships were required and Scotland supplied them. Scotland in the post-war years was prosperous, but it did not develop. The reason is not difficult to discover: the unions were as much to blame as management and any other interest – Clydeside, though busy, was complacent. The Clyde tradition of innovative marine engineering was stuck in old-fashioned, slow, uncompetitive techniques and work practices. Overseas competition badly hit the Clyde shipyards, and light industry had gravitated south to the Midlands and South of England. In the early 1960s, six of Scotland's twenty-five shipyards were forced out of business. A steel strip mill was built at Ravenscraig, but the Scottish motor industry and factories for the production of durable consumer goods were sops by a Conservative government to the Scots: the infrastructure of roads to transport goods was inadequate and transport costs were high, with the result that Scottish workers were worse paid than their English counterparts in order to offset the high delivery costs of the goods they were producing.

Andrew Fletcher of Saltoun

James Hogg by
William Nicholson

Sir Walter Scott by
Sir Francis Grant

Sir Walter Scott receiving George IV in Edinburgh

Queen Victoria and John Brown : Landseer

Mr Punch at the Highland Games

Robert Louis Stevenson

Swanston Village – where Edwin Muir lived and worked

Sir Harry Lauder

R. B. Cunninghame Graham by Jacob Epstein

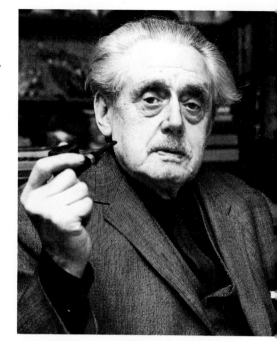

Hugh MacDiarmid

Hugh MacDiarmid's memorial – Valda Grieve (MacDiarmid's widow) with sculptor Jake Harvey

The Royal Caledonian Ball

The Royal Company of Archers

Dame Flora McLeod of McLeod

Billy Connolly

Jimmy Reid

The Edinburgh Festival

*The Edinburgh Festival
Fringe Club*

The Labour government of 1964 promised a great deal, and in 1965 they set up the Highlands and Islands Development Board to create work north of the Highland Line. In 1966 Labour produced its plan to stimulate the economy of Lowland Scotland. New industries such as motor-car production and electronics were to be developed, but meanwhile shipbuilding and coal mining was unprofitable and in decline. Plans to rationalize the shipbuilding industry were drawn up but in practice were found to be uneconomic, and in mid-1966 the Labour government was obliged to deflate the national economy as a whole. Scotland's economy was patched up with temporary dressings, rather than operated upon with the necessary surgical skills that would have given permanent relief to a chronic case of heart failure. The economy continued to decline, and in 1970 the Conservatives won the general election under the leadership of Edward Heath who succeeded in bringing Britain into the Common Market. The Common Market had been held up by its supporters as the answer to Britain's economic ills, but Scotland's economy did not respond. Companies continued to go out of business, and in the yards of Upper Clyde Shipbuilders – an amalgam of several shipyards – the UCS workers staged a 'work-in'.

The hero of the UCS work-in of 1971 was the Communist shop-steward Jimmy Reid who rallied almost four hundred colleagues to participate in the demonstration. The action succeeded, and after fourteen months the government reluctantly agreed to keep the UCS yards open. Reid's view was that the shipbuilding industry was an essential factor in the social as much as the economic life of Clydebank. Both were profoundly interdependent. The argument still continues in the mid-1980s. Clydebank is a touchstone for Scottish pride, for social cohesion, for Scotland's economic survival. But the dinosaurs are, gradually, dying. The hope for the future is the microchip, electronic technology, and the futuristic industries that employ fewer and fewer people. These may create some wealth, but they do not create large numbers of jobs.

Politics in Scotland tend to be coloured by the national belief that the Scots are hard done by in Westminster. The Scots are enduringly suspicious that their special needs are neglected, their traditions subverted, their loyalties either misunderstood or cynically misused, their assets squandered for the benefit of others, and that they are consistently and altogether ignored as a nation within the United Kingdom. In *No Gods and Precious Few Heroes*, Christopher Harvie comments, 'There was an Irish Question in British politics throughout the nineteenth century. It became obsessive after 1880, and refused to disappear even after the setting-up of the Free State in 1921. There was no Scottish Question. Between 1922 and 1964 few specifically Scottish issues preoccupied the Commons for more than a few hours, or Cabinet for as many minutes, even at the pit of the depression. The only one that did, the Caledonian Power Bill of 1936–8, had implications for national defence. This may give a clue to Scotland's unobtrusiveness.' The Scots are not natural revolutionaries.

This is not to say that Scots were not active in politics: the quality of Scottish MPs, however, was not high. Brogan was sceptical about the intellectual capabilities of the ILP members, and Harvie comments that until 1939 'Scottish businessmen were . . . reluctant to go into parliament. Unionist MPs were not distinguished, and the majority of them tended to be drawn from groups – like advocates and landowners – remote from Scotland's economic and social problems.' There was, too, a move away from Scottish constituencies by Unionist front-bench MPs. Scottish politics is not divided solely along class lines. Christopher Harvie points out that Walter Elliot, Secretary of State for Scotland in Ramsay MacDonald's government from 1936–38, was 'conscious of the need to legitimate the Unionists as a party of moderate, statist reform, one that could both incorporate the Liberal tradition and attract the working class.' Conversely, Clifford Allen in 1922 became chairman of the ILP and moved the party to a left-liberal position in order to attract middle-class reformers. However, the Unionists also had to contend with the fact that they had become identified with militant Protestantism.

Catholics tended to vote Labour. Though the Protestant vote was, in fact, split roughly on the British average, nevertheless politics in Scotland acquired a religious as much as a class significance. Interestingly, the radical right had no serious following in Scotland. Though Oswald Mosley counted at least three Scots among his closest confidants, Mosleyite candidates in the 1937 municipal elections were humiliatingly defeated.

Towards the end of World War II, Scottish Nationalism became an issue in Scotland and the SNP won the Motherwell seat in the election of 1945. In 1947, the Nationalist John MacCormick organized a rally of six hundred delegates to a 'Scottish Convention'. These delegates represented the churches, local government, the Co-operatives, and liberal opinion throughout Scotland and in 1948 the Convention approved a Covenant, signed in 1949, demanding home rule within a federal system. Twelve hundred delegates endorsed the Covenant which was signed by two million Scots, but the Labour government rejected its demands though they were prepared to make some cosmetic amendments to the role of the Scottish Grand Committee in Parliament.

In 1950, the Stone of Destiny was snatched by Scottish students from Westminster Abbey – a romantic stroke of Nationalistic fervour that was the last throw of the Covenant movement, though not the last token of Nationalistic aspiration towards Home Rule. Scottish politics quietened down somewhat until the 1960s. Christopher Harvie points to a lack of leadership among the Scots and asks why this should have been so: 'What inhibited leadership? The constraints of Scottish working-class consciousness [*Harvie believes and gives evidence that the Scottish working people were deeply conscious of being 'of a class but not for a class'*]? A relatively open entry into the southern élite, which drew the politically and administratively able away – particularly between the wars? Certainly, for those who stayed, law, local government, education, and the Church offered secure and reasonably influential niches, while MPs who tried to build up a party following in Scotland as well as Westminster ran risks . . .

Stress-based ailments terminated or damaged enough careers to suggest that the peripatetic life damaged party politics – particularly on the Left – more than the other power-bases of Scottish society.'

On the one hand, Scottish politicians of the Left tend to Socialism in its purest form, and those of the Right tend to be drawn from the public schools and universities of England or from the professional classes of Edinburgh. They reflect the split between commercial and industrial Glasgow in the west and professional Edinburgh in the east. Glasgow honours and idolizes a working-class hero, while Edinburgh dearly loves a lord or a lawyer. This may seem to contradict any assertion that Scotland is not a class-conscious or class-based society. Christopher Harvie points out that 'the institutions of Scottish society actually inhibited the development of a positive political class-consciousness. They provided means of "spiralling" out of the working class, and they also created, through the expansion of public intervention, a range of middle-class organizational and leadership roles – schoolteachers, local officials, councillors and MPs, social workers – . . . "a state-sector middle class". This middle class tended to assume leadership of Scottish working-class organizations. Skilled industrial workers, in the 1930s, unable to find work in their own industries, drifted into the general labouring class which was swelled to large proportions but, a generation later, broke up as its more intelligent or confident members either gravitated into middle-class jobs or emigrated. Scottish society was remarkably fluid, and a common culture rather than a class-based culture developed.'

The middle-class Glasgow businessman, remarks Colm Brogan,

is no stranger to the working class. He knows them and understands them. It is not possible for him to live the life of Brahmin-like seclusion from the manual workers which is led by quite a number of London business and professional men. It would never occur to him to claim any instrinsic superiority over the proletariat, nor would it occur to the proletariat to concede him any . . . The fine shades and divisions of the English caste system mean no more to the middle-class man than they do to the riveter in John Brown's or the Govan boiler-scaler . . . The artisan calls no man his superior, but he sometimes finds it difficult to disguise his belief that the unskilled man is his inferior. Life in the slums may have a rich wildness of its own, but the artisan suspects that it is lacking in a due degree of prudence, providence and balance. He may accept it as a political axiom that all that is wrong with the slums is caused by the System, but he has a secret suspicion that some of what is wrong with the slums is caused by the people who live there . . . Nevertheless, in the pub, the tram or on the football terracing, the unskilled man is a brother, and no one would have it otherwise. That is why, although social communication in Glasgow is not always genial, it is always unembarrassed. All sorts and conditions in Glasgow have more in common than they consciously understand.

The principal difference between the classes in Glasgow and Scotland is money. 'It is not a big difference,' says Brogan.

The little pretensions and snobberies of the middle, upper-middle, and upper classes are fairly minor and in any case are liable to be swamped by the common culture which, though it may superficially appear to be rough and basically common-sensical, does not deny the validity of more cosmopolitan values. Brogan properly says that a 'vast number of the London proletariat are blankly unaware of anything beyond their own borough, but there are Glasgow men who may never have crossed the Clyde to Rutherglen but can learnedly discuss the pubs of Hongkong and Shanghai or the proper way of treating native servants in Calcutta.' Scotland's aristocracy lost most of its social and political credibility after the nineteenth-century Highland Clearances when lords of great estate cleared their lands of tenants and gave over their acres to sheep or sportsmen. But upper-class Scots now and again achieve political office – the Earl of Ancram is a Minister at the Scottish Office, George Younger (heir to the viscountcy bestowed on the Younger brewing family) was promoted from Secretary of State for Scotland to Secretary of State for Defence in 1986, and the last Scottish Prime Minster was Sir Alec Douglas-Home, formerly the Earl of Home, who as a Scot achieved some endearing notoriety when he confessed that his understanding of economics depended on his skill in counting matchsticks. Considering the Scots gave the world logarithms, this dependence on manual aids counted somewhat against him.

Even the Queen is liable to get into trouble in Scotland. She is generally well received on her visits to Scotland – her mother is a Bowes-Lyon and was born at Glamis Castle, which counts heavily in her favour, and her regular residence at Balmoral Castle is a plus. But her succession to the throne in 1953 was marked by violence in Scotland. Extreme nationalists such as John MacCormick and Ian Hamilton firmly disputed her right to title herself 'Queen Elizabeth II' there. Since Queen Elizabeth I of England had never been Queen of Scotland, MacCormick and Hamilton argued in court that her proper style in Scotland was 'Queen Elizabeth I of Scotland'. The court said she could call herself what she liked, and found in favour of the Crown. There was some genuine resentment in Scotland after the court decision, and Wendy Wood's Scottish Patriots blew up some pillar-boxes bearing the insignia EIIR. The passions and violence that the question generated in Scotland were, for a while, substantial: and there are many Scots to this day who will insist that the Queen's proper style in Scotland is Elizabeth I of Scotland.

The Scots have always resisted standardization in line with England – centralization of government appeared inevitably to mean that the distinctive character of Scottish institutions – including education, the legal system, certain elements of the banking system, industry, and culture – were likely, at best, to be eroded and, at worst, altogether submerged. Nationalism is a moral issue as much as a political cause, and the Scots are becoming increasingly disheartened and apathetic as their morale, constantly sapped by despair and frustration, continuously declines. Scotland is not an independent state – and

Edinburgh is no longer officially considered as a capital city – but the dreamers of political self-determination continue to fret in their coma. 'The true choice the Scots have is between two dreams,' alleges Tom Nairn. 'One which will destroy them finally, while appearing to redeem them, by shutting them within the prison of an archaic bourgeois nationality, by reinforcing their provincial and Presbyterian society, by clothing the ghosts with flesh. And the other, whose content is revolutionary, and understands that real, meaningful existence can only be won by the destruction of these things.' While clinging to the shreds of nationality, the Scots seem merely to be clustering round a tattered banner – a fairy flag that they hope will give them victory. In reality, the wholesale and haphazard destruction of the Scottish way of life has given the Scots a freedom to reconstruct which past generations of original and daring thinkers and men of action would have seized with relish.

That present-day Scots still possess their passion but have lost their grandiose imagination and the will to fulfil its vision, is perhaps due in large part to their final realization of failure – a failure of leadership in the political arena. The upper class is generally absent, making money or a career in England, the middle class is too busy with domestic detail and preserving its own interests, while the working class is preoccupied with unemployment and the industrial changes that threaten to break it up by splintering its traditional bases. Few care to be bothered with national politics which, since Scotland's interests are perceived to have been relegated to the sidelines by politicians, are regarded as a displacement activity, a matter for pub dispute, an occasion for the exercise of intellectual principles and deeply felt passions, an amusing exercise for an hour or two of the Scottish capacity for rancour and the airing of grudges. Politics have so signally failed to improve the lot of the Scots that political parties and politicians and political manifestos are held in deep disrespect by a nation of cynics who no longer believe there can be a new tune or new words for 'an auld sang'.

This neo-Jacobitism, this lamentation for an industrial glory that has passed, is typical of the Scots who regard themselves as rich in potential but poor in their pockets – a traditional response to a permanent predicament, the blame for which is projected out to be laid at the door of Scotland's immemorial antagonists who, it is thought, have conspired in unholy concert to do Scotland down. The breaking-up of the shipyards and the steelworks is regarded as a calamity akin to the disaster of the Clearances. The political responsibility for Scotland's economic and social despair is generally held to derive from London, from Parliament and the Tory government. The prospect of the return of 'Victorian values', proselytized and evangelized by Margaret Thatcher, is regarded with dismay by those who remember the effect of Victorian values in Scotland in the latter half of the nineteenth century when the Highlands were depopulated and employment and living conditions in the cities were the worst in Europe. The moral precepts of the Victorians, and of Tory politics and big business in the present day, sound hollow to modern Scottish ears. The glittering future of 'Silicon Glen' has not yet dazzled Scottish eyes: microchip technology is interesting, but has not yet proved itself as the salvation of the Scottish soul – it tends to employ women and further erode the traditional role of the Scottish working man as a heroic figure doing daily battle with steel, rivets, large enterprises and striving in the workshop of the world. Dainty-fingered work with the microchip is not Romantic, is scarcely the stuff of legend. The Scottish nostalgia for heavy industry, for masculine status, for heroic achievement, binds the Scots like Prometheus to a rock. The industrial achievements of the Scots in the nineteenth and early twentieth centuries seem, in restrospect, like another Golden Age that has now, in song and fable, been immortalized as solidly in the Scottish imagination as any invention of Sir Walter Scott.

The Scots are at once Romantics and Realists: they are glamorized by their past, or a perception of that past, while at the same time they recognize the difficulties of the present. They look with fearful hearts towards the future. Though lamenting the past, they seek regeneration: the Scots resent stagnation and are prepared to incorporate structural change when it is forced upon them. Their adaptability seems almost limitless, but in fact it is peculiarly Scottish – no sooner has the necessity for change been accepted than the Scots will subtly adapt the results of that change to suit themselves. They impose their character upon it, rather than being fundamentally altered in their own character. This is known as having it both ways. The Scottish character has a genius for synthesis, for reconciling the contradictory: it takes a pride in its own past, while striving to assimilate the present and render it consistent with that past. The heart lies in the past; the mind looks optimistically towards the future; both combine to comprehend the present.

IO

---- ✳ ----

The Lyon Rampant:
the constant Nationalist

I T is not too much to say that nationalism in Scotland is an idiosyncrasy rather than an expression of pure political theory. Nationalism embraces all shades of party political opinion from left to right and, since the Scots have no recent experience of self-determination and self-government, Nationalism is free to adopt policies that it regards as being in the best interests of Scotland – policies that are unlikely to be corrupted or subverted by day-to-day constraints on government. Therefore, Scottish Nationalism has the strong appeal of enlightened and innocent self-interest for most Scots. Nationalism is untouched by political reality or pragmatism: the soul of Scotland is at stake.

Scotland's sense of separate identity can be traced back as far as Roman times, and nationalism was certainly a motivating factor in the Wars of Independence of the fourteenth century. The revolt against England, led by Wallace and Bruce, involved the common people. The Scottish nobility was less enthusiastic and gave little support to the cause. Separateness was reinforced by Continental influences, particularly French and German: while Scotland looked to Europe for inspiration and support, the English remained largely insular. So it is that Scotland has always regarded herself as a European country rather than merely an adjunct to England. As Keith Webb remarks in *The Growth of*

Nationalism in Scotland, 'Although the Scots invaded England and were in turn invaded, there was a qualitative difference between the two acts. It was possible for the Scots to defeat the English on the battlefield, but for the English this did not imply the possibility of permanent subjugation.' The Scots, contrarily, were always likely to be politically and culturally assimilated by the English. The Union of the Crowns in 1603 and the Union of 1707 did, largely, achieve the integration of Scotland and England with no diminution of England's interests.

The modern tendency has been for the Scots to create a historical myth of a Celtic past that serves as a focus to unite a people not noticeably unanimous in anything. The heritage of the past is a glue that binds together disparate, and often contradictory, elements in Scottish history and culture to form a common ground that provides a feeling of nationhood, a sense of Scottish identity developed largely as the result of struggle against immemorial antagonists. There exists, strongly, among the Scots a self-perception that takes heart, colour and mind from the emotional impact of Scotland's heroes, triumphs, and disasters. The figures of Bruce, Wallace, Burns, Scott, MacDiarmid, Fletcher of Saltoun, and a hundred others; the battles of Flodden, Bannockburn and Culloden; the disasters of the Darien Scheme, the '15 and the '45, the Clearances, the decline of the shipyards – all combine, with many another deeply felt perception, to create a body of myth that, however inaccurate in fact, soaks into the Scottish consciousness like Scotch mist. The Scots are saturated by their history, real and imagined, in an immediate way that is incomprehensible to the English who, generally, take their history for granted since they are not oppressed by it.

The Scots may not be depressives, but they have a limitless capacity for being mournful. The old wounds are tenderly licked and salted – a painful, joyless activity. The Scot is too often his own tormentor. He will insist on making the most of his grievances and, when they are no longer to be passively tolerated, he will spring to action. It seems necessary that the Scot should subject himself to intense experience in order to prove to himself that he still has independent life and sensation. The Scottish soul is regularly taken somewhat by surprise, and shaken very thoroughly, by bursts of passionate nationalism. Suddenly, something snaps with a sharp report in the Scottish heart and mind, and the Scots are shaken out of lethargy and complacence. The peat fire, slumbrously smoking, shoots out little tongues of flame. The ashes are raked and the hot, inner incandescence is exposed. On a sudden, the Scots are sparked to remember and rally to their identity. Then Robert Louis Stevenson's words are recalled: 'For that is the mark of the Scot of all classes: that he stands in an attitude towards the past unthinkable to Englishmen, and remembers and cherishes the memory of his forebears, good or bad; and there burns in him a sense of identity with the dead even to the twentieth generation.'

The nationalistic sensation is easily excited because it is so profound. MacDiarmid quoted, approvingly, *The Tractate of Patriotism* by J. S. Machar: 'My Czechdom is the portion in my life which I feel, not as delight and bliss, but as a solemn and inborn fealty.' Scottishness is not something to be boisterously enjoyed as any great pleasure: it is something to be doggedly redeemed from those who seek to subdue or subvert it – usually the English, and those who would make light of the Scottish heritage. It is a perverse but perfervid reaction, perhaps, when the Devil leads a Scot to the roof of the world and offers him dominion over it, that he should choose that barren, hard, sour land of his birth over all the others. The Devil always has one reservation, however – the Scot can have all *but* his own country. Like Cain, he has been deprived of it. The only thing he wants, the Scot cannot easily have. The Scot, like Compton Mackenzie, gazes down and desires his past and his futurity. In 1932, in his Rectorial address to the students of Glasgow University, Mackenzie ended his speech with a fine, mystical flourish:

A few weeks ago upon the Campsie Fells I gazed down at Glasgow. From a mass of dark cloud the sun, himself obscured from where I stood, sloped his golden ladders into that rain-washed city, which lay with all her spires and chimneys, with all her towers and tenements and sparkling roofs, like a vision of heavenly habitations. I have looked down over Athens. I have looked down over Rome. With beauty unparagoned the glory and the grandeur of the past have been spread before my eyes; but in that sight of Glasgow something was added which neither Rome nor Athens could give – the glory and the grandeur of the future, and the beating heart of a nation.

Mackenzie had urged nationalism upon his young auditors in order that they might, sons and daughters of Alba, save their own souls and, thereby, the soul of Man through dedication to their country.

Scottish Nationalism is a periodic phenomenon with at least a 600-year history. It sprang up again after the First World War in Scotland. 'Modern nationalism in Scotland,' wrote Arthur Marwick in 1970, in *Memoirs of a Modern Scotland*,

is made up of two basic ingredients, one best described by the essentially nineteenth-century term, 'Home Rule', and the other nationalist in the fullest sense of the term. Home Rulers stressed administrative efficiency, decentralisation, and the supreme virtue of self-government as an abstract ideal: their aim was a local Scottish parliament within a federal United Kingdom. The mainspring of nationalism is the deep and real fear that Scotland as a separate nation, with a distinct and valuable cultural tradition, is doomed to extinction through emigration and the invasion of alien values, unless she resumes complete control of her own affairs. In practice the two ingredients have been mixed in a pretty dense solution, though on the whole the history of Scottish Nationalism in the twentieth century is of the disintegration of the Home Rule ingredient and the precipitation of the nationalist one.

Marwick links the first phase of the modern Nationalist resurgence to the patriotic stirrings of World War I and to the severe economic depression that followed in the 1920s and 1930s. The second phase, he says, derives from the rather different emotions that were aroused by the Second World War and the hostility aroused by the centralizing policies of the 1940s. This resentment lasted into the 1950s, and the old Home Rule tradition was emphasized. 'The third phase, insistently nationalist again, began sometime in 1962; we are still in its thrall.' Marwick identifies modern Nationalists in all classes and conditions of Scots: Nationalism cuts through class, political, and international lines. Nationalist supporters include lawyers anxious to preserve Scots law (distinct from, but increasingly encroached on by English common law), doctors, teachers, literary men and artists, bohemians, students, the clerical class, and expatriates. The movement towards Nationalism and self-determination is not necessarily Left wing: indeed, Left-wing politicians are often suspicious of a tendency that would reduce the strong support of the Labour Party in Scotland. And Right-wingers who have achieved an overall Conservative Party victory in the polls are in the position of ruling Scotland anyway, whatever the majority vote (normally pro-Labour) in Scotland itself.

The Nationalists of the late 1920s and early 1930s were not hot-headed firebrands. Some of them, the public orators and figureheads such as Compton Mackenzie, Hugh MacDiarmid, John MacCormick and R. B. Cunninghame Graham, were colourful, kenspeckle creatures with charismatic appeal. But someone like Lewis Spence was resolutely subfusc and bowler-hatted. The Nationalist movement, though it aims to set up a Scottish Parliament in the Royal High School in Edinburgh, is Glasgow-based in inspiration and its idealistic support. Glasgow students are usually in the vanguard of Nationalist support. Mackenzie, in 1932, pointed this out to Glasgow University students: 'though we must acclaim Edinburgh as the capital, the stern and masculine parent, Glasgow is the metropolis – the mother city. No other city is so representative of the whole country, and what is true of Glasgow is true of Glasgow University. Every criticism which is levelled against it may be levelled against Scotland itself. The virtues, faults, hopes, fears, ambitions, and dreams of the country as a whole are more completely expressed in this University than anywhere. Its very position in the midst of a crashing industrial turmoil and yet always within sound of the two voices of liberty, the voice of the sea and the voice of the hills, is a prefigurative symbol of our country's future.' Glasgow is the melting pot of Highlands and Lowlands, the crucible in which it is endlessly hoped the nation will be reborn.

The reality of the Scottish Nationalist supporters came as a shock to the young George Scott-Moncrieff in the early 1930s. His disenchantment was sudden:

> I think I was quite ready at 22 to man the barricades, and I remember my disappointment when I first made the journey from Edinburgh to Glasgow and met the leaders of the SNP [*Scottish National Party*]. Glasgow at that time was still firmly bowler-hatted. I rather think there was a special Glasgow bowler hat, distinctive in its relationship of brim to bowl. It was certainly not worn jauntily, and worn soberly, the bowler gives men a sad, dull appearance, hard to identify with the plumed helmets that the romantic mind associates with a brave cause. The grave, aspiring politicians donned their bowlers and took me out to coffee in an oppressively over-oaked coffee room, where conversation lapsed in mutual discontent.

The Nationalist movement of the 1930s was not only political: the dream inspired and fed a national renascence of art, letters, and the higher things of the mind. It seemed an urgent aim to sweep out all traces of what George Scott-Moncrieff happily called 'Balmorality'. MacDiarmid's poetry was one of the triggers, perhaps prompting Compton Mackenzie's wider vision of Scottish nationalism as a force for the salvation of the soul of man. MacDiarmid's poetry, while at one level being particularly addressed to the Scots in a vernacular language in order to stir the sense of Scottish particularity, and to provoke a Scottish renaissance, an awakening of Scottish consciousness, on another level spoke to the aspirations of mankind at large, assuming and creating common bonds. MacDiarmid was certainly European in his vision, only partly through his feeling of being not-English.

The thought occurred to George Scott-Moncrieff, as it may have done to others, that far from being different, the Scots may in fact be very like everyone else – with one notable exception. 'Three people said to me at different points: "You Scots – you are not like the English, you are like us." One was Austrian, one Norwegian, and the third French, and it seemed to me that it could only mean that the English were the most *different* people in Europe: doubtless an accident of history rather than race.' One draws from this comment the inference that the Scots consider themselves to be truly European, in direct contrast to the English who generally oppose any view that would conflate them with the countries of Europe.

Hector MacIver dispiritedly described the result of Scottish Nationalism in the 1930s, and the comparative failure of the accompanying Scottish renaissance to fulfil all that had been wildly expected of it, as having been 'like farting against a hurricane'. Scott-Moncrieff, from a perspective of forty years on, considered it now 'easier to see the thought and aspirations of the Thirties in their place, as part effect, part cause, of a process of change that could be the hope and inspiration of a post-British Scotland, a Scotland that is once again European.'

The European influence continues, of course, but more to the point in the modern world is the influence of America, Japan, and other expansionist countries which provide capital, technology, and work ethics for economically depressed or undeveloped countries throughout the world. American and Japanese investment in Scotland is economically significant and culturally important.

The second objection to self-determination is that, in addition to becoming a fiefdom of supra-national corporations, Scotland rampant would once again become detumescent in the grip of the Holy Willies. 'The real question for Scotsmen,' remarks Arthur

Marwick, 'is not whether an independent Scotland would be viable, but whether it would be bearable . . . Still certain, most of them, that there is a life after death, Scotland's urban middle class sees little need for a life after dark . . . it is not the wild men of Scottish nationalism who are to be feared: it is the dull men of unchanging Scotland.'

Nationalism speaks seductively to the Scots, promising redemption: the past, that broad highway, will lead to final glory. Suffering will be justly rewarded, and romantic fantasy will be converted to the new reality of a Golden Age. Myth will be made manifest. Scotland will grasp the thistle and be, finally, what it has always perceived itself to be in its inner heart – rich, successful, powerful, a nation among nations, respected for all those virtues that have unaccountably failed to save it in the past. Those virtues of canny-eyed Calvinism, of penurious economy in things small and great, of moral purpose, of chauvinism, of driving ambition, are all part and parcel of Scottish self-denial. The Scots congratulate themselves on their self-restraint: on their virtuous impotence. Wicked energy, deriving from sinful inner chaos, might well have tumbled empires, ruined princes, laid waste a world. Scotland's potential for disorder has been channelled by religion, rigorous conditions of life, and self-control into positive achievement – so the Scots maintain, pointing with some justifiable pride to their influence in the wider world. Repressing their capacity for destruction, they have created empires, supported princes, and fashioned a world that, if there were any justice, would now recognize and reward the Scottish contribution.

Failing such recognition and reward, the Scots have become mistrustful of the world and their self-confidence has somewhat faltered. The Scots dimly feel that they are not loved. Nationalism gives the Scots a certain self-respect and the opportunity to redeem their international standing. Tom Nairn, a contentious Scottish historian, lambasts modern Scottish Nationalism as opportunistic and self-serving, narcissistic and introverted, cautious and self-interested (when it might have been impetuous and noble) and dominated by a dull bourgeoisie. He is not convinced that Scottish Nationalism is a truly spontaneous, revolutionary movement inspired by an upsurge of popular feeling, but rather that it is a populist movement created by alliances to fight old, traditional enemies. He may be right to assume that sentiment for the homeland, resentment against alleged exploitation from outsiders, and a desire to keep the riches of the country for the Scots themselves, are the principal moves behind Nationalism. Nairn criticizes the chauvinistic impulse from the standpoint of Marxism, more or less, and regrets the lack of true revolutionary spirit among the Scots who cling to their past with a tenacity that inhibits progress towards 'the great dreams' of a society wholly restructured.

Tom Nairn's words of stinging reproof, calling for new myths, in 1970, fell on deaf ears – *Invisible Country* by James Campbell, published in 1984, is still calling for new myths without much hope that they can be invented or sustained. We like our old ones too much to let them go – they are as numbing as a shirt of stinging nettles. The old myths itch, and we idly scratch at them, but we do not think to divest ourselves of a painful but comfortingly familiar irritation. Gordon Wilson, MP, present leader of the Scottish Nationalists, is quoted as saying, optimistically, that 'there may be a bit of post-1979 depression floating about, but you'll never take the big idea away from us. The big idea is still there.' The big idea of a Scottish Parliament, of Home Rule, of independence, of self-determination in all essential matters, of cultural renewal, of the sad, provincial stupor of Scotland being suddenly galvanized into vital life, has been a big idea for God alone knows how long. There have always been bounds set around Scotland from, very likely, Roman times, inhibiting free expression, free trade, free love, free whisky and whatever else the Scottish heart and mind so urgently craves but is prepared to do very little to obtain.

The Scottish National Party may seem like a vehicle for salvation to some, but for more radical spirits it appears only to be a fast train back to the hell of the past. To Tom Nairn, in concert with Arthur Marwick, it appears that the 'odious, grudging tyranny of the older generations over youth which distinguishes Calvinism from civilization will naturally be reinforced after independence . . . This evil *mélange* of decrepit Presbyterianism and imperialist thuggery, whose spirit may be savoured by a few mornings with the Edinburgh *Scotsman* and a few evenings watching Scottish television, appears to be solidly represented in the Scottish National Party. . . . As far as I'm concerned, Scotland will be reborn the day the last minister is strangled with the last copy of the *Sunday Post*.' The *Sunday Post* being a particularly smug, pious, reactionary newspaper giving comfort to almost the entire country, reinforcing its readers in their cosy prejudices, sentimentalism, romanticism, and self-satisfaction. There is nothing quite like the *Sunday Post* for bringing a flush of patriotic pleasure or radical rage to the cheeks of its supporters and detractors.

In *No Gods and Precious Few Heroes*, an account of Scotland from 1914 to 1980, the historian Christopher Harvie in his Introduction quotes appositely from *The Leopard* by Giuseppe di Lampedusa:

Lampedusa's Prince characterized his Sicily as punch-drunk, crippled by climate and recurrent invasions, a country that could only be a senile spectator of the nineteenth-century industrial world. It was the perceptive comment of a man – Lampedusa himself – drawn from an older stratum of society yet powerfully affected by the main current of twentieth-century thought, Marxism. But it was fundamentally pessimistic: modern industrialization and class-formation were too much for the ingrained traditions of the country; and qualities of consciousness, however perceptive, were not enough to combat this; the intellectuals solved their problems by moving out. If there can be little quarrel with this analysis of one type of decadence, then something analogous to it applies only too accurately to Scotland: two centuries of industrialization have done the work of 2,500 years of Sicilian subjugation.

Edwin Muir, in the 1930s, would have had no quarrel with this view of Scotland in decline. There was little doubt in Muir's mind that the traditional life of the Scottish people was inevitably disintegrating owing to the lack of any 'visible and effective power to hold it together'. No such problem affected the English, he observed: England would not cease to be itself. 'But all that Scotland possesses is its style of life; once it loses that it loses everything, and is nothing more than a name on a map.' Muir, not being a preservationist for the sake of it, was obliged to consider whether the Scottish way of life was in fact worth preserving and, if so, what could be done to conserve something judged to be of value. His opinion was that the Scots could only decide the question for themselves, but that they could not solve it unaided: 'the understanding and help of England are needed. It would be foolish to claim that the Scottish style of life is inherently better than the English; in most ways it is less admirable; but it is a style with laws of its own, which it must obey if it is to achieve anything of genuine worth.'

Scotland today is perhaps not a notably oppressed country, but it is a disappointed country, uncertain of its national identity. It relies on regrets, recriminations, and resentments to rally itself – but it is easily seduced by promises of short term gain, as though, once given a leg up, with one bound Jock will be free. A letter to the *Scotsman* on 15 January 1985 said, among other tart things, that 'Scotland will not achieve independence and would not know what to do with it anyway until it regains its self-reliance in an atmosphere of pride and self-knowledge.' Well, the Scots have pride enough when they take what is offered as something less than their due, and self-knowledge is not lacking, though there is a stern reluctance to acknowledge bitter truths that can be more palatably wrapped in sugary romanticism. The Scots blame others more than they are able to blame themselves – this projection of national resentment is sometimes based properly in fact, but too often it is a self-denying fantasy. On the analyst's couch, the Scots would not be allowed to get away with it for a minute – but they have got away with it for several hundred years, to their own considerable confusion.

Scottish Nationalism, the fitful desire for it, the bureaucratic and political struggle for it, the focus it provides for possible amelioration of discontent, is perhaps a form of displacement activity. Since the Scots cannot, or will not, cease to cherish their history and take pride in their national identity, Scottish Nationalism has become a symbol of Scottish adulthood. That the Scots are different, that they have their own particular needs and desires that stem from a particular culture (or two cultures, Highland and Lowland), and that the national identity can only, or best, be continued by self-determination, is an argument common to most peoples who wish a greater say in their own affairs. Like the Basques, the Scots have a decent case. Unlike the Basques, Scots do not resort to violence – though there are some wild men on the fringes of the Nationalist movement – to gain their ends. Yet the Scots survive, at home and abroad. They have a genius for survival that resides in the Scottish character and informs the manifestations of that character. Anything antithetical to that character is rejected or, by a process of assimilation, altered to suit it. By and large, the Scots lead a quiet life. To the extent that they are not naturally revolutionary, they are left to themselves – the result being that the English and others who would subvert, it is said, the Scots, are ignorant of Scottish potential, history, culture, and passions. A Scot never likes to be ignored or underrated: Nationalism may be a convenient means of asserting himself and involving himself in the subtle, tricky, art of getting what he wants by making a proper nuisance of himself. The undergraduate spirit of protest, deeply felt, but also offering an exciting alternative to the dull business of getting on in life, pervades Scottish Nationalism.

Nationalism has somewhat sunk into dilapidation after the high hopes in the 1970s of a Scottish Parliament and a substantial measure of self-determination in administrative and financial matters. Nairn turns to Europe and the world for inspiration, for the hope of salvation for Scotland, while Hector MacIver turned, in a different manner, equally to the wider world. He, too, saw that Scotland was a disparate, disputatious, divided country. Karl Miller describes the view of MacIver who

> was a living reproof to the Nationalist conception that Scotland was racially or ethnically homogeneous and distinct . . . He was aware that the one country of Scotland held a mixture of races, and at least two languages and two cultural traditions, and he may have felt in the end that if Scotland could contain the Western Isles, in however casual and improvident a fashion, then the British Isles could contain Scotland. He was incapable of indulging in the half-smiling pantomimes of race hatred that certain Nationalist writers went in for, and made no bones about the fact of the Scottish diaspora, the dispersal of native talent throughout the world. His friends Louis MacNeice and Dylan Thomas were not despised for living, despite their blood, in London: and Dylan Thomas was not despised for despising Welsh Nationalism. Neither of them was treated as if he were some Celtic spy who had been posted south to poison the wells of the Spoken Word in Portland Place.

In America, Europe, and elsewhere, Scottish Nationalism is regarded as rather a joke, good for a bit of humour. Scotland is not Ireland: the Scots have stolen the Stone of Destiny from Westminster Abbey in 1951, signed a grandiloquent Covenant in 1948, elected some Scottish Nationalist MPs to the House of Commons and the European Parliament; but the Nationalist movement is sporadic, fitful, and – once seen to be in decline – lapses into somnolence. Only a handful of leaders remain today, flogging hopelessly at the dead horse of the Scottish imagination in an effort to rouse it to some semblance of life that will carry them, like Uncle Tom Cobbley and all, triumphant to Westminster and, thence, in secession, to Edinburgh. The Scots, failing to get all that they want all at once, tend to give up the attack and see little point in defence in defeat. James Campbell, towards the end of the journey through Scotland that he describes in *Invisible Country*, remarks:

> 'Despised . . . ridiculed . . . sneered at . . . and ignored.' The Scottish inferiority complex; it is at once reassuring and daunting to discover that it has a long and distinguished pedigree.
>
> Scotland – and Edinburgh in particular – copes with present disablement by making the most of the small glories of the past. The capital city's former dignity has gained the force of a myth, but a myth which, instead of strengthening the people's feeling for the present, acts as compensation for it. Except on those rare occasions when the nation functions autonomously – such as at football matches – it is difficult for the Scots to believe in their country as having will and appetites of its own. It is, indeed, forced to feed off the past, an indulgence which has given us Scottish nostalgia, tartanry and Kailyard literature, Sir Harry Lauder, 'a music hall song and a few bad novels'.

II

———— ✳ ————

A nation theological: from Calvin to the Knoxplex

HELL is not what it was. In the mid-eighteenth century in Scotland it was a very real and painful prospect to young James Boswell: 'The eternity of punishment was the first great idea I ever formed. How it made me shudder! Since fire was a material substance, I had an idea of it. I thought but rarely about the bliss of heaven because I had no idea of it. I had heard that one passed one's time there in endless praise of God, and I imagined that that meant singing psalms as in church; and singing psalms did not appeal to me. I should not have wished to go to heaven if there had been any other way of not going to hell.' Between the two twentieth-century world wars, Norman Maclean, a popular liberal Evangelical minister, harrowed hell by declaring that 'Man's place is not fixed unalterably in death; if he carry with him the power of choice and will; if in the depth of hell it be still in his power to say "I will arise and go to my Father."' Free will, rather than predestination from birth to be damned or saved, was a serious matter on which many Scottish ministers chose not to preach. As T. C. Smout puts it, 'How could a Protestant religion survive in its traditional forms if God was truly Love?' Justice was what the Scots had been conditioned to accept, fair but cold. If Charity was to be brought into the equation, with the prospect of forgiveness and redemption, then the after-life might not be precisely as confidently reported from the pulpit.

The Scots in 1560, at the time of the legal establishment of the Reformation, true to their character, adopted the logical system of Calvin. The English, true to theirs, tempered Calvinistic austerities and comfortably compromised. From the sixteenth to the nineteenth centuries, says Smout, Scotland was regarded by churchmen as 'a new Israel, its inhabitants a second chosen people of the Lord'. From the evangelizing mission of St Columba to Iona in the middle of the sixth century, the Scots have regarded themselves as virtually the first among the elect of God.

The characteristic stubbornness and tendency to go to logical extremes was already established in the nature of the Scots, but religion ingrained it so deeply that Calvinism and the Scottish character have come to seem almost synonymous. Religion was a stern discipline that set its mark on generation after generation and still retains a hold on the Scottish conscience. The Scots have become imbued with a persistent guilt over the slightest infractions of Calvinist morality. But such an uncompromising religion could not have taken root had it not appealed strongly to the hearts as much as to the minds of the Scots. Its austerities suited their lives, and it became an intellectual delight to establish principles and give logical, rational explanations for them. It was about the only delight Calvinism did have to offer: mostly, it reprobated all pleasures. The Scots profoundly distrust all pleasures of the senses. Drink numbs the senses, and that may partly account for its popularity. We know, surely, that if we have not suffered before pleasure, we shall certainly suffer as a result of it: best to eschew it altogether, or to drive out guilt by excess in which may be found oblivion.

Hector MacIver, in a collection of essays entitled *Scottish Country*, published in 1935, wrote: 'As interpreted by the Presbyterian ministers of the Hebrides, life is identified with asceticism and repression. The crucifixion of the body is the monotonous theme of all their discourses. Drinking, dancing, music and recreation are officially condemned. But these gentlemen in their fanatical and destructive campaign forget that such taboos cannot be imposed on country people, whose nature it is to set more store on human values than ascetic ones. And the more their human wants are denied them, the more they tend to excess.' Karl Miller commented, in 1970, after quoting this passage in *Romantic Town*, that '"Asceticism and repression" are no joke, but a painful and stubborn reality, which counts for more than the lack of cultural institutions has done, and which breeds the "violent dreamed escape" – in the words of another poet, Thom Gunn – through drink or through a strenuous, murderous sexuality, a wiring into women.' Miller also remarks that 'Romanticism is associated historically with the challenge to the Church's authority which developed during the nineteenth century. The pursuit of the clandestine and the forbidden, and of excess, is romantic.'

That authority was widespread. Until the 1870s, the Church supervised education, it was a social venue (often, in rural districts, the only regular community meeting place), it administered Poor Relief until 1845, was involved in banking, and generally busied itself with all aspects of everyday life – though not in any genial manner. The ministers of the Church were regarded by their congregations as remote, austere characters readier with a word of warning and reproof than with an ear to listen or a mouth to encourage. The Church exercised and retained considerable power over the lives of most Scots until after World War II. 'The Church' implies a monolith – but the Scots have ever been active dissenters, schismatics, and intellectual heretics. The history of church politics in Scotland is complex, but briefly: the established Church of Scotland was widely supported numerically at the beginning of the nineteenth century. Roman Catholics were mostly to be found in some Highland parishes, Aberdeenshire, and among Irish immigrants. Episcopalians were mostly upper-middle class: it was fashionable to be Episcopalian, but they were few in number and inconsiderable as a social force. Evangelism fired the minds and hearts of Congregationalists who were few in number, and there were scattered bodies of Quakers, Baptists, Methodists, and seceders from the established Church who continued to be Presbyterians.

The Evangelicals, in the early years of the nineteenth century, began to assert themselves against the dominant Moderates of the Church of Scotland, influenced by English revivalists such as Wilberforce and Simeon. Both parties were orthodox Calvinists, though the Evangelists were narrower in their beliefs and fervid in their enthusiasm, looking back to the seventeenth-century Covenanters, martyrs all, for lessons in intolerance and faith. The Evangelicals ardently and urgently wished to reform society as a whole, and to that end would brook no intellectual deviation – the Moderates might seek to save an individual; the Evangelicals were out to save a nation. The Evangelicals appealed strongly to the rising urban middle class, exhorting them to respect the laws of political economy, discourage trade unionism, dedicate themselves to moral and material improvement (much the same thing, in the mind of the middle class and the Evangelicals: 'The gospel of wealth but echoes Christ's words,' declared Andrew Carnegie), devote themselves to self-interest and self-help, and thereby, as shining examples, inspire the working class to traditional virtue of the simpler sort – thrift, sobriety, continence, and personal responsibility. The middle class heard what it wanted to hear and enthusiastically supported the Evangelicals in their crusade to redeem Scotland from moral and economic bankruptcy. To the credit of the Evangelicals, they also laid equal stress on philanthropy – on the improvement of community morals and conditions, a creed that inspired the social consciences of Carnegie, Collins, Quarrier, and Peabody. By 1834 the Evangelicals dominated the governing body of the Church of Scotland, the General Assembly.

The government, less fired by Evangelical zeal, refused to contribute to the maintenance or extension of the godly work. Funds were not forthcoming to build new churches. Additionally, Evangelicals had been frustrated by the laws of Parliament in their desire to restrict the right of landowners to appoint their own nominees to the ministry of the Church. The Evangelicals seceded to form the Free Church of Scotland, to be financed by voluntary subscription. Since philanthropy was encouraged among its supporters, the Free Church of Scotland drew a great deal of income from its middle-class congregations and established not only its material but its moral credit. The Evangelicals all but destroyed the Moderate Church of Scotland. Not until 1929 were they reconciled and reunited. These storms were of the greatest interest to the Scots: in 1851, a third of the population could be found in one or other of the churches on a Sunday. By 1900, attendance had substantially dropped and by the 1950s only about twenty per cent of the population regularly attended church services: still a good number, but indicative of a continuing falling away from the Church. Gradually, the Church of Scotland has dropped its immoderate beliefs in favour of liberal Protestantism: though there is still a body of opinion that attributes the drop in Church attendance to the integration of the beastly doctrines of Darwin, the Biblical scholarship of Andrew Bruce Davidson, who in the latter part of the nineteenth century influenced two generations of divinity students by his literary and historical criticism of scripture, and George Adam Smith, who in 1902 was tried for heresy when he suggested, among other things, that Genesis was not an accurate historical record. He was acquitted of the charge.

Roman Catholicism was barely tolerated in Scotland after the Reformation, and all but died away until, in the eighteenth century, not more than 30,000, mostly in rural areas, remained loyal to their faith. But Irish immigrants in the mid-nineteenth century increased the Catholic population to about 146,000. By 1951, there were three quarters of a million (fifteen per cent of the population) Catholics in Scotland. There was, and continues to be, some secular and religious resentment against Catholics in Scotland. Most of the bigotry is confined to football matches, but marches by Protestant Orangemen are perceived by Catholics to be, and no doubt sometimes verifiably are, provocative and inflammatory of religious division which too quickly becomes social division. Catholics maintain their own schools in Scotland, and – despite the move towards ecumenism (bitterly opposed by religious bigots among extremist Protestants) – generally keep themselves to themselves. Episcopalian churches thrive and are not resented unless they move towards the introduction of elaborate ritual. But they are supported, as has been suggested, mostly by middle-class Anglo-Scots and the Episcopalian support in Scotland may be reckoned at not more than five per cent of the population – if that. It would be unfair to suggest that pious Episcopalians attract new Scottish members to their congregations because they offer social advantage, but that perception, in the minds of some Scots, is ineradicable.

Church-going is confined, to a large extent, to women and children. Children are still sent in significant numbers to Sunday School, though their parents may not regularly attend Sunday services. Male church-goers are, normally, middle class and devoted to the conventional morality of thrift and self-help, or wish to make a contribution to the community through service to the presbytery and church organizations. Over-emphatic piety is neither expected nor encouraged. But convention, as a motive for church attendance, is dying out with the corresponding diminution of the Church as a significant force in urban areas. The Church maintains strong and good relations with the community in rural areas where, possibly as a result, community attendance is stronger and more regular. The Church now rarely talks to its congregations *de haut en bas*: indeed, makes an effort to be relevant to current social conditions and its ministers spare no effort to act as unofficial social workers. Intellectually, the Church has reconciled its doctrines, more or less, with modern philosophical, scientific, and scriptural thought. It actively seeks to influence government thinking on crucial matters of wide general concern – it pronounces, in the forum of the annual General Assembly of the Church of Scotland, on politics, the nuclear threat, social morality, and – vitally – the relationship between Church and State. The Church of Scotland, like any other significant pressure group, is regularly consulted by the government and no doubt its views are taken into account. That it is listened to, sometimes sympathetically, sometimes sceptically, is a tribute to tradition rather than an acknowledgement that the Church still controls the hearts and minds of the Scots. It may occasionally oblige them to think, but it no longer has a monopoly of influence.

Statistics about church-going, however, tell us very little about the residual effect of the Reformation on the Scottish psyche. That the original impact was profound, and not only confirmed many Scottish traits of personality but accentuated them and gave them an outlet for expression, is certain. No less certain is the fact that the disturbance of the Scottish psyche has not yet run its full course. In her weekly *Scotsman* column, Dr Anne Smith recently discussed the advantages the Scots might obtain from thorough psychoanalysis, with particular reference to an examination of the connection between Calvinism and guilt. 'Beyond the shadow of a doubt,' she remarked, 'it will be found the Knox Syndrome is at the root of all our major national afflictions, from tooth decay to alcoholism. Our morbid national craving for cakes and ale, in short, is a neurotic response to the Knoxious injunction to virtue which all Scots suck in with their mother's milk ... I asked a friend, an American artist (no Scot would touch the job) to design for me a series of postcards with titles like "Flashing John Knox", "The Monstrous Regiment of Knox", and "The Nightlife of J. K." She had never heard of the National Scourge, and I had, on my conscience, to explain to her that these postcards would be seen to be blasphemous, for in the Scottish psyche John Knox and God are one and the same.'

John Knox was the leading militant Protestant of the Scottish Reformation, in constant conflict with the Roman Catholic Mary Queen of Scots. He suffers, perhaps in the comparison: as Sellers and Yeatman, authors of *1066 and All That* might have put it, Mary was historically wrong but romantic, while Knox was right but repulsive. Knox was largely responsible for uniting those Scots of later generations who were joined together in a doleful national identity that found expression in Calvinism and cold comfort in Predestination. Stevenson, writing about Knox in the latter part of the nineteenth century, commented: 'A new creed, like a new country, is an unhomely place of sojourn; but it makes men lean on one another and join hands.' But there was no room for anyone who would not join hands: like Freud, who suffered no criticism of his views on the ground that he had first to establish a bridgehead before permitting attack on his principles and doctrines, so the Scots permitted not the slightest yielding against the forces that might defeat or encroach upon them. George Mackay Brown, in *The Broken Heraldy*, reflects sadly on the sudden changes brought about by the Reformation in Orkney. 'In earlier times the temporal and the eternal, the story and the fable, were not divorced, as they came to be after Knox: they used the same language and imagery, so that the whole of life was illuminated. Crofters and fishermen knew what Christ was talking about, better perhaps than the canons and prebendaries of St Magnus, because they bore the stigmata of labour on their bodies – the net let down into the sea, the sower going forth to sow, the fields white towards harvest.' Then there developed the idea of progress. 'Suddenly the violent change to Calvinism was thrust on them. Their sacraments were forbidden and squandered; their altars and images put down; black preachers solemnly impressed on them that their strivings towards the consummation of heaven would avail them nothing, since either their salvation or their damnation was sealed before the beginning of the world. . . . Poets followed priests into the darkness. It is almost impossible, at a distance of four centuries, to estimate the catastrophe that Calvinism brought to Orkney (and to the rest of Scotland).' Edwin Muir, as much as George Mackay Brown and many other Scottish writers, bitterly resented the influence of Calvinism over Scotland, its life and its people. And yet, and yet, as Moray McLaren points out, 'our Reformation was, though it may not have been conceived by us, made by us, fashioned after our own ideas,' and it was Knox, a Scotsman, who so efficiently proselytized the basic tenets of the Reformation in Scotland. 'He was vehement in affection, as in doctrine,' says Stevenson. 'Knox was not one of those who are humble in the hour of triumph; he was aggressive even when things were at their worst. He had a grim reliance in himself, or rather in his mission; if he were not sure that he was a great man, he was at least sure that he was one set apart to do great things.'

This is true of very many Scotsmen who, despite personal misgivings, have carried the lantern of enlightenment (as they conceive of it) into many dark and daunting places. The lantern of Knox's own analysis, says Stevenson, 'did not always shine with a very serviceable light; but he had the virtue, at least, to carry it into many places of fictitious holiness, and was not abashed by the tinsel divinity that hedged kings and queens from his contemporaries.' Knox never doubted that he was right, that his interpretation was correct, that the burning word would smoke out falsehood and error. As Alastair Reid remarks, 'There is a sense in which the Scots are never wrong about anything, which, translated, means that they shut from their minds any thought of an alternative to their own way of life. National infallibility is not anything to admire, although its persistence into this turbulent present may be admirable, as were kamikaze pilots in the Pacific.' The Scots do tend to be stoical about fate, and accept third or fourth best as inevitable, while reflecting that they have at least avoided fifth or sixth best. 'That things could be worse is a woeful substitute for the hope that they could be better,' writes Alastair Reid – 'that human life is bearable seems to me to fall miserably short of the possibility of its being fruitfully enjoyed.' Like the feeling of nationality, the Scottish religious sentiment is a solemn thing to be observed with a grim relish.

The theology and morality of the Presbyterian Church of Scotland is perhaps losing a little of its firm grip on the Scottish psyche – it is not too much to say that the Church is making efforts to relax it, and many Presbyterian ministers are very much more socially conscious and humanitarian than, say, fifty years ago. Certainly, militant Protestantism that sets its face against ecumenism and maintains a resolute sectarianism is on the decline in Scotland. Dr Steve Bruce in a recent book, *No Pope of*

Rome, claims that the Scottish culture is now largely secular and that militant Protestantism has no bedrock of support that can be rallied against Catholics in Scotland. The doctrines of Calvinism have been moderated, and the polite conventions of the bourgeoisie have socialized working-class entrants into the ministry, weaning them from their Orange origins which they perceive as a reactionary working-class phenomenon.

> If Protestantism survives, [*says Dr Bruce*] it will be in a 'ghetto' in small isolated communities, separated from the main culture either because of geographical features (as in the case of the Highlands and Islands) or because a group of people have chosen to build their own social institutions to preserve their faith and identity. There is no widespread anti-Catholicism just waiting for the right sort of leader. Scotland is no longer a country in which the country is informed by strongly held Protestant principles. In some urban areas, young Protestants and Catholics still fight, but even this violence is considerably less than it was in the days of the 'Billy Boys' and the 'Norman Conks'. It is just a boy's game. And isolated in the geographical peripheries, older people believe that the Pope is the anti-Christ and that the health of a society depends on keeping the Lord's Day. But most Scots are not part of either of these cultures. They see the young bloods of the Scottish Loyalist movement as unprincipled thugs; they see the Highland Calvinists as quaint oddities. Most Scots live in a secular society.

Since church-going is very much in decline, Scottish morals have been relaxed in line with those of most Western Protestant societies. Young people may now live together without the convention of marriage, illegitimate children are not, generally, held to be disgraceful, it is possible to work or shop on a Sunday, the licensing laws and hours are liberal and civilized: almost the sole exception to this softening of moral outrage is the position of homosexuals in Scotland. Their activities are still, under law, illegal though in practice the laws against the sexual activities of two consenting adult men in private are a dead letter – such men are not usually prosecuted unless their activities give rise to public offence. God's judgement on those reckoned to be sinners is not invoked very readily nowadays except by the editor of the *Sunday Express* and the more reactionary readers of the *Sunday Post*.

To give a flavour of pre-permissive days, it is instructive to turn to the diaries of John Mill, a pious and devoted minister of the mid-eighteenth century. He recorded many and wonderful instances of the lax morals of a decadent world and the divine retribution which, inevitably and gratifyingly, they inspired. In 1753 he was appealed to by a parishioner to rebuke another for taking the name of God in vain and imprecating damnation on the petitioner. Mill upbraided the offender and warned him that he was likely himself to be damned unless he sincerely repented. The blasphemer told Mill he had repented, according to his ability, of his awesome crime, but betrayed himself when, wrote Mill, 'he bought a dram and, offering to take it without a blessing asked, I checked him. The fellow trembled, and was in great confusion, which made me suspect he had lied in saying he had sought pardon from God, and was adding sin to sin rather.' The next morning, Mill was informed that the imperfect penitent later 'gave loose reins to daft mirth; and going out, was suddenly struck dead at the peat stack.' This was too good to waste: at the first opportunity, Mill 'laid the whole matter, as it stood, before the congregation, warning all thereby to guard against that heinous sin, as they would wish to escape God's righteous judgement.'

Despite his best efforts, Mill found his parishioners 'so immersed in the body and world that the most rousing sermons and awful alarming providences make no impression on their blind heads and obstinate hearts.' Pestilential fever in 1758, a winter of ice and snow, and famine, failed to turn the hearts and minds of his flock towards respectful contemplation of God's judgement: there were more immediate matters to be considered – 'everyone looking about them how breaches might be made up in the loss of husband, wife or child, etc.' Mill himself was afflicted with sciatica, but took a leaf out of the Book of Job, and submitted to God's wisdom: 'I desire to kiss the rod that smites. He does not afflict, nor grieve the children of men willingly, nor for His pleasure, but people's profit, to make them partakers of His holiness that they may share in His happiness. And blessed be His great and glorious name who was pleased to open my eyes to read in my sin the punishment.' This apparently comfortless philosophy much consoled him in his pain.

1788 was no better a year. The best crop for seven years had merely encouraged the people who 'were publickly warned to beware of abusing it to God's dishonour, as they had done in 1781, by fidling and Ranting, gluttony, Drunkenness, and all unclean abominations, the usual concomitants thereof, and thereby provoke a just and holy God to send sore judgments on the land, by famine and a plague, to sweep such obstinate vermin off the earth into the pit of destruction.' These warnings of apocalyptic judgement were regularly issued in times of glut or of famine – the God of the Presbyterians was a difficult God to please. The want of the spirit of God operating within his flock to their betterment was a continual disappointment to Mr Mill, their good shepherd, who deplored and denounced, ever observing the machinations of the Devil in the souls of the hard-pressed Scots.

When not actively struggling with the Devil, ministers of the Church beguiled their leisure moments by considering fine points of theology to propound to their congregations. 'We may take as a fair exponent of old Scottish theology Professor Blackwell of Aberdeen,' writes H. G. Graham in *The Social Life of Scotland in the Eighteenth Century*, 'who in various works which are long forgotten presents to the world an orthodox scheme of the Universe.' Mr Graham smacks his lips with relish as he approaches this imaginative and thorough theologian.

In his theological works he shows himself as inquisitive and energetic in investigating still higher matters. In giving an account of the origin of the Universe he writes down the 'motions' and 'resolutions' of the Council of Trinity like a clerk writing the minutes of a meeting of Presbytery.

He tells how the Deity did from all eternity enjoy perfect blessedness in the 'contemplation of His own perfection'. But the Divine Mind 'presently' found that He could get 'an additional revenue of glory by creating rational creatures who should sing eternal hallelujahs.' 'A motion was made' to this effect in the Council of Three-in-One; and 'the aforesaid great motion was agreed to (Job. xxxv.7, Rev. iv. 11),' – so states Dr Blackwell, who attributes to the deliberations of the Trinity the procedure of the Presbytery of Aberdeen. He next describes how the 'great decreed moment' arrived for 'eternity to give place to a parenthesis of time'; how matter was created out of nothing; he shows how angels were created in the third heaven, 'of which the firmament is the coarser side of the pavement'; 'these angels are the rational creatures' who are created largely to sing 'eternal hallelujahs' to delight the Trinity and, in order that their movements through space may not be impeded, their garments are made loose. The earth was then formed with the vegetables and the beasts thereon; but in time the Trinity discovered a great blank in the architecture of the world – which, it is curious, had not been foreseen. To adjust this difficulty, a Council of Three-in-One assembled, and man was created: firstly, to declare God's perfections; to be a 'covenanting party to transact with the Trinity'; to bring wild beasts to subjection 'by the stateliness of his person, the majesty of his countenance, and the carefulness of his voice'; and lastly, to prevent angels supposing all things were created for themselves, to 'produce double return of declarative glory to God'. According to this scheme and all of those old schemes, everything was made and designed to give glory and honour and praise to the Deity, while in the other world angels and men have their employment through eternity, singing praises and hallelujahs . . .

The Fall of man was the subject of endless ingenuity to justify the ways of God to men; and it was the unfailing topic of every sermon from every pulpit. It was proved by preachers how 'extremely kind' it was to make the fate of all future generations depend on Adam's conduct. 'What could be more kind,' it was urged, 'than for the Creator to accept the obedience of one man in the room of millions, and instead of exacting perfect obedience from each individual? What could be more fair than to make a covenant with a being formed perfect, and therefore the most likely to keep the bargain, than to require it of each and all, who would be more likely to break it? Surely if all mankind had been present in the garden of Eden, they would unanimously have agreed to such a proposal, and have chosen Adam as their representative.' It is thus that Professor Blackwell makes the difficulty vanish.

Would that all difficulties had vanished so prettily, but the kindness and generosity of the implacable Creator was not much emphasized: justice was His inevitable reward for saint or sinner, and no pleas in mitigation were accepted. Confession could not redeem error or obtain absolution, and to suppose that it could was considered Popish hypocrisy.

It is little wonder, considering the emphasis placed on hell-fire, sulphur, and certain damnation, that the Scots have been preoccupied with the subject of death, what Stevenson called 'the great change'. Their translation from one condition to another was a matter of much concern, and a certain art grew up around it. In *Picturesque Notes on Edinburgh*, Stevenson remarked that, 'setting aside tombs of Roubilliac, which belong to the heroic order of graveyard art, we Scots stand, to my fancy, highest among nations in the matter of grimly illustrating death. We seem to love for their own sake the emblems of time and the great change; and even around churches you will find a wonderful exhibition of skulls, and crossbones, and noseless angels, and trumpets pealing for the Judgement Day. Every mason was a pedestrian Holbein: he had a deep consciousness of death, and loved to put its terrors pithily before the churchyard loiterer; he was brimful of rough hints upon mortality, and any dead farmer was seized upon to be a text. The classical examples of this art are in Greyfriars.'

Humbler, but no less affecting intimations of mortality were preserved and ornamented by one Robert Paterson who was born at Haggisha, near Hawick, in 1715. After marriage, he followed the gloomy trade of a monumental mason. He was a violent Presbyterian and Anti-Jacobite. Unfortunately, his stone quarry lay in the path of Prince Charles Edward Stuart's army retreating from England, and Mr Paterson, for some piece of impertinence, was swept off with the troops after they had plundered his house.

He is next heard of as a follower of the Covenanting martyr Richard Cameron, and devoting himself to the maintenance and restoration of the gravestones of Covenanting heroes. Where a stern and spotless Presbyterian hero lacked a stone, Paterson would supply one from his own yard, graced with an epitaph of his own devising. In 1758 he deserted his wife and five children, the eldest of which discovered him soon afterwards working on a nearby tombstone. His virtuous discipline had become a mania: he remained deaf to pleas for his speedy return to his family, and for forty-three years thereafter he haunted kirkyards in search of the martyrs' tombs.

His melancholy figure, mounted on a white horse, became a familiar sight. When in Galloway one time, Paterson happened to call at a house where young Walter Scott was being entertained. Scott naturally enquired who this mournful old party might be, and in a burst of happy inspiration, his hostess replied, 'Old Mortality.' And so, through the writings of Scott, he became.

With somewhat larger pretensions, the tenth Duke of Hamilton, who flourished between 1767 and 1825, prepared for immortality by building a mausoleum for himself, his forebears, and his descendants. Augustus Hare, in *The Story of My Life*, published in 1900, lovingly describes this monument to mortality: in the park of Hamilton Palace (now demolished)

is a huge domed edifice something like the tomb of Theodoric at Ravenna. It was erected by the last Duke for himself, his son, his grandson, and his nine predecessors. 'What a grand sight it will be,' he said, 'when twelve Dukes of Hamilton rise together here at the Resurrection!' He lies himself just under the dome, upon a pavement of coloured marbles and inside the sarcophagus of an Egyptian queen, with *her* image painted and sculptured outside. He had this sarcophagus brought from Thebes, and used frequently to lie down in it to see how it fitted. It is made of Egyptian syenite, the hardest of all stones, and could not be altered; but when dying he was so haunted by the idea that his body might be too long to go inside the queen, that his last words were, 'Double me up! double me up!' The last drive he took had been to buy spices for his own embalming. After he was dead, no amount of doubling up could get him into the mummy-case, and they had to cut off his feet to do it. The mausoleum is a most strange place; and as you enter mysterious voices seem to be whispering and clamouring together in the height of the dome; and when the door bangs, it is as if all the demons in the Inferno were let loose, and the shriekings and screamings around you are perfectly terrific. Beneath lie all the house of Hamilton in their crimson coffins, which you survey by the light of a single tallow candle.

To Hare, who took a certain morbid interest in such things, all this was wholly satisfactory.

Revelations of the life hereafter were not all of hell-fire and sulphur: more subtle tortures might be approached with dread. One of her friends, asking Miss Meenie Trotter of the Mortonhall family how she was, received the reply, 'Very weel – quite weel. But, eh, I had a dismal dream last night; a fearful dream! Of a' the places in the world, I dreamed I was in heaven! And what d'ye think I saw there? De'il hae't but thoosands upon thoosands o' stark naked weans! That would be a dreadful thing, for ye ken I ne'er could bide bairns a' my days.' In this considerable alarm at being surrounded for all eternity by a host of naked cherubim, she died shortly thereafter.

Few Scots now, except the most hidebound in the Highlands

and Islands, believe in Predestination, in the elect and the damned, in eternal brimstone or harp-plucking for the greater glorification of God. But the legacy of Calvinism remains a potent force – the pursed lip and the gimlet eye still reprobate deviations from the norm of bourgeois sensibility, and pride silently covers a multitude of indiscretions. But shameful little secrets are the very stuff of small-town and village gossip. In 'Borderlines', an essay contributed to *Memoirs of a Modern Scotland*, Alastair Reid notes that the people of the Scottish Border country 'are all instinctive custodians of a *status quo*, protective towards themselves and one another, censorious according to a public morality which they maintain ruthlessly but understand only imperfectly: it makes them at worst into fearful gossips, at best into fearful nay-sayers with an infallible eye for the flaws in any argument. Even more, it makes them extremely difficult to identify as individual people . . . an individual is less a separate entity than a function within a community; people have meaning, not in themselves, but in a context.'

Reid has prefaced these comments with the opinion that, 'Whether from a collective guilt or fear or shame, the private self gets irretrievably buried, and the few who prevail are labelled as eccentrics or "characters" and granted licences which allow them to be at once outrageous but ineffectual, the stuff of fresh anecdote . . . Spontaneity is immediately suspicious, private feelings a cause for shame; one is still told, by people wearing pain on their faces: "Oh, we can't complain." Whatever it stems from – the Protestant ethic, pride, guilt, the fear of being found out, the notion of human life as something to be tholed or endured – this inborn attitude seems to me intolerable, unfruitful and certainly unfulfilling.'

Presbyterianism, Protestantism, Calvinism, or what have you, has put its mark on the Scots who still, generally, bow their heads to any condemnation of their unconsidered, frivolous activities as wasteful, if not nowadays positively sinful. Reid is surely right to say that eccentricity – that is to say, any deviation from a vaguely understood but definitely felt norm of social behaviour – is tolerated so long as it does not threaten, so long as it occurs only on the periphery of everyday life. The Scots need a definite occasion in order to express joyfulness, spontaneous glee, ebullience – whether at a *ceilidh*, a wedding, a Burns' Night Supper, or on New Year's Eve. They need a reason, or a licence, to be gay and spirited. And of course, since such occasions are not frequent, the Scots tend to excess when given a pretext for pleasure. Even in their recreations, the Scots are not light.

12

---- * ----

The Thistle looks at a drunk man: bards and booze

THE lyrical qualities of poetry and strong drink, and the lyricism intoxicants induce, are combined in Scottish life. The annual feast to celebrate the national poet, Robert Burns, on 25 January is the most striking instance of the association of bards and booze. 'In Scotland,' states Stevenson, 'all our singers have a stave or two for blazing fires and stout potations: – to get indoors out of the wind and swallow something hot to the stomach, are benefits so easily appreciated where they dwelt!' In less cosy mood, he remarks: 'A Scot of poetic temperament, and without religious exaltation, drops as if by nature into the public house. The picture may not be pleasing, but what else is a man to do in this dog's weather?' Robert Benchley, in his urgent desire to 'get out of these wet clothes and into a Dry Martini', might have understood the Scots in this particular aspect of their attitude to drink.

Passion, one of the predominant characteristics of the Scots, is most effectively liberated by drink. In an Edinburgh pub selected more or less at random by Moray McLaren in the 1930s, 'The faces of the drinkers pleased me; most of them were intelligent; and this quality, predominant through the passion and the violence of the expressions which they assumed as their owners discussed, jeered, condoled, expostulated or extravagantly

praised, prevented that death-like looseness which so fright-
eningly descends upon the more torpid, the less vital faces of
those Anglo-Saxons who have abandoned themselves to some
form of dissipation.' Edwin Muir also remarks the difference
between Scottish and English drinkers: 'Scottish people drink
spasmodically and intensely, for the sake of a momentary but
complete release, whereas the English like to bathe and paddle
about bucolically in a mild puddle of beer. One might put this
down to a difference of national temperament or of national
religion or to a hundred other things; there is no doubt, in any
case, that the drinking habits of the Scots, like their dances, are
far wilder than those of the English.'

The Scottish pub as a forum for passionate debate struck
Moray McLaren very forcibly:

I caught something of the conversation around me. It was,
though forced out in jets of speech, really remarkably intelligent and, for a public-house discussion, what was so extraordinary, each disputant did not merely pursue his own train of
thought, moving farther away from his opponents', but paid
some kind of grudging attention to what was said to him and
made an attempt to deal with his opponents' points. The glory
of the English pub argument is that it gives wings to the
imagination, to the latent poetry of the race. Each arguer,
though there be as many as a dozen, floats off on a particular
line of thought: the only effect of the other's speech is the
murmuring stimulation of sound to moving thought. The sense
of it has no importance. In this way are the poets made.

Things are radically different in a Scottish saloon bar: 'Scottish
argument – and some of the best of it has taken place in Scottish
pubs – is coherent and contained in one channel, one direction.
Though the disputants may fight, struggle, cry out with impatience, or surrender angrily, they cling together and are impelled,
one furious group, in the same way by the same wind of thought.
In this way are the theologians and philosophers made.' Theology

and philosophy spring from the same well of *aqua vitae* as poetry, of course, and are animated and illuminated by drink so that alcohol, taken to console the spirit, enables a man to summon the more profound comforts of philosophy, theology and poetry. Boswell, offering an apparently general but in fact peculiarly personal apologia for drink, in his guise as 'The Hypochondriack' contributing several essays on the subject of drink to *The London Magazine* in 1780, prefaces his comments with the declaration: 'I do fairly acknowledge that I love Drinking; that I have a constitutional inclination to indulge in fermented liquors, and that if it were not for the restraints of reason and religion I am afraid I should be as constant a votary of Bacchus as any man.' Like his friend Dr Johnson however, reason and religion were not sufficient restraints upon a character that could only be abstemious since it could not be temperate. Boswell now and again put himself on a water diet, but inevitably turned again to the bottle.

'An Hypochondriack', says Boswell, 'is under peculiar temptations to participate freely of wine. For the impatience of his temper under his sufferings which are sometimes almost intolerable, urges him to fly to what will give him immediate relief... To have the mind fairly disengaged from its baneful foe [*black distress*], even for a little while, is of essential consequence. For it may then exert its latent vigour, and though hurt by its rough deliverer, be able to get the better of what pressed it down before in abject submission.' As a specific against depression, drink is a convenient method of rallying the spirits and increasing the gaiety of social life in Scotland. In this respect, the attitude of the Scots to drink is not unique, but their reputation as hard and purposeful drinkers exceeds the merely recreational.

In *The Glasgow Story*, published in 1952, Colm Brogan writes: 'I am told that during the Prohibition period American cinema audiences were apt to laugh and cheer at any mention or glimpse of Glasgow on the screen. They knew Glasgow as a city which produced whisky they could drink with confidence that their stomach lining would remain more or less where it was before... Glasgow may have the reputation of being a reliable whisky-

producer because it also has the reputation of being an enthusiastic whisky-consumer.' The liberality of the licensing hours and
the softer, Southern attitudes encouraged by the brewers who
have opened wine bars and tarted up their Glasgow and Edinburgh pubs, have – over the past decade, since the mid-1970s –
diminished the intense, spasmodic consumption of drink that
formerly characterized Scottish drinking habits. But the Scottish
reputation for regular blind-drunkenness persists. There are still
falling-down drunks to be found in the streets of small and large
Scottish towns on Saturday nights, belligerently squaring up to
the world if still on their feet, or grappling with it physically if on
their faces in the gutter.

Drunkenness was never confined to the peasantry, compensating as quickly as possible for the testing conditions of Scottish life.
Judges appointed to the Court of Session after 1800, says Lord
Cockburn in his *Memorials*, were conscientiously sober on the
bench, but their colleagues of the preceding generation were
accustomed to indulge in a judicial practice 'at which even their
barbaric age used to shake its head'. These gentlemen

> had always wine and biscuits *on the Bench*, when the business
> was clearly to be protracted beyond the usual dinner hour . . .
> Black bottles of strong port were set down beside them on the
> bench, with glasses, carafes of water, tumblers, and biscuits;
> and this without the slightest attempt at concealment. The
> refreshment was generally allowed to stand untouched for a
> short time, as if despised, during which their Lordships
> seemed to be intent only on their notes. But in a little, some
> water was poured into the tumbler, and sipped quietly as if
> merely to sustain nature. Then a few drops of wine were
> ventured upon, but only with the water. But at last patience
> could endure no longer, and a full bumper of the pure black
> element was tossed over; after which the thing went on regu-
> larly, and there was a comfortable munching and quaffing to
> the great envy of the parched throats in the gallery. The
> strong-headed stood it tolerably well, but it told, plainly

enough, upon the feeble. Not that the ermine was absolutely intoxicated, but it was certainly sometimes affected. This however was so ordinary with these sages, that it really made little apparent change upon them. It was not very perceptible at a distance; and they all acquired the habit of sitting and looking judicial enough, even when their bottles had reached the lowest ebb.

The Circuit courts had slightly different habits to those of Parliament Square in Edinburgh. In country districts, the 'temptation of the inn frequently produced a total stoppage of business; during which all concerned – judges and counsel, clerks, jurymen, and provost, had a jolly dinner; after which they returned to the transportations and hangings. . . It was a common remark that the step of the evening procession was far less true to the music than that of the morning.'

The Scottish pub is a dour, driech, businesslike development of the old coffee houses, clubs, and bothies that flourished in the eighteenth century. These were the products of a convivial, drinking society – particularly in Edinburgh – and class was no barrier to one's welcome reception among wits and cits, solid traders and spendthrift youths, judges and clerks, men of law, men of letters, men merely of leisure, and great lords. The ten o'clock curfew of the early eighteenth century was so regularly disregarded that, in later times, the topers tippled on until the small hours in cellars and dives where the chief expense was the expenditure of time which, since the drinkers were happy, was perhaps not wasted.

Women did not generally join the men in their refections, but they were not necessarily excluded – the likes of Jeanie Maxwell, later to be Duchess of Gordon, bundled up her skirts without compunction and descended to the oyster cellars where she drank as much porter and ate as many oysters as any man, and afterwards danced in her high-heeled shoes. Punch and brandy followed the unsteady steps of the dance, and nobody thought any the worse of Jeanie Maxwell except, perhaps, the stately Lady

Minto, who sniffed, 'the misses are the most rotten part of society'. The expense of candles and brooms was not great in these dark, dirty underground dens, but nothing very much happened to offend modesty: social life was pure compared to London standards of the period.

Drinking in Scotland used largely to be a sociable business. The first thing one was offered on crossing the threshold was a dram, and a dram was the last thing to be offered on departure; to refuse was tantamount to spurning one's host's bread and salt, to rejecting hospitality. A vestige of the custom remains today in the tradition of 'first-footing' on New Year's Eve. Few people now carry a fish and a lump of coal, to ensure the host's nourishment and warmth throughout the coming year, but it is a brave man who will refuse to take a drink from his guest's bottle or omit to offer a dram from his own to the visitor.

Drinking became less sociable in the nineteenth century and early twentieth century, taking a taciturn mode. Carlyle, having spent several hours in the company of Emerson without a word having passed between them, declared it one of the best nights he had spent with anyone. Hugh MacDiarmid described succinctly the conditions in which he preferred to drink: 'Like a high proportion of my country's regular and purposive drinkers, I greatly prefer a complete absence of women on occasions of libation. I also prefer a complete absence of music and very little illumination. I am therefore a strong supporter of the lower- or lowest type of "dive" where drinking is the principal purpose and no one wants to be distracted from that absorbing business.' The public house, in MacDiarmid's view, is not a sociable forum. 'We do not like the confiding, the intimate, the ingratiating, the hail-fellow-well-met, but prefer the unapproachable, the hard-bitten, the recalcitrant, the sinister, the malignant, the sarcastic, the saturnine, the cross-grained and the cankered, and the howling wilderness to the amenities of civilization, the irascible to the affable, the prickly to the smooth. We have no damned fellow-feeling at all.'

The cold comfort of the traditional Scottish pub bears little relation, even now, to the atmosphere of easy, warm, comfortable intimacy that the brewers have tried to encourage in their particular attempts to woo women into the social life of the public house. It is a daunting thought for a woman to enter a Scottish saloon bar unaccompanied by a man, particularly outside the urban centres of Scotland. According to one set of statistics, only one in four will dare. She can enter a hotel lounge without great trepidation, without compromising her virtue, and order a drink at the bar; she can enter one of the novelty wine-bars on her own with perfect confidence; and any pub decked out with velvet banquettes and flock wallpaper is normally open territory – no hard-grained Scot would be seen dead or dead drunk in an environment decorated, apparently, with all the taste of a Hungarian confectioner.

The Scottish pub *pur sang* is a howff, and nothing more. A wooden pew used to be a luxury and linoleum an affectation. All that was necessary was a bar counter and, at floor level, a narrow sawdust-filled trough that served a multiple function as ashtray, litter-bin, and cuspidor. The walls were generally painted cream that was allowed to fog to yellow and finally to brown, and usually dripped with a clammy condensation. Moray McLaren was lucky to meet a clutch of intelligent, argumentative drinkers in an Edinburgh pub – the level of intellectual debate, though passionate, is not high and the subject nowadays is less likely to be politics, philosophy, or theology than last Saturday's football game. The great questions will be examined and pronounced upon, of course, on request – there is nothing upon which a Scot does not have a firm opinion or, more usually, a prejudice. Anyone wishing to get down to brass tacks in a Scottish pub is likely to find himself nailed to the wall with them.

MacDiarmid attributes the lack of fellow-feeling in a Scottish pub to the Scottish scorn for mere emotion and sentimentality: 'we . . . are solely concerned with passions,' he declared. Mac-Diarmid the poet spoke and wrote from passion, and to the extent that the Scots are all passionate, they may all claim to be poets and indulge that passionate poetic temperament freely. It is the passionate temperament, after all, that is addicted to, and responds to, strong drink. 'In short,' said MacDiarmid, 'we are all poets (all true Scots – that is, all Scots not encased in a carapace of conventionality a mile thick) of *l'humour noir* and, as William Blake said: "All poets are the devil's party."'

The Licensing (Scotland) Act of 1976 was preceded by the Clayson Committee Report which recommended reform of the liquor licensing laws in Scotland. Those of England and Wales are still unreformed and it is difficult to see the Scottish experiment as other than a pilot scheme for the eventual liberalization of the licensing hours in the rest of the country – though there is still diehard opposition to change. In the past ten years the pattern of Scottish drinking has changed. The Scots, now able to obtain a drink at a bar twelve hours a day or more, no longer feel the desperate need to sink as much liquor as possible in as short a time as possible before being thrust out on the inhospitable street by a clock-watching publican. Crime statistics of liquor-related offences prosecuted by the police have shown a marked drop, though the figures probably reflect police activity over the past ten years more reliably than the level of public drinking. A Conservative Member of Parliament remarked in early 1985 that there is 'more evidence of the economic and social benefits, and we have evidence of a substantial reduction in drunkenness and lawlessness in Scotland. The gloomsters, the doomsters, the killjoys and the dead-handers cannot brush off the Scottish experience.'

Draught and canned lager has replaced whisky as Scotland's favourite tipple. It is perhaps a myth that late-twentieth-century Scots are more addicted to whisky than to other drinks. In 'The Dour Drinkers of Glasgow', published in the United States in 1952, Hugh MacDiarmid suggested that 'in Glasgow pubs today at least 90 per cent of the drinking is of beer – and mere "swipes" at that; "beer' that never saw a hop. I can remember the time when it was the other way about. What beer was consumed was used simply as a "chaser" to the whisky in precisely the same way as a "boilermaker" in New York. For, of course, you get drunk quicker on whisky plus water than on neat whisky, and whisky and soda is an English monstrosity no true Scot can countenance at all.' The recent recession has a good deal to do with the decline in whisky-drinking in pubs – the meagre shot of whisky you get for your 6op or thereabouts (the 1986 equivalent of a dollar) is enough for a mouthful, merely. But lager is heavily promoted in the press, on television, and through sports sponsorship by the brewers and it is a drink, too, that women can enjoy. The Scottish ale and lager market is worth more than £700,000,000 a year (approximately a billion dollars).

That statistic may seem, on first inspection, alarming – but it accounts for less than the 1983/84 average figure of £7.20 (about $10–12) spent weekly on drink by the average Scottish family. The figure for the UK as a whole in 1983/84 was £7.08. In 1973/74 the average Scottish family spent £2.39 on drink in a week, compared with the annual UK average of £2.03. According to these statistics, published by the Department of Employment, supplied by the Family Expenditure Survey, the Scots spend only pennies more per family on drink than the average for the entire United Kingdom. Generally, the level of alcohol consumption nation-wide has been falling, not only in Scotland. The only drink, apart from lager and beers, to show an increase in sales has been wine, a product formerly disregarded by the Scots except on special occasions.

Dr Clayson, a retired chest physician and former president of the Royal College of Physicians of Edinburgh, recommended in his Report that parents should be permitted to take their children into the public bar of a public house and that pubs should provide 'family facilities' so that children (under the age of eighteen) could be introduced to the social uses of alcohol under parental control. The House of Commons when debating the Licensing (Scotland) Bill would have none of it – the suggestion did not even merit consideration by the legislators. The then Secretary of State for Scotland, William Ross, stated that the introduction of children into the public bar of a public house would not be in line with current Scottish drinking practices. In vain, did Clayson protest that he was thinking of social conditions twenty-five years or more ahead, in the year 2000.

The *Glasgow Herald* commented, in March 1985, that the 'Scots have traditionally had an ambiguous attitude to drink, producing the most famous of all drinks and gaining a reputation for devotion to it, while simultaneously holding it in pious disregard . . . We should remember that alcoholics are a small minority of drinkers and that the Scottish level of alcoholism is not notably higher than in many other European nations . . . The facts are that most people in Scotland with experience of pubs and clubs believe that drinking has been civilized now that Scots have the opportunity to enjoy a leisurely drink and that we are not only drinking less but becoming noticeably less drunk, at least in public.'

Hugh MacDiarmid considered that the 'Scottish climate – not to speak of the soot-laden, catarrh-producing atmosphere of Glasgow in particular – makes us traditionally great spirit-drinkers.' Now that the air is cleaner, allowing the public buildings of Glasgow and Edinburgh to be washed and to gleam, now that central heating is a substitute for the inner warmth of whisky, now that health education has taught us the benefits of moderation in all things, it seems likely that Scotland's reputation will rest more on its competence as a whisky-producer rather than its capacity to consume the national product. The response of the distillers to this situation is to export Scottish whisky and to glamorize it as a chic drink guaranteed to enhance not only one's social standing but one's sexual success. Cheer without inebriation still seems incomplete, and one's appreciation of whisky in the modern world gives one a certain cachet among the cognoscenti.

This image of whisky as a civilized drink among the aspiring and upper classes is fairly recent. From the middle of the eighteenth to the end of the nineteenth century, the upper classes drank wine (claret and hock, principally), brandy, and ale. When the tax on port was less onerous than on claret, the Scots drank port. Whisky, or a spirit distilled from grain, was drunk mainly by the working classes to relieve the rigours of industrial life in the slums. Neil Gunn commented:

One wonders why those who were (and still are) repelled abhorrently by whisky were not infinitely more repelled by the social conditions which let whisky act so revealingly. One would think that whisky had been the *cause* of the state of the poor, that it had built the slums and ensured the poverty, that it was the whole monstrous creator of that economic hell ... One may readily have patience with the women who, being realists, condemned the drunken horrors they saw. But with the so-called social and temperance reformers, as with the religious and political rulers, patience is less easy, for it is natural to expect that they would have made some effort to see through the effect to the cause, and once having seen, to have become the people's impassioned leaders against the savagery of a system that produced such appalling results.

As the social order improved, Gunn thought, so drunkenness lessened. But he remained committed in his anger against those grandees of the 'owning or governing class' who supported a social order in which every man was divinely ordained to his appointed place by a righteous God, and those figures of the establishment who relentlessly 'hunted and persecuted such "friends of the people" as, haunted by humanity's vision of liberty and fraternity, dared raise a voice in the people's favour.' It is salutary, in view of the statistics on drink-related offences and the decline in alcohol consumption by the average Scots family in 1983, to recognize that Gunn was probably right to consider that Scots social intemperance was 'only a phase', the result of appalling social conditions. Drinking in Scotland may be a matter of temperament, or a response to the weather, or be inspired by a traditional conviviality on certain occasions such as Burns' Night, New Year's Eve (Hogmanay), and the odd Saturday night out, but in a period of increasing unemployment it may become a simple displacement activity like smoking or eating to excess. The Scots have a sweet tooth (their consumption of sweets and choc-olate is greater *per capita* than most other nations) and when whisky or beer is too expensive they take readily and with lip-smacking appreciation to fortified, sweetened, cheap wines which would be intolerable to a sophisticated palate. It is perfectly easy and inexpensive to get dead drunk on a bottle of 'red biddy' and still feel virtuous that one has kept off 'the hard stuff'. Such drinking kills time and the senses at no great expense.

A peculiar view of sobriety was taken by an eighteenth-century Scottish judge, no mean toper himself, when, presented with the drunkenness of the defendant as a plea in mitigation of his crime, he cried out: 'If he did this when he was drunk, what might he not do when he is sober?' This interpretation has some validity, perverse though it may sound. The Scots, particularly the Celtic Scots, are thought to be passionate and impetuous, their senses liable to be inflamed in a moment. Drink, in these circumstances, may be considered a useful depressant. It is the sober man, liable to go to a logical extreme, who requires the medium of alcohol to restrain his enthusiasm and put it into some perspective. If his senses are indulged by liquor, they are likely to be dulled to his own benefit and that of society. As an argument, it has an almost plausible charm. The world, to the Scot, is a dramatic place. 'Among the tea-rooms of Princes Street there are places more strange than a dream,' thought Edwin Muir. 'They excite or depress the senses to the limit of endurance, and pour non-alcoholic drinks on the resulting commotion. The pubs are, in comparison, civilized and humane institutions.'

The tea-rooms of Edinburgh (alas, no more) were centres of gossip and speculation conducted *sotto voce* by middle-class votaries of Lipton's tea and MacVittie's teacakes, in the middle of the morning or afternoon, where reputations rose and fell as regularly as the cup was lifted to the lips and replaced in the saucer. Verdicts of social life or death were passed among the tables, as among jurors. Characters were blackened amid the snowy napery, tarnished as easily as a silver knife could cut through sponge cake. The damage was done by the faintest raise of an eyebrow or the slightest sibilant of an indrawn breath. A well-nigh imperceptible nod of the head, and the dropping of eyelids a fraction of an inch, cut as deep as the blade of a guillotine across some hapless neck. These tea-table Mesdames Defarge, cosy in their cashmere and tweeds, felt the joy of battle race in their veins, the pride of prejudice thump in their hearts, and the bile of justice wash in their stomachs. Little wonder that only the most intrepid dared approach the tea-table with utter confidence, righteous in their spotless rectitude.

In a public house, the conventional restraints can at least be momentarily set aside and beer or whisky may quickly calm the perplexities, vexations and anxieties of gut-gripping everyday life. A stiff drink mercifully fuddles the brain so that it is not obliged to contend clear-headedly with the world and its manifold demands. 'Whisky had made us what we are,' wrote R. H. Bruce Lockhart, '. . . It is our release from materialism, and I often think that without it we should have been so irritatingly efficient that a worse persecution than the Hebrews ever suffered would have been our fate.' The clear-headedness of the Scots, it would appear on one interpretation, is too exhausting a characteristic to be consistently maintained – the material world is too much with the Scots, and their escape from it is to consider it through a faint haze of alcohol which renders it, for the time being, tolerable. Under conditions of severe trial, alcohol may be a short-term means of escape (if not survival), temporarily deadening otherwise over-active senses. In a too-vital world, dullness is a wonderfully quiet, healing condition.

Temperance has never been a Scottish virtue. Drinking habits, though they have moderated in recent years, reflect the Scottish tendency to pursue some desirable commodity or state with passionate energy. If oblivion is what is most desired, then the Scot knows how to obtain it. In this respect, he is like the Russian or the American, both of whom have strong heads for strong drink and are not so affected by it as other nationals more accustomed to drink wine or less fiery spirits. The reputation of the Scots for whisky-drinking is, as has been noted, largely a thing of the past. The Scots are proof of the Thomas Jefferson notion that 'No nation is drunken where wine is cheap, and none sober where the dearness of wine substitutes ardent spirits as the common beverage. Wine is, in truth, the only antidote to the bane of whisky.' Jefferson was a connoisseur of fine French wines, and perhaps spoke as a dedicated oenophile. But in Scotland, the eighteenth-century tax on claret obliged the Scots to turn to port and to liquor. One might be tempted to blame Scottish drunkenness on the English who imposed the tax on wine. As a generalization, it has a certain charm.

Since drinking has become more recreational rather than a desperate and absorbing preoccupation, the Scots do indeed drink more wine than before. Partly, this is due to the influence of foreign travel and a general gentrification of the populace who are more exposed, and more responsive, to novelties. 'The northern nations,' wrote Boswell, 'are more addicted to the use of strong liquors than the southern, in order to supply by art the want of that genial warmth of blood which the sun produces.' Vodka, slivovitz, gin, aquavit, poteen and whisky are all products of northern climates, and it can be no coincidence that, at some time or another, the northern peoples have all had a reputation for drunkenness. The Scots are not unique in this respect, and nowadays their unjustified reputation as a nation of dedicated dram drinkers probably belongs more properly to the Russians who throw off glasses of vodka immoderately.

The problem the Scots are said to experience with drink is not one of alcoholism or alcohol abuse. Most Scots learn at an early age how to drink moderately and continue to do so, with pleasure, for the rest of their lives. The problem may be that hard drinking and high thinking never came to terms. The Presbyterian conscience reprobated drink, but the natural gaiety of the Celtic Scot required whisky. Whisky induced, it was thought, a careless attitude to life, a fecklessness that was no use to anybody. The thoroughness, too, with which the Scot took to things was thought to make him a certain drunkard if spirits so much as touched his lips. Abstinence was, then, the only means of avoiding intemperance and the sure ruin of self, family, and, by extension, the entire social order. This logical progression still convinces many Scots who regard the figure of John Barleycorn as a fifth horseman of the Apocalypse.

Temperance, if not a typically Scottish virtue, was a magic word among the nineteenth-century reformers. In the early years of the nineteenth century, the Scots certainly merited their reputation as hard and consistent drinkers: viciousness, however, was not the motive – rather, the Scots used drink as an aid to conviviality, and the occasions of compliment and kindness were many and varied. From 1830 to 1839, average annual *per capita* consumption of whisky in Scotland was twenty-nine pints. This figure implies that many men drank more than twenty-nine pints, since women normally consumed less and children were not hardened or copious drinkers from infancy. By 1939, a century later, average *per capita* consumption had dropped to four pints per annum. The number of pubs per head of population dropped almost correspondingly, and the incidence of drink-related criminal convictions fell from 103 per 10,000 of population per year in the first decade of the twentieth century to 27 in 1930–1939. Modern-day levels of whisky consumption are rising, but the forces that restricted alcohol consumption in the nineteenth and early twentieth centuries persist. The Evangelicals, crusaders for morality and teetotalism, have been replaced by evangelical doctors and health experts, proselytizing fitness for sports and enhanced levels of performance in everyday life.

Consumption of drink was curbed by several factors – the Forbes-Mackenzie Act of 1853 closed licensed premises on Sundays and obliged the pubs to close at 11 p.m. The Methylated Spirit Act of 1855 hampered the manufacture and distribution of meths for consumption, and in the 1860s police were enabled to enter and close unlicensed shebeens. Tax on spirits was introduced, and between 1853 and 1860 the spirit duty was almost doubled. Duty continues to rise annually. It has been pointed out that these measures mainly affected the working man, restricting the pleasures of the poor. The middle class could, of course, become quietly and secretly sodden in the comfort of their own homes any time they liked. This was not so easy for the working man, who lived with his family in two rooms – three at the most – in squalid conditions, and who escaped from the claustrophobia of his life into the pub leaving the wife and bairns at home with little to do but get irritable with each other. But the middle class, and the respectable working class, were not ignored. Among them the reformers, piously engaged on the Lord's work of salvation, tapped a rich vein of Scottish sanctimoniousness.

John Dunlop, a Greenock magistrate, and William Collins, a Glasgow publisher, founded organizations in 1829 dedicated to wiping out only the drinking of spirits. Wine they left pretty much aside since it was not an urgent problem for the working class. England, in 1830, saw the first movement for total abstention at Preston in Lancashire. It was the English who favoured total abstention, while the Scots drew back from complete teetotalism and calls for prohibition. The Church of Scotland and the Evangelicals were at first suspicious: the established church did not care for the 'enthusiasm' of the reformers, while the Evangelicals distrusted a movement that did not rely wholly on Jesus as the medium of salvation and gave most of the responsibility for saving himself from drink to the individual and his willpower. The Catholic community was very little affected by the appeals of the temperance societies and continued, in the eyes of the moral majority, to be uproarious. This strengthened, of course, the popular prejudice against Catholics and, particularly, Irish Catholics in Scottish cities.

Drink was popularly supposed to lie at the root of all squalor and degradation in working-class life. Those of the respectable working class who gave it up, prospered mightily in their self-conceit. The middle class gave up drink in public at least, but at very little hardship to themselves – they had not often frequented howffs and shebeens and pubs, or roistered the night away in Leith Walk or in Blackfriars Wynd. For a while, the temperance societies were all the rage – a type of mass hysteria infected the poor and the rich alike, and many the pledge was given that, to the credit of the more strong-willed, was kept. The effect was perhaps not unlike the campaign against smoking today: temperance societies waged a successful propaganda war against alcoholic drink of all kinds by entertaining while cautioning prospective converts. Charismatic speakers filled public parks and halls; the Band of Hope caught children young and dwelt, disarmingly, on cheerfulness rather than horror. Exciting public demonstrations of a quasi-scientific nature were held – alcohol poured on gunpowder caused an explosion; what, then, could a ball of whisky not do to the gut when it hit the stomach lining? These tactics succeeded for a while, and were remarkably influential in changing the collective view of drink as a harmless recreation into suspicion of it as a brain-maddening demon that wrecked lives, homes, and prospects not only of material improvement but spiritual salvation. The Scots, always receptive to doom-laden pronouncements, drank the words in and experienced the intoxication of the call to virtue.

Propaganda combined with fiscal and legislative measures by the state to reduce the level of alcohol consumption – evangelizing could not have succeeded alone. Initially, the temperance movement believed that teetotalism could reform society, but drinking was slowly perceived to derive, in the most part, from the intolerable conditions of society. An echo of the problem may be heard today in Glasgow, Edinburgh, and Scottish towns: the incidence of glue-sniffing and drug-taking among the young, at all levels of society, though particularly among the unemployed and disadvantaged, is reaching crisis proportions. In Edinburgh particularly, there is great concern about the risk of hepatitis, AIDS, and other diseases spread by indiscriminate sharing of needles among addicts who mainline in the notorious 'shooting galleries' of the city. A serious, concerted effort by parents, charities, social services, the churches, and government health agencies to deal with the drugs problem by rehabilitation and education of addicts and young people exposed to risk, seems merely to scratch at the surface of an epidemic rooted – if the Scottish experience of drink is anything to go by – in poverty, despair, profound pessimism about the probability of any improvement in social conditions, and cynicism. The overall decrease in the level of consumption of alcohol in Scotland is owing to many things – the impulse to virtue, the cost of whisky, improved recreational facilities, improved housing, liberalization of licensing laws, and better health education. But the increase in drug consumption and dependency, in glue-sniffing in schools, in smoking and valium-consumption among women, and in crime associated with drug misuse and poverty, does not point to any miraculous improvement in the physical and spiritual health of the Scots. Drink was a symptom of social malaise, but drink as the manifestation of an old, underlying dissatisfaction among the Scots is but one of many Hydra heads: the monster itself has not been fully recognized or tackled.

13

---- * ----

The clash of cultures:
MacDiarmid and Lauder

THE Scots derive most of their popular modern culture from
the working class and the myths of their history. Burns, the
ploughman poet, was the natural man of the fields, the Romantic
who, when he attempted to adopt upper-class modes of speech
and deportment, became artificial – so it is alleged: his entry into
polite Edinburgh society is regarded with some mistrust by his
partisans. The tall, bearded, shambling figure of the comedian
Billy Connolly is the Glasgow 'hard man', the iconoclast and
cynic, foul-mouthed and pugnacious, the hero of the shipyards.
Harry Lauder, the popular music-hall comedian, raconteur
and singer, was the penurious, soft-hearted, canny but kindly
Kailyarder. Hugh MacDiarmid was the tough, socialistic
visionary, romantic and hard-headed, a charismatic introvert (at
home as much in his own thoughts as on a public platform), poetic
yet practical, who attempted to give their cultural heritage to the
uncomprehending Scots.

As in Ireland, so in Scotland the most acclaimed and the most
mortifying (to the middle-class and respectable working-class
mind) artistic achievements of modern culture have taken their
cue from the heroisms and tragedies of the dispossessed, the
disadvantaged, the poor of the slums and the tower blocks, of the
windy spaces of once teeming shipyards and steelmills, of the

stony land, and of Scotland's heritage of despair and defeat. A recent television play *The Holy City*, by Bill Bryden, a Scottish playwright, portrayed the return of Jesus Christ in the guise of an unemployed Glasgow man who played out the passion of Christ in the city – but not often is such a terrible beauty born from a myth, and many Scots were shocked that Christ should have been portrayed as a cross between a lay preacher, social worker, socialist trade union official, and rabble-rouser clearly agin the government. One Scottish critic, Allan Massie, inveighed against the play as 'an image as sodden with Romantic nostalgia as any Victorian painting of a wounded Highlander after Culloden'. But the Scots, tender in their sensibilities, are as easily shocked by gritty reality as critics are by soft-headed and soft-hearted Romanticism. The Scots cling to the familiar, the banal, the cosy and the immediately comprehensible. Their traditions are imperfectly understood, and therefore may easily be exploited and debased. It is worth repeating that the Scots' perception of themselves is complacent.

It is not quite true to say that when a Scot hears the word 'culture', the first thing he reaches for is his kilt. But probably the last thing he reaches for is his wallet. On 28 August 1983, during the annual Edinburgh Festival, Dr Alistair Dunnett, a former editor of the *Scotsman*, published a remarkable article in the *Glasgow Herald*. It was titled, 'Can Edinburgh be saved from the shrivelled minds?' and the author did not shrink from writing, pungently, what many had begun to think. Looking at Edinburgh's cultural history from the mid-1950s to the early 1980s, Dunnett could not 'recall a single worthy stroke of civic imagination. Edinburgh is in a terrible decline: not even a violent decline but a dull sunset without the sun. The city has become

> "A withered beldame now
> Brooding on ancient fame."

Not even brooding on ancient fame, because the people concerned with the present destiny of Edinburgh do not seem to have much idea of what the ancient fame was and how to hold and enlarge it.'

It is as though the Scots, and Edinburgh councillors in particular, have become deracinated, or worse, disoriginated. 'Know whence you came,' says the black American writer James Baldwin. 'If you know whence you came, there is really no limit to where you can go.' Dunnett laments, 'By this time there should have turned up in post-war Scotland and, one would have hoped, from Edinburgh, some voice expressing the search for the Scottish renewal. Not a word!' There is currently some vitality in Glasgow, but the Scottish mind still has to reach back some two hundred years to the mid-eighteenth century for evidence of the last, and greatest, flowering of Scottish intellectual genius in Edinburgh when there was

the tremendous explosion of intellectual curiosity and declaration from a group of able men who suddenly found themselves going all together. It was the Enlightenment, and it staggered Europe to the heart. Edinburgh swarmed with able world figures innovating, arguing, inventing, understanding. 'I can go down the High Street of Edinburgh,' said one of them, 'and take 50 men of genius by the hand.' One of the reasons that made it possible was that they all – Scots, tough as nails, full of argument and debate – suddenly turned and all went in the same direction. They backed each other up. Nothing like it had been seen since Athens, and nothing like it has been seen anywhere since. What are the chances of an action replay? It can't be done artificially. You can't set it up by seminar. But here and there, who knows, there may be men and women waiting to take their opportunity.

Dunnett, in spite of all strictures, remains mildly, a shade wistfully, optimistic.

The official contribution of money, resources and encouragement by the city to the Edinburgh Festival is generally perceived by the 'culturati' to be 'pitiful, unbelievable'. Dunnett believes the tight-fistedness, feather-mindedness and lead-heartedness of Edinburgh councillors to be 'probably the meanest story in the world, and not just the artistic world . . . It must have been this kind of sustained and shrivelled mind which in the end scunnered John Drummond and made him quit. You cannot go round the globe purporting to be director of the world's greatest International Festival of Drama and the Arts and be always apologizing.' Ingenious reasoning, close to sophistry, was the response of Timothy Mason, director of the Scottish Arts Council, who met the egalitarian arguments of Scottish critics of the Edinburgh Festival with the suggestion that arts such as opera and dance are not intrinsically elitist.

Mr Mason reminded the Scots that artists, though they may themselves form a kind of elite, are also workers whose products are available to all. From the humblest spear-carrier to Dame Kiri te Kanawa, no lilies of the field they, but toilers in the vineyard like the rest of us. The work is the thing, the product quite something else. It is not done for fun, but, rather, with serious artistic intent, which makes it morally OK. Effete little cliques are not gladly regarded in the East of Scotland, just as 'the more delicate aesthetic pretensions' (to quote William McIlvanney) do not thrive on the West coast, and suggestions from the 'culturati' that all is not well in the arena of the arts are not kindly received by the civic authority. George Kerevan, an Edinburgh councillor and convenor of the council's theatres and halls sub-committee, declared that carping attacks on councillors' philistinism only proved that there is an arts establishment in Edinburgh and that its guerrillas and subversives should take warning: 'we declare war on it; we will abolish it; we will democratise it. If you feel threatened by that statement you know which side you're on.' The emphasis of the arts in Edinburgh should be on people actually doing things, he thought, rather than on grandiose plans for an opera house. The saga of Edinburgh's proposed opera house (generally and satirically known as 'the hole in the ground' since nothing has been erected over the excavations) gives grief and pain to Dr Dunnett. 'One finds it difficult to tell foreign friends the story of the opera house . . . It sounds to them like a bad joke. It is.' Councillor Kerevan envisages, instead of a temple to bourgeois culture, travelling exhibitions going into culturally deprived areas (he does not consider central Edinburgh in this category, evidently) and artists in residence throughout the city, thirled and thrilling to salaried employment and productivity deals no doubt.

At this level of debate about the arts in Scotland, the Edinburgh Festival provides a valuable focus for national political dispute. 'We love a "guid-ganging plea", we relish and digest a good argument. Judge after judge', remarked Robert Louis Stevenson, 'must utter forth his *obiter dicta* to his delighted brethren.' The arts are particularly satisfactory as a subject for debate, since politics and theology can be introduced and, like cannon, employed to annihilate an adversary who might temporarily hold the field with the elegant cavalry of culture, liberal thought and civilized values. Like Knox, characterized by Stevenson, Edinburgh councillors boldly shine their uncertain lanterns 'into many places of fictitious holiness' and are not abashed by the tinsel divinities (those wantons, the Muses) they find there.

The Festival is supportable to Edinburghers because it considerably enriches the city and its citizens financially, if not morally or aesthetically. The ideal would be that the activities and the visitors they attract should cause as little inconvenience as possible to the lieges. It was decided to move The Book Festival in 1985, after its successful debut in 1984, because it made a noise and a mess in the gardens of Charlotte Square, to the disturbance of the political and legal establishment in the surrounding handsome Adam buildings. That books should have suddenly displayed themselves as vivacious, as having a life beyond the library shelf or the bookshop, perhaps shocked some citizens. But militarism makes a noise, and the lights and commotion of the Military Tattoo on the Castle Esplanade are not reprobated – though, curiously, by a judicial quirk, the noise of erecting seating for spectators was held to constitute a nuisance, an infringement of a nearby property-owner's right to quiet enjoyment of her flat in Ramsay Gardens. Fifes and drums, bagpipes and the clatter of boots, however, at ten o'clock at night when sober citizens are abed, was judged reasonable and permitted to proceed without legal hindrance.

The civic mind would prefer to diffuse the lights and commotion over a wider area: a recent suggestion was that Fringe groups (participants in the unofficial Festival which now greatly exceeds the official Festival in vitality and size) might care to consider the charm and convenience of church halls in Gilmerton, Corstorphine, Musselburgh, or Leith, outposts of suburban Edinburgh beyond which culture becomes merely a suffix for agri- or horti-. But most prefer to remain in town for the three weeks of the Festival. The glamorous epicentre around which the critics and grandees whirl remains irresistible: the workers are sociable and gregarious, and enjoy the company of their own kind who are more likely to be found at the Festival Club or the Fringe Club, tossing down champagne, than winding down with a bag of chips and a bottle of beer on the seafront at Portobello after a particularly demanding performance of *The World in a Teacup* – perhaps *in* a teacup.

The irony of the Edinburgh Festival is that the Scots consider themselves Europeans, and the Festival is a European event. It is not English, and it is not especially Scottish. There's the rub: Europeans we may be, but first we are Scots. We cling to our parochialism, however briefly we may be glamorized by a fairy procession of the Muses and their raggle-taggle attendants passing like a rabble of gypsies through the town, endlessly peripatetic as they make their tour of Edinburgh, Salzburg, Venice, cities all which will repossess their streets and revert to insularity and rain.

The general idea most visitors have of Scottish culture is the image promulgated by the Scottish Tourist Board which, like any such body in any other country of the world, naturally picks out the traditional and the picturesque, the colourful and the photogenic to present to its prospective customers. Castles in Scotland are repositories of historical relics and evocative of historical events in much the same way as castles in Spain or châteaux in France; Highland dancers partake of the same quaintness as Morris dancers or Georgian folk dancers; haggis and whisky are promoted with the same enthusiasm, and consumed with the same cautious adventure, as blinis and vodka in Russia or fondue and glühwein in Austria. This does not matter too much so far as tourists are concerned, but it matters a great deal more when the Scots themselves come to believe wholeheartedly in their myths, like Alice gazing through the looking-glass and taking the reflection for reality. Hugh MacDiarmid, a Borderer and patriot, writing in *The Scottish Chapbook* in February 1923, opposed the sentimentality of some Scots as 'belonging to a type of life that has passed and cannot return [*as*] a sort of museum department of our consciousness'.

In his introduction to MacDiarmid's *Aesthetics in Scotland*, the poet Alan Bold suggests that MacDiarmid's aim was to make Scots 'no longer to see themselves as others saw them but to wake up to new possibilities'. MacDiarmid himself wrote, 'The mass of the people will react all right if they get a chance. It is the stupid conservatism of their self-styled "betters" that is the danger . . . Amateurism has always been the curse of the arts in modern Scotland – amateurism and, along with it, the inveterate predilection to "domesticate the issue" . . . the progress of the Arts in Scotland is dependent upon . . . the wider appreciation and striving after the highest possible standard.' He thought it especially true of Scotland that 'the national tradition has been hopelessly fragmented or driven underground and very few people, if any, possess a complete knowledge of it.' He was critical of the Scottish 'common sense' school of philosophy and, says Bold, 'wanted to undermine the traditional scepticism of the Scottish people and make them believe in the spiritual qualities he himself expressed as an artist.'

MacDiarmid, a self-proclaimed 'man of the people', nevertheless was attacked by fellow-Scots who regarded his approach to literature and the other arts as elitist and high-faluting. It took a long while for Modernism, which MacDiarmid recommended, to percolate through the Scottish mind and, indeed, it (and the following schools of thought) has never been fully assimilated. It is only in recent years that Art Nouveau and the architecture and design principles of Charles Rennie Mackintosh and his associates have been appreciated at their true worth in Scotland. MacDiarmid was, of course, a complicated man and his complexity did not endear him to the Scots. He dismissed 'most people' as 'the feck' who disregarded his calls to them to experience the sublimity of spiritual values. Bold comments,

The man of the people who castigated 'the feck' was also (at times) a Scottish Nationalist and a card-carrying Communist with an abiding interest in 'Social Credit'. The result was not so much inconsistency as complexity arising from his vision of a world in which the new saviour of society is the artist who leads the people ever upwards into increasingly subtle aesthetic spheres. In 'Aesthetics in Scotland' he combines his intellectual elitism with a belief in the untapped resources of the Scottish people. He categorises 'the man in the street and his wife' as culturally underprivileged and looks forward to the day when the spiritual light of the Scottish Renaissance will dawn in Scotland so that all Scots will be in a position to comprehend their own culture.

Shock tactics were required to stimulate Scottish tradition and to reanimate a Scotland which had laboured for too long under a defeatist attitude of mind and way of life. 'In all his work,' says Alan Bold, 'MacDiarmid stressed the quality of Scotland as a nation that could build an artistically assertive future by recalling the giants of the past and putting the present under powerful aesthetic pressure.' The shocks MacDiarmid administered to 'the man in the street and his wife' were taken as personal affronts by the outraged Scots who have yet to forgive him not only for his work but his cantankerous personality. It is rarely wise to attempt to tell a Scot what is good for him, particularly in the high-and-

mighty tones MacDiarmid was thought to adopt when evangelizing his traditionalist/modernist artistic and political points of
view. The non-cerebral Scot is more than content with the poetry
of Robert Burns and the 'Border Ballads', and has little time and
nothing but uninformed scorn for anything he regards as preten-
tious or not immediately comprehensible in terms of sentimental
realism. MacDiarmid had his work cut out to stimulate the
comfortable intellectual slothfulness of platitudinous 'common
sense' that refuses to respond cerebrally to a work of art. Among
the generality of Scots, there is a scanty audience for any word
that will not appropriately grace a greeting card or any picture that
will not agreeably decorate a chocolate box. The natural scepticism of the Scots is easily undermined by sentimentality, and that
scepticism forms an almost impenetrable barrier against any
unfamiliar or challenging form of expression.

Yet there are a few unguarded entries into the Scottish psyche.
The startling success of *The New Testament in Scots*, published in
the early 1980s, is a recent example of a significant work of art, or
literature, long in the making and profoundly scholarly, adopted
with enthusiasm by the Scots. This lively rendering of the Bible
into the vernacular is at once a reclamation of broad Scots, the
traditional language of the streets, and a sop to the vanity of the
'man in the street and his wife' who regard their everyday culture
as something precious, peculiar to themselves, worthy of pres-
ervation, traditional in the commonsense mode and therefore accessible and still useful, and expressive of their basic chauvinistic
patriotism. There are writers who use, consciously and creatively,
the vernacular Scottish speech – William McIlvanney, Fred
Urquhart, Alasdair Gray, Liz Lochhead, Anne Smith, Agnes
Owen, and James Kelman, to name but a few living Scottish
writers at random. And Scotland has her novelists and poets who,
though they write without resort to broad Scots, are nevertheless
distinctively Scottish in their attitudes and modes of thought –
Ronald Frame, Douglas Dunn, Allan Massie, Robin Jenkins,
George Mackay Brown, and that constitutional exile, Muriel
Spark.

Neither Edinburgh nor Glasgow can point to anything resembling the theatre district of New York's Broadway or London's Shaftesbury Avenue: theatre is confined to rather small, established theatres which, like the still controversial Traverse Theatre in Edinburgh (founded by an American), retain a faintly impromptu, *ad hoc* feeling. Most of the large urban theatres are given over to pop concerts, pantomimes, the occasional theatrical comedy, and performances by a travelling ballet or opera group. Traditional classical music attracts regular audiences in Glasgow and Edinburgh, and there are a number of distinguished Scottish musicians and conductors who are able to export their talents. Scotland also produces, regularly, marketable pop stars who find it necessary to make their names and fortunes in London or Los Angeles. And Scotland can claim as her own a clutch of distinguished modern artists – Ian Hamilton Finlay (who is equally a poet), John Bellany (who fulfils MacDiarmid's hopes by using Celtic imagery in his work which has an international reputation), Alexander Moffat, Barbara Rae, Will Maclean, Lys Hansen and Steven Campbell – to cite, again, names more or less at random.

The arts, both traditional and experimental, do flourish in Scotland, albeit against considerable pressures towards conformity to Scottish social ideals or towards expressing traditional Scottish platitudes. The audience in Scotland for modern writing, painting, dance, music, theatre, or any form of unconventional fine or applied art is not large, and a Scottish artist, while necessarily drawing on the experience of being a Scot, must direct his or her work towards a wider national UK or international market. The successful Scot in Scotland is the artist who wraps a commonplace Scottishness around himself like a bolt of tartan, broadens his accent, adopts national prejudices as truisms, and hams up the characteristics of the Scots as if his life, and not merely his livelihood, depended upon it. The figure who evoked MacDiarmid's deepest despair and most profound disgust was Sir Harry Lauder, the singer, comedian and raconteur who, in his homespun manner, has come to personify all the canny chauvinism of the cast of the Scottish Kailyard.

Lauder perpetually roamed in a gloaming that never was on land or sea, but was artfully painted on a backdrop in music halls throughout the world. Equipped with a knobbly stick and a flat bonnet, he marched indefatigably to the end of the road, into terminal romanticism. In a volume of short homilies, entitled *Ticklin' Talks* (published by D. C. Thomson of Dundee, publishers of *People's Friend* and the *Sunday Post*), he discusses the everyday challenges of life, such as 'Auld Freens' (Old Friends); 'Folks That Get My Goat' ('The highbrow is not a man with a big forehead. He is usually an individual obsessed with a big idea. That big idea is – himself.'); 'My Day's Darg' ('My Day's Work' – 'I have now lived over 22,265 days [*written in January 1932*]! Gosh, that mak's me feel as if I were Methuselah! Every one o' them has been packed with interest. And on every one o' them I've been busy.'); 'Gi'e Me The Lass That's Plump!' ('Take plenty of exercise, eat cannily, be sparing wi' the chocolates, and there'll be nae fears o' you becoming unwieldy. You'll just be that buxom, sonsy, cheerful body we men a' like to see. As I've said already, I like a womanly woman. Nane o' your walking-stick for Harry Lauder!')

In an essay, 'Books I'd Like Fine to Read Again', Lauder recommends a second reading of the Bible, the poems of Robert Burns, 'Self Help' by Samuel Smiles, and – for deeper moments, the philosophy of Marcus Aurelius. A biography of Abraham Lincoln should be a constant companion ('the more I know about old Abe the better I like him'), and among novels Lauder particularly enjoyed were *Sorrel and Son* by Warwick Deeping and *Hatter's Castle* by A. J. Cronin. But, above even these, J. M. Barrie interested Lauder ('I can see the folks in those cottages and kirks o' Thrums and hear them speak, and because I'm an Angus man I the more enjoy being in their company.'). In his literary discourse, 'Looking for a Lass', Lauder quotes a letter from a woman who had seen him in a theatrical performance: 'I am quite a stranger to you, Sir Harry, but the other night the glint of your eye made my heart palpitate. You made me feel romantic. And at forty, too!' Sir Harry comments, 'I can imagine hearing my young friends saying: "Oh, isn't that mushy, isn't that sloppy!" But I merely tell them they use modern slang for feelings that can never be eradicated from ordinary humanity. What they object to is that people should express their inmost thoughts. They don't like those who wear their hearts on their sleeves. Well, we are as God made us. And some of us are more emotional than others.'

Well, yes, up to a point, Sir Harry. The Scots are deeply emotional, though often they will vehemently deny it with all the passion of that emotional nature. They don't much care for the heart freely bleeding on the sleeve, but have an insatiable taste for the artificial heart strapped to the forearm and made to beat by means of a rubber bulb, hidden in the pocket, pumping air into it so that it palpitates madly and inexhaustibly. Lauder's speech was picturesquely vernacular, a form of language readily accessible to his Scottish audiences who used it themselves in everyday life. But it was not the language of Scotland that MacDiarmid longed for and strove to use naturally in his work. He had nothing but scorn for those Scots 'who have seldom got beyond mere dictionary-dredging to achieve the illumination which I have called *satori*.' MacDiarmid defined 'satori' as 'an illumination, a sudden awakening'. This awakening to the true meaning and value of the Scottish tradition was hampered by the activities of Lauder who entrenched a sentiment that never went back beyond the Reformation and had become stuck in the Kailyard. Lauder's choice of the Bible and Burns as favourite reading is telling: Edwin Muir considered that 'Burns is a very Protestant poet . . . He certainly had no affection for the God of Knox, yet he himself had no other, except on occasion an eighteenth-century abstraction. His ribaldry, blasphemy, libertinism and sentimentality are all Protestant and quite narrowly so.' In his re-moulding of Scottish folk songs, Burns went past the Reformation in sentiment but, says MacDiarmid, 'his work in renovating and redefining Scottish folk songs . . . wasn't his proper business at all.' MacDiarmid

wanted to escape from the provincializing of Scottish litera-ture. I wanted to carry on the independent Scottish literary tradition from the time that Burns died, for it didn't seem to me that anything of value had been done in between. I wanted to carry forward the reintegration of the Scottish language, taking it a great deal further than Burns had taken it, and at the same time to carry forward the tradition politically . . . I think the main problem I faced was the appalling nostalgia that had afflicted Scottish writers and the Scottish reading public since the death of Burns. Everything was propitious for a forward move in Scottish letters had it not been for that backward-looking characteristic.

Nostalgia is not merely confined to language: it informs every facet of Scottish culture. Two letters to the *Scotsman* and the *Glasgow Herald* on 25 and 17 January 1985 remarked on the display the Scots make of themselves on television late at night on Hogmanay. The television programmes celebrating the occasion of the New Year are mainly for home consumption, and take the form of decorous and decorative studio parties attended by well-dressed suburbanites who have turned out to be regaled with wine and whisky and diverted by dancers, comedians, balladeers and groups of folk singers. Writing of 'the humiliating Scottish New Year TV programme', Florence Russell refers back to the day, long before the birth of Harry Lauder, when James VI and I 'abandoned Scotland to take his court and courtiers and other Scottish gentry on the make, to London,' and 'appeasement of contemptuous foreigners began'. Today, says Ms Russell, 'sycophantic Scots latch on to the hostile stereotypes and make money waggling their tartans in showbiz.' J. Derrick McClure of Aberdeen agreed with Ms Russell: 'With a national culture and national achievement worthy of the respect and admiration of all civilized States, we choose to assert our Scottish identity by presenting ourselves to the rest of the world as pathetic buffoons . . . To quote Fionn MacColla, will we never wake up?' These two letters spoke forcefully against what was perceived as English domination of Scottish culture: 'are we to accept that the Scotland of the past is gone beyond recall, let our national achievements be either totally forgotten or credited to England, and resign ourselves to the final disappearance of the Scottish identity?'

In February 1985, Colin Campbell of Benbecula was writing to the *Glasgow Herald* to protest that the BBC and the IBA (Independent Broadcasting Authority) are 'overtly political in their unrelenting pursuit of a "one-nation" image of Britain and of course this "one-nation" image is predominantly English.' Scottish culture, Campbell claims, is ignored and swamped by American and English products:

> Scotland's national instrument gets 20 minutes a week on Radio Scotland. The clarsach gets nothing. Hundreds of bands, orchestras and ensembles play unencouraged. Scores of choirs sing unrecorded. Scottish opera and ballet are largely ignored in favour of broadcast performances by their better endowed English sisters, and the rest of the arts in Scotland likewise receive derisory broadcasting coverage. The great Gaelic inheritance is locked away in secure sub-regional pockets where it cannot impinge upon the brash Anglo-Saxon cultural monopoly. And the Scots see all this, cringe in their impotence and dwindle in national self-esteem to the size of the splintered images so beloved of TV title artists.

This is an extreme view, but it has some validity.

Television is perceived as a strong cultural tool. Scotland has no independent broadcasting organization, although it possesses regional radio stations and two television stations within the IBA, Scottish Television and Grampian, both of which provide regional news programmes and current affairs documentaries as well as light entertainment and some drama productions. Stuart Hood, in 1970, lamented 'The Backwardness of Scottish Television' in an essay that could be reprinted today without significant amendment. As a distinguished broadcaster, he spoke out boldly in *The Listener*:

Scotland does have certain cultural and moral traditions but they are part of a broken-backed culture. Its Renaissance was late and blighted. Its only claimant to the title of Renaissance prince died at Flodden. Its Gaelic culture was destroyed along with the social system that nurtured it. Its Age of Enlightenment came when the pull of London was already overwhelming: . . . The 19th century began with sentimental Jacobitism and ended in the Kailyard. The 20th century saw Gaelic poets writing in a language fewer people spoke with each decade; other poets engaged in the fruitless attempt to keep alive the dialects of Lowland Scotland as a vehicle for serious literary work.

This, then, was the situation when television entered the social and cultural arena and, says Hood, the BBC in Scotland failed in its duty to reflect the life and culture of the nation in all its diversity. He explains this by referring, first, to the fact that the BBC spoke to the Scottish people *de haut en bas*, 'in the accents of the manse. The BBC was and is, by its nature, respectful of established centres of power, but its Scottish Region was notorious for its subservience to the Scottish Establishment. It bowed low to St Andrew's House, to the Kirk, to the Glasgow civic authorities, to the great Highland landowners and the great Clydeside industrialists.' It must be said that the BBC in Scotland has taken its cue from the BBC in London and is nowadays a great deal more free-spoken about social, moral and cultural issues than it was even ten years ago. In a recent series of interviews of prominent persons by large groups of Scottish schoolchildren, the questions were allowed to be penetrating, direct and – to some senior, shockable ears – bordering on the impertinent. It was refreshing, however, to find that Scottish schoolchildren, normally uncommunicative and unresponsive, had at last found their tongues and allied them to their wits.

But there is still resistance in Scotland, though not so much by the media, to unpalatable representations of Scottish life. Too regularly, after exposure of some dispiriting social problem, the telephone lines will be jammed by viewers calling not merely to complain about being distressed but anxious to point to elements in Scottish life that, being pleasant and wholesome, the broadcasters have wilfully disregarded. This is not merely an appeal for balance (that holy thing) but a disinclination, bordering on refusal, to be made aware that Scotland is not the terrestrial paradise. The Scottish viewer in general would prefer programmes featuring 'sentimental Scottish singing by young men in full Highland fig' (that *nice* Peter Morrison, for preference). 'It is easy in Scotland', says Stuart Hood, 'to be seduced by pretty pictures and the kind of facile romanticism that goes with them.' It was easy for STV in the early days, comments Hood, 'to blanket the industrial belt of Scotland with entertainment which lacked roots even in the urban culture of the area.' Part of the continuing problem is the difficulty 'in accustoming the Scottish public, which at its worst can be ineffably smug, to seeing honest inquiries into Scottish society and to co-operating in the effort to discover the truth.' On the drama front, Hood considers the 'enemies of realistic drama on Scottish themes will as always be sentimentalism and the fear that honest plays might give Scotland a bad name.'

This refusal to face harsh reality is a constant. The Scots live with it, but are reluctant to acknowledge that there might be a cure for it other than battening down the hatches, putting on the blinkers, and stoically enduring. The Scots shake their fists at the BBC and IBA on comparatively trivial matters which are blown up as grievous affronts to the national dignity. The BBC in particular takes pains to instruct its newsreaders and announcers in pronunciation, but they can never get it right to the satisfaction of Scottish viewers. The Cairngorms are regularly called 'Ken Goams', according to R. A. Howieson who speculated on the identity of this noble Scot in a letter to the *Glasgow Herald*. BBC announcers who can, with enviable ease, twist their tongues round names like Khomenei, Quatar and Popieluszko, seem incapable (according to Harry D. Watson, in a letter to the *Scotsman*) of pronouncing Forfar as other than For-*Fahr*, Brechin as Br*eck*in, and Greenock as Gr*enn*ock. Conversely, of course, there is some consternation among the English at the introduction of radio or television announcers with regional accents. Welsh is more or less acceptable as an accent, Irish is generally risible, but a Scots accent infuriates listeners disproportionately. A Scots accent is, generally, only acceptable in comedians and as an aid to establishing a stereotyped Scottish character in a radio or television play. Mr Watson also noted some curious inaccuracies of description: 'One night not so long ago, when the blizzards in the South-east of England [*in the winter of 1985*] were at their worst, BBC weatherman Bill Giles assured his nationwide audience that "we" were in for more of the same, but not to worry, as the icy weather would soon be moving up north.' Later, sitting reading his 'quality' Sunday newspaper, Mr Watson noted an Oxford graduate describing Dunbar's '"obscure poem" *Lament for the Makaris* as apparently part of the "wealth of English literature". The same paper carried a letter from an Edinburgh reader, complaining about a recent map consigning Glasgow to the Solway Firth. And wasn't there a story a few weeks ago about a Church of Scotland "vicar"?'

These gnat-bites, in sufficient quantity, irritate the Scots almost beyond endurance. It is perhaps a reflection of the Scots' insecurity that they should be so easily provoked by slights to their nationalistic *amour propre*. Their anxiety to preserve their little patch from foreign taint also involves repelling all mutineers against the 'commonsense' commonplace traditions of nineteenth- and twentieth-century Scotland. Attitudes perceived as insulting are not readily forgiven, particularly if they are broadcast by Scots whose loyalty to the country may not be in question but whose attitude towards the Scots may be regarded as questionable because it is questioning. The thickness of Scottish skin against the weather and as a carapace to protect conventionality and the homely virtues is wonderful in its density. But the merest pinprick can, mysteriously, penetrate to wound the Scottish pride if the barb is verbal or literary. Thrums may be the fictional invention of J. M. Barrie, but it is the national village in which too many Scots still live. Sometimes, however, the introversion of Thrums becomes too much for the national consciousness to endure, and forthright speaking becomes not merely a duty, it becomes a pleasure – an attitude not uncommon among Scottish moralists. National scandals, however minor, are often representative of national preoccupations and the scandal of a proposed memorial to Hugh MacDiarmid in early 1985 provoked some lively internecine conflict among the Scots.

Normally, monuments to national heroes (or, at least, national figures) are erected with pious goodwill and solemn lessons are taken from the life of the dedicatee. The commission of the monument is often a convenient occasion for dispute, but rarely does the character of the person in whose honour the monument is to be raised come into question. By the time he is to be honoured, his rough edges have been smoothed away and he is regarded as a gratifying (if not always wholly venerable) ornament to the life of the nation. The consternation in the Border town of Langholm over a monument to MacDiarmid is comparable in some respects to the outrage over Epstein's monument to Oscar Wilde. Neither memorial nor dedicatee were well regarded. MacDiarmid died in 1978. A national appeal for funds for a memorial to his memory was successful and a sculptor, Jake Harvey of Melrose, was commissioned by the Scottish Sculpture Trust to create a monument in the form of an open book in bronze standing more than ten feet high and fifteen feet across. The resulting piece of work was described by Councillor Robert Robinson, at a meeting of Dumfries and Galloway planning committee, as 'a hideous thing . . . If it were an Oxo sign we would all refuse it.' It was narrowly refused, by a six to five vote of the committee, and Langholm breathed easy, secure in the faith that they would not have to view the memorial sculpture, which was to have been sited a mile outside the town, as a daily reminder of the son of Langholm who had offended the civic dignity of the town by referring obliquely, in his autobiography, *Lucky Poet*, to the sexual proclivities of a local citizen – mercifully unidentified. The ungrateful reference was thought to reflect badly upon the moral standing of Langholm as a whole. 'The refusal is another example of the Scots spitting in the faces of their own great men,' said a representative of the Scottish Sculpture Trust. 'This must be seen as a national disgrace. We are not talking about planning permission for a garage or a shed, but a memorial to a major national figure, made by a major Scottish sculptor.' The sculptor himself remarked, 'I can take criticism of my own work, but this [*refusal*] shows a failure to understand MacDiarmid's significance.'

Alan Bold, editor of MacDiarmid's letters and his biographer, wrote in the *Scotsman*: 'there has been in Langholm a history of hostility to MacDiarmid, prompted by a few bawdy anecdotes in his autobiography *Lucky Poet* (1943). On the basis of a couple of jokes, a handful of local citizens have held a grudge against the great man. It is astonishing that the poet who put Langholm on the cultural map of the world should be treated, albeit by a few folk, as a disgrace to the community rather than as a writer whose praise of his birthplace ensures the town's immortality.' Mac-Diarmid had indeed lavishly praised Langholm, and he loved it with a passion. Forty years later, old grudges still rankled and festered. The *Glasgow Herald* commented (magnanimously, since MacDiarmid had also insulted that newspaper in *The Company I've Kept*):

The MacDiarmid row in Langholm has been off and on now for 20 years or so. He was never offered the freedom of the town, an honour which went instead to the first man on the moon, Neil Armstrong, whose connection with Langholm was tenuous to say the very least. Yet the publicity of that honour put Langholm on the map, perhaps more than MacDiarmid would have done. For Langholm to continue to resist recognising the greatness of MacDiarmid now smacks of small-town pettiness. Borderers, and Langholmites in particular, are a thrawn lot but this latest snub smells of perversity. MacDiarmid, the Langholmite who referred to his home town as 'my touchstone in all creative matters' was many things:

thrawn, harsh, critical, and liable at all times to literary combustion. But he was never small-minded.

The Scots are perhaps properly suspicious of poets, who strive to tell the truth in matters small and domestic as much as in matters large and cosmic: they are perilous beings, as much a danger in love as in hate. Alastair Reid provides a personal clue to the Borders, when he writes that the Borders 'are a way of life that expects acquiescence and does not brook contradiction, yet all this implicitly, for the Borders are anything but self-conscious, and never talk of themselves except in pawky clichés of self-congratulation. When I was innocent of speech and thought, I had no quarrel with the place at all, and revelled in the countryside and even in the taciturnity of the town, which made its rules for behaviour indelibly felt beyond words. But it was when words began in me, and the stirrings of a separate consciousness, that I began to separate myself from the community and look for the few people I could find who said things I could not expect, and who would answer questions rather than brush them aside.' Poets are persons who deal in words, who say things one could not expect, and who attempt to answer questions that, disquietingly, others may not even have thought existed. To have been a poet at all may have been Hugh MacDiarmid's error, in the eyes and ears of his fellow-Borderers and to the discomfiture of the smug moral majority of the Scots who are easily satisfied with arts that seek to soothe and please and reinforce their preconceptions. In *Aesthetics in Scotland*, MacDiarmid in 1950 shot at the pretensions of the newly established Edinburgh Festival, combining a democratic instinct with artistic elitism and adding a gratuitously insulting reference to the Jews which sorts indefensibly as a parallel but logically, as he saw it, with his own professed nationalism:

The Scottish dichotomy between experience and consciousness – the dissociation in our midst between energy and sensibility, between conduct and theories of conduct, between

life conceived as an opportunity and life conceived as a discipline – cannot be healed in the Edinburgh Festival way. Our
national culture suffers from all the ills of a split personality.
The Edinburgh Festival's high prices excluding most of our
people, together with its importation of foreign art and artists
and the virtual exclusion of our own, simply accentuates this
schizophrenia . . . It would seem now that some of our better-
off people, in compensation for backward cultural conditions
and a lost religious ethic, are developing or pretending to
develop through this Festival, a supreme talent for refinement
just as a certain type of Jew, in compensation for adverse social
conditions and a lost national independence, developed a
supreme talent for cleverness. The one must inevitably be as
flashy and meretricious as the other has been.

MacDiarmid was surely right to see Scottish national culture as
split in the ways he described, because the Scots themselves are
so split, but he was perhaps off-beam and opportunistic when
condemning the Edinburgh Festival for being a world focus for
the arts of all nations: the Edinburgh Festival is an international
festival and, as such, is not specifically a Scottish festival. Edinburgh is merely the picturesque forum for an international festival
of the arts. There is, of course, an argument for an Edinburgh (or
a Glasgow) Scottish Festival, and perhaps one day we will get it.

Then, of course, we will have a lively national debate on the
place of Gaelic culture in the current state of the arts in Scotland.
In Sorley MacLean's view, 'Scottish Gaelic song is the chief
artistic glory of the Scots, and of all peoples of Celtic speech, and
one of the greatest artistic glories of Europe.' About 6,000
separate Gaelic melodies have been collected by the School of
Scottish Studies, together with most of the words of the songs.
Unfortunately, as Stuart Hood has pointed out, fewer and fewer
Scots in each succeeding generation speak Gaelic as their first
language. Only the efforts of folklorists of the late nineteenth
century preserved the oral folk tales of the Scottish West Highlands: the most significant and readable collection, recently

reprinted in paperback, being a word-for-word translation of oral sources by John Francis Campbell.

The study of Gaelic culture is nowadays almost entirely an academic exercise, though efforts are being made to revitalize the study and practice of the language, the musical instruments of the West Highlands, the dances, the music, and the arts and crafts of the Highlanders. But it has little or no impact on the ordinary, modern Scot who cannot understand a word of Gaelic. The Welsh language and culture is very much more integrated into the everyday life of the Welsh people than the Gaelic into the lives of even the Highland Scots, and the process (outside the far North-West and the Islands) of distancing ourselves from it has gone too far to be reversed. The traditional songs of the weavers have largely fallen into desuetude, along with the traditional machines across which they crooned the old songs in time with the movements of their hands. When the language of the Gaelic stories and songs is no longer spoken or sung, the tales, and the poems, and the music no longer develop in their place of origin, the arts of narrative and song-making may only be preserved as library and archive material. But they remain, fortunately, as material to be adapted by modern writers and artists such as the English writer Alan Garner and the Scottish painter John Bellany. It is encouraging to note that the Scottish Education Department, the Scottish Arts Council and the Scottish universities provide funds and facilities for the publication of books, magazines and records in the Gaelic language, and that some ministers in Edinburgh, Inverness, in the Western Isles and in Canada still preach to their congregations in Gaelic.

In general, the cultural life of the Scots is not a matter that engages their deeper passions or their profoundest intellect. The Scots do not respond as robustly as the Italians to opera, as intellectually as the French to literature, as devoutly as the Germans to music, or as avidly as Americans to the cinema. Voltaire remarked that it is difficult to paint when one's feet are cold, which is why the Scots may prefer wild dancing to less energetic art forms. Their country, folk, and Highland dances are nevertheless highly disciplined: one maladroit dancer in a set can ruin the symmetrical, almost geometric, beauty of a complicated group dance. There is strict order even in apparent chaos: the conventions are traditionally honoured and observed in Scottish national arts, and it is difficult even for the most determined iconoclast to break off and improvise his own steps when the rest are hoofing it in strict formation in time to the piper's tempo. The piper, in Scotland, calls the tune and plays it according to his own sense of fitness.

Much of the foregoing may seem a little harsh: the Scots can point to native artists and patrons, to considerable works of art, to great art collections, to rich cultural traditions, and to the energies that are currently directed towards the creation, originality, and wide dissemination of the arts in Scotland. MacDiarmid quoted the art historian and critic, Ian Finlay, who noted that

> our best constructive minds have taken up engineering and only sentimentalists have practised art. We are largely (the world has assessed us rightly) a nation of engineers. Let us realise that a man may still be an engineer and yet concerned with a picture conceived purely as a kind of engine which has a different kind of functional power to an engine in the ordinary sense of the term. Here then is what we Scots have – a terrific vitality combined with a constructive ability unequalled by any other nation. What more do we need? – merely sufficient analytical power to clear away the maze of sentimentality and accepted 'artistic' values which obscure our ideas of Art.

MacDiarmid went on to comment:

> All the things by which Scotland has captured the world without losing its own soul, have been its most indigenous, exclusive and inimitable things. I mean on different levels such things as Scotch whisky, our tartans, our traditional Scottish dances, and our pipe music. True, some of these are still inadequately or wrongly appreciated. Piping, for instance; not

only among foreigners, but amongst most of our own people, knowledge of piping is limited to strathspeys and military marches and to 'smart fingering' and far too little is known of one of the greatest glories of Scotland, the *Piobaireachd*. All that means is that there is in these matters room to grow – room for creative developments, better informed appreciation, and fundamental exposition.

In the European traditions of the arts, Scotland – as a European country – has too rarely reached the highest standard. But in her native traditions – which include engineering – Scotland has arts that are known and practised throughout the world, and not only by Scots.

14
＊

Caledonian salt:
the sardonic Scot

ACCORDING to Don Roberto (R. B. Cunninghame Graham) the Scots possess 'the saving grace of humour, that humour which as far surpasses wit, as whisky beer, and which, rising superior to climate and the terrors of the Calvinistic faith, has made North Britons kindly in their hardness, and rendered them easier of endurance to foreigners in spite of all their angularities than the majestic and pure-blooded cis-Tweedian Celto Saxon.' If this is true, then the Scottish sense of humour must, at its height, rise above all vicissitudes and regard them from a lofty eminence, beyond despair, beyond the merely temporal. But the Scots are not generally Olympian in their scepticism, cynicism, and pragmatism. 'Our attitude is not inhuman,' said Hugh MacDiarmid. 'We are experienced men of the world. We like what we like to be a little grim – in keeping with the facts of life, and loathe facile emotions. We cherish no illusions ... if our risible faculties are moved at all by the human spectacle, the movement only adorns our faces intermittently with some sort of *risus sardonicus*.' It was this reluctance to crack a full grin except out of politeness that perhaps prompted Sydney Smith to observe, 'It requires a surgical operation to get a joke well into a Scotch understanding. Their only idea of wit ... is laughing immoderately at stated intervals.' The Scots perhaps paid Sydney Smith the compliment of taking his witty sallies seriously and as worthy of proper consideration.

A grim graveyard humour is the Scottish genius, often as earthy as the sod that will inevitably cover us all. The just reward is the basis of much of our humour. At the last judgement, the Scots will cry out, faced with hell-fire, 'Lord, Lord, we didna' ken!' and the Lord will look down and remark, affably, 'Ay, weel, ye ken noo!' We are galvanized by the ghastly into a grudging smile and a quiet satisfaction that none of us can escape being satirized to our benefit. The moral aspect of Scottish humour is very strong, particularly as the targets are often the sacred topics of religion, drink, sin, and our own virtues.

The true Scots humour is not sentimental. 'The Scottish temper ... is little known abroad,' wrote MacDiarmid. 'Our internationally famous comedians purvey a very different account of us. The sorry joke is that so many Scots believe the latter and model themselves all too successfully on it.' This was a swipe at Sir Harry Lauder whose music-hall caricature of the typical Scot has set the mould for foreign images of the Scottish character and appearance. We should all, according to the Lauder model, be small, bow-legged, fond of a dram, tight-fisted, sentimental, kilted, crowned with a tam-o'-shanter bonnet, and maudlin. We should be a nation of grotesques. Lauder himself was, ironically, typically Scottish – industrious, pious, glad-handed, emotional, and – for his efforts – prosperous, everything his stage-image promised except for the redeeming fact that he was a man of great financial generosity. Audiences shrieked with pleasure, and wept with abandon, captivated by his Kailyard virtues that appeared pleasingly simple and sincere: as, indeed, they probably were. Lauder's antics produced broad, self-satisfied belly-laughs from his audience, in direct contrast to the traditional black Scottish humour that resulted merely in an appreciative, self-congratulatory smile for the pay-off line that confirmed some thrawn characteristic of the Scots.

The native astuteness of Scottish children is no whit inferior to the sharpness of their elders. In *Scottish School Humour*, the reminiscences of a Buckie schoolmaster, C. W. Thomson, published in 1936, the author refers to the developing personality of a type of Scottish child who is, at an early age, 'on guard in defence of his own rights and liberties. Asked to write a line of As, he does nothing. When asked why, he replies, "Ye'd be telling me to do a line of Bs next!"' If he has had some little beginnings of 'education' before going to school, he is distinctly supercilious. Such a one was asked, on arriving home after his first day, how he had liked the school. 'It's no much o' a place yon! A wife didna ken hoo to spell CAT, an' I tellt her.' Thomson gives an instance of youthful Scottish matter-of-factness which, one dearly hopes, is not apocryphal: 'A boy of distinct ability was rather a problem to his friends in the matter of choosing a career. His mother wished him to be a minister, his father a merchant, his uncle a farmer, his brother an engineer. Finally, to test his propensities, they decided to place him in a room containing a Bible, a half-crown, an apple and a knife. According as he read the Bible, caressed the half-crown, ate the apple, or used the knife, he was to be a minister, merchant, farmer, or engineer. At the end of a few minutes they entered, and found him sitting on the Bible, with the half-crown in his pocket, peeling and eating the apple with the help of the knife. So they made him a lawyer.'

The traditional Scots sense of humour is subtle, sharp, pithy and dry. It aims to wound, if directed at an individual or an institution, rather than content itself with a cautionary slap on the wrist. The humour of the Scots is succinct, but oddly the pun is rarely a feature of Scottish wit. The rarity of the pun makes a good one outstanding – Edwin Muir described Scottish writers as 'men of sorrow and acquainted with Grieve'. Even rarer in Scotland is the lengthy 'shaggy-dog story' of the English; and the English delight in slapstick is unlikely to please the Scots who will find it too broad for their taste, which is more likely to be diverted by the quick improbability of farce which at least has a sort of logic that is central to the extremes of the plot. In its spontaneity, Scots humour is akin to the quick, ruthless wit of the East Coast of the United States – some student of literature will perhaps some day write a thesis on this interesting similarity. An English journalist in New York, fumbling for an address, attempted to excuse her disorientation by explaining, with a winsome smile, 'I'm English' – as if those magic words nowadays cut any ice in any part of the world. 'Well, get over it, lady,' was the cab-driver's response. In its severity, in its practicality, that reply is very Scottish. As Henry MacKenzie ('The Man of Feeling') wrote to Elizabeth Ross in 1770, 'In Scotland we can be very bitter in our Wrath, seldom jocose in our Satire; We can lash an Adversary, but want the Art of laughing at him . . .' The Scots can tell a joke, and it can be well received, with no apparent indication that the thing has been done. The effect is rather like an audience sitting with the profoundest satisfaction through a silent period in the minimalist music of John Cage and then leaving without having applauded. At its best, Scottish humour is dead-pan, po-faced. The teller of the joke will not indicate that the joke has been made; it is up to the listener to take it or leave it. The Scottish sense of humour is the sane side of Scottish romanticism – since the Scots have severe difficulty in finding the middle way, since they do not possess the English ability to compromise, they oscillate between two extremes: 'You Scots', wrote Barrie, 'are such a mixture of the practical and the emotional that you escape out of an Englishman's hand like a trout.'

Scottish humour relies heavily on sarcasm: the Duke of Argyll, responding to the German Queen of George II who had asked about the character of Highland lairds, informed her: 'They are like the German princes, very poor and very proud.' There is a touch of the magisterial, if not the majestic, about such a remark. It has the dryness of nobility about it, much like the *sotto voce* asides one associates with academic high tables at the older, grander universities. The Scots, even in the humblest ranks, possess this caustic and iconoclastic wit based on the realities of Scottish life: 'Coming from hell, Lauchlan,' remarked a Highland shepherd passing an acquaintance coming from the Established Church as he was going to the Free Church. 'Better than going to it, Rory,' replied Lauchlan pleasantly. Even the children have it: a boy was being interviewed by a farmer for a job as a farm labourer. 'Have ye got a written character?' The boy said he had, but it was at home. 'Bring it wi' ye on Friday and meet me here at two o'clock.' When they met again, the farmer inquired, 'Weel, ha'e ye got your character?' 'Na,' said the boy. 'But I've got yours, and I'm no' comin'.' Both these exchanges are wholly satisfactory – in neither case is there room for compromise, and both sides of the dialogue are neatly balanced. Balance is the thing, very often, in Scottish humour: 'There's anither row up at the Soutars,' reported Willie Wilson to his wife. 'But it's nae sae bad. When the wife gets in her tantrums, she aye throws a plate or brush, or maybe twa or three, at Sandy's heid. If she hits him, she's fair pleased, an' if she misses him, he's fair pleased. So there's aye some pleasure to a'e side or the ither.'

The desiccated humour of the Scots is perhaps most aptly expressed in the famous story of the Edinburgh divine who, shaking out his umbrella, complained to his beadle, 'I'm wat, I'm wat.' The beadle comforted him, 'Dinna vex yourself, minister, ye'll be dry enough in the pulpit.' The pulpit is a favourite target for Scottish wit, though much of it is handed down from there. Mr Shirra of Kircaldy, much given to parentheses from the pulpit, happened to be reading one Sunday from the 116th Psalm of David. '*I said in my haste, all men are liars,*' he recited, adding, 'Indeed, Davie, if ye had lived in this parish, ye might ha'e said it at yer leisure.' Tact was never the strong card of the old Scottish ministers, but they were painfully honest. Discovering that news of the death of one of the Georges had not reached him before praying for the King in his last sermon, a Highland minister stood up the next week in his pulpit and frankly admitted, 'it was a' lees I tell't ye last Sunday.' Discretion was, nevertheless, occasionally required. The Revd Neil McVicar was determined, after Bonny Prince Charlie's victory at Prestonpans in 1745, to pray for George II and, in his way, for the Prince. Before a congregation of armed Highlanders loyal to the Prince, he prayed: 'Bless the King! Thou knowest what King I mean. May the crown sit long on his head. As for that young man who has come among us to seek an earthly crown, we beseech Thee to take him to Thyself and give him a crown of glory.'

There was no confounding the old-style ministers: two reckless youths accosted the famous Revd 'Watty' Dunlop to give him some glad news – 'The devil's deid.' 'Is he?' said Mr Dunlop. 'Then I maun pray for twa fatherless bairns.' The same Mr Dunlop was confronted one night in the churchyard by several youths who hoped to frighten him by rising up from behind tombstones dressed in gravecloths. 'Is it a general risin'?' asked Watty, 'or are ye just takin' a daunder yer lane [*taking a walk by yourselves*]?' The fear of God (and the Devil) was stronger in the Scottish mind than any terror the graveyard might hold. The dead would rise at the proper time, and not before. An old Glasgow shoemaker was sitting by the bedside of his dying wife who knew her fate but wished to be reassured on certain matters in this life. 'I ha'e been a guid wife tae ye, John.' 'Oh, middlin', middlin', Jenny,' replied John non-committally. 'Aye, I've been a guid wife tae ye, and ye maun promise to bury me in the kirkyard at Stra'von, for I couldnae rest in peace among unco folk in the stour and smoke o' Glesca'.' 'Weel, weel, Jenny, I'll dae this for ye – we'll pit ye in the Gorbals first, and if ye dinna' lie quiet there, we'll tak' ye tae Stra'von.'

Scottish epitaphs are often an occasion for bleak humour. Robert Burns is said to have composed this one for himself:

> Lament him, Mauchline husbands a',
>   He often did assist ye!
> Tho ye had bidden years awa'
>   Your wives [*wad*] ne'er ha'e miss't ye.
>
> Ye Mauchline bairns, as bye ye pass
>   To school in bands thegither,
> O tread but lightly on the grass,
>   Perhaps he was your father!

From the churchyard at Aberdeen comes this remarkably frank testamentary verse:

> Here lie the bones of Elizabeth Charlotte,
> Born a virgin, died a harlot.
> She was aye a virgin at seventeen,
> A remarkable thing in Aberdeen.

George MacDonald, in 'David Elginbrod', appeals to the Lord for mercy rather than justice in this 'do-as-you-would-be-done-by' plea:

> Here lie I, Martin Elginbrodde;
> Hae mercy o' my soul, Lord God,
> As I wad do, were I Lord God,
> And ye were Martin Elginbrodde.

The afterlife, if conditions were favourable, was thought to be a place of rest and good content. It was expected that one would be gladly welcomed by one's dear departed family and friends – some of whom would, one might think, merely add another terror to death. But Dean Ramsay tells of the urgent desire of friends of a dying Scottish woman to pass on messages to their own family. The response of the old woman was, at best, grudging: 'If I see them, I'll tell them. But dinna' expect I'm gaun clank, clankin' about heaven lookin' for your folk.'

Death, according to the lights of the disgraceful Lord Braxfield, was often too good for defendants haled before the bench of the courts in Edinburgh. 'Ye're clever chiels, but you'll be nane the waur o' a hangin',' was Braxfield's bracing farewell to those he sentenced. His colleagues were no better. The cruel wit of Lord Kames was indulgently described by his biographer, Lord Woodhouselee, as 'due to a certain humorous manner' and as 'the pleasing relaxation of a great mind'. The great mind of Braxfield was pleasingly relaxed when, having to sentence a friend with whom he had regularly played chess, he sent him to the gallows with a merry chuckle: 'That's checkmate tae ye, Mattie!' In a political case, it was pleaded in defence to Braxfield that 'all great men had been reformers, even our Saviour himself'.

Braxfield was equal to this spurious appeal: 'Muckle he made o' that. He was hangit.'

The ludicrous Lord Eskgrove, a contemporary of Braxfield's and his successor as head of the Criminal Court, was on one occasion confronted by a woman of great beauty who appeared, veiled, before him as a witness. Eskgrove proceeded to give her this exposition of her duty: 'Young woman, you will now consider yourself as in the presence of Almighty God, and of this High Court. Lift up your veil, throw off all modesty, and look me in the face.' An example such as this, of unconscious humour, is much treasured in Scotland.

Scottish satire was discussed by Robert Louis Stevenson in 'The Satirist', an essay which considered the subject from both sides:

> After all, I thought, our satirist has gone just far enough into his neighbours to find that the outside is false, without caring to go farther and discover what is really true. He is content to find that things are not what they seem, and broadly generalises from it that they do not exist at all. He sees our virtues are not what they pretend they are; and, on the strength of that, he denies us the possession of virtue altogether. He has learnt the first lesson, that no man is wholly good; but he has not even suspected that there is another equally true, to wit, that no man is wholly bad. Like the inmate of a coloured star, he has eyes for one colour alone. He has a keen scent after evil, but his nostrils are plugged against all good, as people plugged their nostrils before going about the streets of the plague-struck city.

Having considered this to be unreasonable, Stevenson admitted that the Satirist might not be unwise.

> He does not wish to see the good, because he is happier without it . . . He has the forbidden fruit in his waistcoat pocket, and can make himself a god as often and as long as he likes. He has raised himself upon a pedestal above his fellows; he has

touched the summit of ambition; and he envies neither King nor Kaiser, Prophet nor Priest, content in an elevation as high as theirs, and much more easily attained . . . He has not risen by climbing himself, but by pushing others down. He has grown great in his own estimation, not by blowing himself out and risking the fate of Aesop's frog, but simply by the habitual use of a diminishing glass on everybody else. And I think that his is a better, safer, and a surer recipe than most others.

Stevenson is 'giving the headsman a mouthful of his own sawdust', but much of what he has to say applies to Scottish humour. We satirize our own virtues and often expose them as hypocrisy; we cynically impute base motives to the finest actions because we know ourselves to be base; we tend to be suspicious of innocence because we ourselves have lost it. The type of Scottish humour that rejoices in Jock Tamson getting the better of the laird or his master relies for its effect not so much on the nobility and canniness of the underdog as the pride of the master who is, for his own benefit, humbled. But Tamson, in his way, is equally prideful – he calls no man 'Sir' but God, the King, and perhaps the Prince of Wales (though their right to such an address is by no means certain).

The worst example of innocence being cruelly mocked, of a simple nobility of spirit and ambition (laced with a good dose of conceit) being brutally put down, is found in the treatment accorded to William McGonagall. Hugh MacDiarmid was surely right to rage at the miserable fate he suffered at the hands of his countrymen. 'William McGonagall,' says MacDiarmid, 'was not a bad poet; still less a good bad poet. He was not a poet at all, and that he has become synonymous with bad poetry in Scotland is only a natural consequence of Scottish insensitivity to the qualities alike of good poetry and of bad.' McGonagall was, quite simply, unique. He knew nothing of poetry: 'His productions know nothing of grammar, the rubrics and the accepted devices of versification.' MacDiarmid, with relish, proceeds to the attack: not against McGonagall, but against those who would judge him in terms of literature. 'So far as literature has been concerned, the idea of Burns as a "ploughman poet" has been fatal. Scotland has suffered since from an endless succession of railwayman poets, policeman poets, and the like. The movement was in full swing when McGonagall was caught up in it [*in the late nineteenth century*] . . . It is not surprising that McGonagall thought – or was easily persuaded by one of his friends or more likely one of his tormentors – that he could do as well as any of these.' As well? Better!

Where McGonagall differed from all these working-man poets was that he knew nothing of poetry – nothing even of the execrable models they copied, nothing of the whole debased tradition of popular poetry in which they operated. He was quite incapable of all their stock *clichés*, their little flights of fancy, any indication whatever of play of spirit, anything like their range of subject-matter, and, above all, of any humour. He, in fact, heartily despised them and all the common attributes and graces of their verses, which he regarded as trivial and unworthy of his portentous Muse. But he stuck fast by the fundamental ingredients of the great Dundee recipe for sound family literature – a love of battles and an incontinent adoration of kings, queens, members of the royal family, the nobility, and the leading officers of the army and navy; in short the recipe which has made modern Scotland what she is. Knowing his own perfect loyalty and integrity in these great matters, the 'slings and arrows of outrageous fortune' to which he was continuously subjected were incredible to him. He deserved better – in fact, there was nothing that he did not deserve. He was sustained through all his miserable career by this unwavering consciousness of his high deserts and enabled to regard all his calamities as a series of monstrous and inexplicable injustices.

McGonagall was certainly misunderstood – he misunderstood himself, fatally, and suffered for his misapprehensions. It is his fate to have become an object of scornful hilarity, of a 'wholly vicious and unintelligent facetiousness – the flower of which is the "Scotch coamic" and the typical "Scotch Joke."' MacDiarmid regards McGonagall as 'the Ossian of the ineffably absurd' and, as such, 'he has entered upon immortality'.

William Power, in *My Scotland*, describes a performance by the bewildered McGonagall in the Albion Halls in Glasgow:

> He was an old man, but, with his athletic though slightly stooping figure and his dark hair, he did not look more than forty-five; and he appeared to have been shaved the night before. He wore a Highland dress of Rob Roy tartan and boy's size. After reciting some of his own poems, to an accompaniment of whistles and cat-calls, the Bard armed himself with a most dangerous-looking broadsword, and strode up and down the platform, declaiming 'Clarence's Dream' and 'Give me another horse – Bind up my wounds'. His voice rose to a howl. He thrust and slashed at imaginary foes. A shower of apples and oranges fell on the platform. Almost before they touched it, they were met by the fell edge of McGonagall's claymore and cut to pieces. The Bard was beaded with perspiration and orange juice. The audience yelled with delight; McGonagall yelled louder still, with a fury which I fancy was not wholly feigned. It was like a squalid travesty of the wildest scenes of *Don Quixote* and *Orlando Furioso*. I left the hall early, saddened and disgusted.

This was not humour, this was the literary equivalent of bear-baiting – bard-baiting, perhaps.

McGonagall is held up to ridicule as a Scottish character by English comedians (notably by Spike Milligan) who appear on stage in sagging kilts, large and improbably flat tartan bonnets, boots and braces, and proceed to intone, in suitably exaggerated Scottish accents, choice examples of McGonagall's verses. This performance is invariably greeted with enthusiasm – as much by the Scots as by the English. And still the Muse indefatigably prods improbable poets. Most recently, the Renfrew poetaster Walter McCorrisken (who styles himself the 'World's Worst Poet') applied to the Scottish Arts Council for registration on its list of new writers. He was politely refused a certificate of respectability on the grounds that a committee of the Council decided his work did not meet the required criteria, including a requirement that the writer can command a fee and that his work is widely acknowledged in terms of quantity and quality. 'I am finished as a poet,' commented Mr McCorrisken. He had left his job at Glasgow Airport and had been classed as a self-employed poet which meant, he said, that he was not entitled to State benefits. As his earnings dropped, he became more disillusioned. His sole comfort is that his poetry, though generally disparaged, has 'made quite a few people happy over the years.' After publishing a 'slim volume' and making several television appearances, McCorrisken described his new status before the crushing blow delivered by the Scottish Arts Council:

Ah'm still a modest poet
Though Ah've become a star
Ah still like ma modest food
Totties, mince and caviar.

The *Glasgow Herald* commented sagely, 'Mr McCorrisken, it would seem, has been caught up in his own contradictions. Lack of recognition would surely have been welcomed by a man who tried to be awful. Otherwise his works could be misconstrued as good, even if it was recognition that he was good at being bad.' It would not be the first time a Scot had been hoist by his own petard, a victim of his own contradictions.

Dean Ramsay, whose book of *Scottish Life and Character* has given pleasure to generations and furnished many an after-dinner speaker with unattributed anecdotes, talks of Scottish pleasantry 'which is sly, and cheery, and pawky' and 'depends a good deal upon the vehicle in which the story is conveyed'. A majority of Scottish jokes, witticisms, pleasantries and stories depend for their effect upon dialect. 'There is nothing less exportable than a national sense of humour,' said MacDiarmid, and very likely he was right. The Scottish dialects are far from dead or dying, and Scottish eccentricities of character persist: so, therefore, do characteristic Scottish jokes and the Scots sense of humour. This type of humour, wrote Ramsay, did 'not always proceed from the personal wit or cleverness of any of the individuals concerned in them. The amusement comes from the circumstances, from the concurrence or combination of the ideas, and in many cases from the mere expressions which describe the facts. The humour of the narrative is unquestionable, and yet no one has tried to be humorous. In short, it is the *Scottishness* that gives the zest.' Ramsay tells the story of a traveller asking a countryman if he was on the right road to Dunkeld. 'With some of his national inquisitiveness about strangers, the countryman asked his inquirer where he came from. Offended at the liberty, as he considered it, he sharply reminded the man that where he came from was nothing to him; but all the answer he got was the quiet rejoinder, "Indeed, it's just as little to me where you're gaen." English malice would have resulted in the traveller's being given wholly wrong directions, but the Scottish instinct is merely to be stubbornly unhelpful in the face of discourtesy, not wilfully misleading.

There is the story of a Scottish gentleman out walking with a friend, who happened upon a large hole in the ground – a sort of quarry. Stopping, the gentleman remarked, 'I took several thousand pounds out of that hole.' Proceeding a little further, they came to another hole. 'I put it all into that one,' he said. The humour here proceeds not from any wit, but from the dry, matter-of-fact view of things peculiar to the Scots. Matter-of-factness becomes ruthlessness on occasion. A Scottish crofter's wife hurried off to get veterinary attention for her sole asset – a cow. The vet, knowing her husband was seriously ill, asked whether he was any better. She declared him to be at death's door, and impatiently hurried the vet along: 'I can get anither husband soon enough, but God knows where I'd get anither coo.'

The traditional rivalry between Scotland and England has given rise to as many jokes as insults. The best jokes are, of course, also insulting. The general view is that England's most admirable men are probably clever enough to have been Scotsmen. But no matter how eminent and learned an Englishman, he will get his comeuppance if he doesn't mind his manners. Dr Johnson, being offered a dish of hotch-potch by a Scotswoman in London, gruffly complimented it as 'very good for hogs, I believe.' 'Then let me help you to a little more,' said the lady, heaping Johnson's plate. A party of Englishmen, travelling between Edinburgh and Stirling, gave it as their opinion that 'no Englishman could settle down in such a region.' Looking out the window of the railway carriage at the rain, their Scottish travelling companion snorted and pointed a little beyond the line: 'a gey wheen o' yer countrymen cam here mair than five hunder year ago, and they're no' thinkin' o' leavin'. Ye could say they're weel settled.' 'Where's that?' asked the Englishmen. 'Bannockburn,' said the Scotsman. Nelson's famous signal to the fleet at Trafalgar, 'England expects every man to do his duty', vexed two Scottish sailors. 'No a word about puir Auld Scotland,' said one. 'Nae Scotsman need be tell't tae dae his duty,' said the other. 'That's jist a hint tae the English.' A Scotsman found a picture of John Knox hanging in a dark lumber room in an English house. Taking offence at the treatment of a national hero, he nevertheless reined his temper, remarking only that he considered the situation very appropriate, 'for if ever a man could throw light on a dark subject, that was the man.'

The Scots do not lack aplomb in company. In *Thistledown*, a book of Scottish humour compiled by Robert Ford, can be found a story cherished from the days of James VI and I. At a dinner given by Lord Harewood, an English general got to his feet and said, 'Gentlemen, when I am in my cups, and the generous wine begins to warm my blood, I have an absurd custom of railing against the Scotch. Knowing my weakness, I hope no gentleman of the company will take it amiss.' For a moment there was a thoughtful silence, until a Highland chief, Sir Robert Bleakie of

Blair Athol, rose to his feet and remarked, 'Gentlemen, I, when I am in my cups, and the generous wine begins to warm my blood, if I hear a man rail against the Scotch, have an absurd custom of kicking him at once out of the company. Knowing my weakness, I hope no gentleman of the company will take it amiss.' The general did not, on this occasion, follow his usual custom. The courteous answer that, if it does not exactly turn away wrath, at least renders it futile and impotent, is characteristic of a type of Scottish humour. There is a politeness about the Scots that simultaneously damns and disarms their antagonists, rendering them speechless at an innocent insolence which, inscrutably, is indefinably offensive. A farmer who was much addicted to swearing was one day driving along a country road, when one of the wheels of his vehicle ran across a large stone in the middle of the road. Just at that moment, an old Highlander was passing, and the farmer shouted, 'lift that stone and throw it to hell.' 'Not at all, not at all,' said the Highlander, obligingly lifting the stone and throwing it to the side of the road, 'if I threw it to that place it would only be a stumbling block in your path again.'

It is, finally, difficult to be too harsh about the sentimentalism of the Scots because, as James Bridie observed, the Scots probably see through it. 'A great deal of what is called Scotch sentiment *is* funny. To anybody who knows the people who indulge in it, Wallacethebruceism, Charlieoverthewaterism, Puirrabbieburnsism, Bonniebonniebanksism, Myainfolksism, and Laymedoonandeeism, those not very various forms of Scottish Sentiment, are very comical indeed. The Scot himself, greeting heartily beneath his bonnie briar bush, has been known to smile through his tears.' May we detect, there, a gleam of satire, of the moon glinting on the teeth of the fox grinning as he sights the poultry yard? Even the apologist cannot wholly suppress the killer instinct when it comes to the subject of Scottish humour.

15

*

The passionate Scot:
the puritan and the phoenix

I STOOD upon one of the eastern spurs of the Pentland Hills and looked down upon that prospect which quite suddenly and completely discovers the 'North' to the traveller walking from England . . . I seemed to comprehend the whole race in my imagination. I thought of all the Scotsmen in innumerable pubs all over the world, getting drunk as only Scotsmen can do; of the shy, clumsy youths newly arrived in London and making, almost passionately, the same absurd mistakes – which only Scotsmen can make; of the Scotsmen on humorous picture postcards; of the Scotsmen rising to the head of great businesses; of the Scotsmen hopelessly failing; of the Scotsmen being super-sensitively offended; of the Scotsmen being offensively and unwarrantably rude; of the Scotsmen conducting tediously logical arguments with Englishmen who will not listen: of the Scotsmen making the most barefaced appeals to the emotions, to which everyone cannot help listening; of the Scotsmen in music-halls; of the Scotsmen in musical comedies; of the Scotsmen in romantic dramas; of the Scotsmen being religious; of the Scotsmen being ponderously atheistical; of those being coarse, those being 'refined', those being sloppy, those most charmingly courteous and those being beyond words ridiculous.

I recognised in a flash the strong national emotion which combines all these different people, and which is the force behind all their so different but violent actions. I thought of all the nonsense that has been written about Scotland and the Scots, and though I realized how difficult it is to understand them, I surprisingly found myself being angry as I thought of the stupid, uncomprehending abuse which the Scots themselves have in some ways done so much to deserve, and of the far more painful sentimental slobbering over them which they have done nothing to deserve.

Moray McLaren, *Return to Scotland*

The Scots have maintained a proud, passionate defence of their way of life for centuries – it has not much profited them at home. Medieval cartographers sited Scotland out on the rim of their *mappamundi* of the flat earth, diametrically opposite to 'Paradise' which they supposed to lie in the region now known to be occupied by Sri Lanka, and at the furthest remove from Jerusalem, the centre of the Christian world. This may have given confidence to Cleveland, a poet of the early seventeenth century, to describe Scotland as the nearest approximation to hell on earth, and to suggest:

> Had Cain been Scot, God would have changed his doom,
> Not forced him wander, but confined him home.

The Scots have ever laboured under yokes of their own devising. Like Job, they have been sore-smitten but grateful for small mercies. That they were among the elect of God yet put to an extremity of trial, has always puzzled the Scots.

The Declaration of Arbroath in 1326, Scotland's Declaration of Independence twelve years after the battle of Bannockburn when the English were routed, specifically refers to the proud claim of the Scots to have been almost the first to have been chosen to be called to the holy faith of Christianity, 'though we were almost in the outermost parts of the earth' – a reference to St Columba's evangelical mission to Iona. This was considered an honour and attention paid by the King of Kings personally to the Scots, who have been cognizant of it ever since and have enrolled the activities of the Saint among the myths of Scotland. It did not occur to the Scots, perhaps, that they might have merited Columba's most urgent prayers for their conversion from the state of wild and proud barbarism that had so thoroughly disconcerted and disgusted the Romans. Later, more perceptive divines like Knox atoned for this prideful self-congratulation by declaring that the Scots were pretty surely damned even if they mended their ways that were so distressful to God and His ministry.

Religion, like cold showers and other expedients for sublimating natural passions, is thought to have contributed mightily towards the improvement of the Scots. But that innate passion was merely diverted into other channels, away from the pleasures of the flesh and into the more serious business of maintaining moral standards and the intellectual development of the mind. Passion features prominently as a characteristic of pre-Reformation Scotland, in its history and in the demands made upon the Scots by the savage nature of the land. Passion is a characteristic of Celtic culture as immortalized in song and fable, in its art and artefacts. Sentimentality was a nineteenth-century invention, an attempt to soften the grim struggle for existence in a land that Sydney Smith, in the eighteenth century, characterized as 'that garret of the earth – that knuckle-end of England – that land of Calvin, oat-cakes and sulphur.' When Scott had done his work, when he published *The Lady of the Lake* in 1810, the Scots, like Byron who awoke one morning to find himself famous, awoke to the idea that they had become suddenly Romantic. Hearts and minds on both sides of the border perceived, suddenly, the romantic and pathetic possibilities of North Britain.

It is this self-perception among the Scots, that they are noble and ill-used, that they are at the mercy of forces beyond the remedy of bravery and morality, that renders the Scots apathetic. Sentimentality is, at heart, foreign to the Scots, though they use it unashamedly and abuse it cynically. It is too easy for the lachrymose Scot to fall into the pathetic and bathetic cliché that his heart is in the Highlands and pines for a 'little grey home in the West', while reaching for his bottle or his Bible. The modern Scot must make some effort to pull himself together. He must recognize that passion is his predominant characteristic.

Moray McLaren, also in *Return to Scotland*, declared that the Scots

> are a passionate race. Their failings and their virtues spring from their ample passion. Their very caution is a passionate caution; and this is the quality which the inhabitants of the old and new town [*of Edinburgh*] share. The gloom, the restraint of the well-to-do spring from a passion to conserve what has been passionately won. The really terrifying abandonment of a group of Scottish men to the ecstasy of drink comes from the same disturbing quality. The awkwardness of gesture and speech, that can mar the intercourse and manners of both, are the signs of a violent and still imperfectly controlled impetuous nature. The shyness, the rudeness, the tenderness, the loyalty, the friendliness, the caution, the meanness, the generosity of the race have as their motive force the passion which underlies the whole Scottish character, and which is the danger as well as the proudest gift which it possesses. There is no one so upright as the Scots puritan: no one so abandoned as the Scots libertine. Both have as their salvation a deep generosity of spirit and their heritage fine, clear working brains.

Hugh MacDiarmid uncompromisingly stated, in *The Dour Drinkers of Glasgow*, 'We have no use for emotions, let alone sentiments, but are solely concerned with passions.' And Robert Louis Stevenson thought that one of the greatest Scots, John Knox, 'like many men, and many Scotsmen . . . saw the world and his own heart, not so much under any very steady, equable light, as by extreme flashes of passion, true for the moment, but not true in the long run.' Passion is, of course, a dangerous and unpredictable characteristic, but better than the stifling dullness of sentimentality or bourgeois virtue that finds its most brilliant achievement to be respectability.

The Scottish way of life, determined by the Scottish character, would be a success if it made the Scots happy. It does not – the Scots grumble and fret, and succeed only in making their problems worse. That the Scots are discontented is to state the obvious. The problems accumulate and regularly precipitate catastrophes. The Scots regard this periodic process with a fatalistic eye: in their hearts, they cherish their triumphs as much as they grieve for their tragedies, and in the Scottish mind there is no doubt that the country can, like the phoenix, rise again from the ashes. But so long as the Scots rake the ashes for signs and portents of future greatness, attempting to perceive the prospect of glory among the embers of the past, the mythical, miraculous bird will grow cold in the egg as the Scots, dust-sifting through history, burn their fingers yet again and retreat to a corner to suck them.

Bibliography

BARR, ANN and YORK, PETER, *The Sloane Ranger Handbook*, Ebury Press, 1982

BOLD, ALAN, *Modern Scottish Literature*, Longman, 1983

BOSWELL, JAMES, *Journal of a Tour to the Hebrides*, Oxford University Press, 1978

— *Boswell's Column*, edited by Margery Bailey, Kimber, 1951

BRANDER, MICHAEL, *The Emigrant Scots*, Constable, 1982

BROGAN, COLM, *The Glasgow Story*, Frederick Muller, 1952

BRUCE LOCKHART, SIR R. H., *Scotch*, Putnam, 1951

BRUCE, STEVE, *No Pope of Rome*, Mainstream Publishing Co., 1985

BURNS, ROBERT, *The Poems and Songs of Robert Burns*, Collins, 1952

BURTON, J. H., *The Scot Abroad*, Blackwood, 1898

CAMPBELL, ANDREW and MARTINE, RODDY, *The Swinging Sporran*, Wolfe Publishing, 1973

CAMPBELL, JAMES, *Invisible Country*, Weidenfeld & Nicolson, 1984

CHAMBERS, ROBERT (ed), *The Biographical Dictionary of Eminent Scotsmen*, Blackie & Son, 1853

COCKBURN, LORD HENRY, *Memorials of his Time*, Robert Grant, 1946

— *Circuit Journeys*, Byway Books, 1983

CROSLAND, T. W. H., *The Unspeakable Scot*, Grant Richards, 1902

CUNNINGHAME GRAHAM, R. B., *Success*, Duckworth, 1902

— *Progress*, Duckworth, 1905

— *Rodeo*, edited by A. F. Tschiffely, Heinemann, 1936

DAICHES, DAVID, *Glasgow*, André Deutsch, 1977

FIEDLER, LESLIE, *Love and Death in the American Novel*, Jonathan Cape, 1967

FORD, ROBERT, *Thistledown*, Alexander Gardner, 1914

FUSSELL, PAUL, *Caste Marks*, Heinemann, 1984

GILBERT, BIL, *Westering Man*, Athenaeum, 1983

GRAHAM, HENRY GREY, *Scottish Men of Letters in the Eighteenth Century*, A & C Black, 1901

— *The Social Life of Scotland in the Eighteenth Century*, A & C Black, 1899

HAMILTON, IAIN, *Scotland the Brave*, Michael Joseph, 1957

HARE, AUGUSTUS, *The Story of my Life*, George Allen, 1900

HARVIE, CHRISTOPHER, *No Gods and Precious Few Heroes*, Edward Arnold, 1981

HOGG, JAMES, *The Private Memoirs and Confessions of a Justified Sinner*, Introduced by John Wain, Penguin, 1983

JAMIESON, DR JOHN, *Dictionary of the Scottish Language*, edited by Johnstone, Longmuir and Metcalfe, Alexander Gardner, 1912

KIGHTLY, CHARLES, *Folk Heroes of Britain*, Thames & Hudson, 1982

LAUDER, HARRY, *Ticklin' Talks*, D. C. Thomson, no date

MACDIARMID, HUGH, *Aesthetics in Scotland*, Mainstream, 1984

— *The Uncanny Scot*, MacGibbon & Kee, 1968

— *Scottish Eccentrics*, George Routledge, 1936

MACKENZIE, AGNES MUIR, *Scottish Pageant*, Oliver & Boyd, 1950

MACKENZIE, COMPTON, *Hunting the Fairies*, Chatto & Windus, 1949

MACKIE, J. D., *A History of Scotland*, Penguin, 1982

MACLENNON, RODERICK, *The Scottish Highlander*, Eneas Mackay, 1905

MACLEOD MALLOCH, D., *The Book of Glasgow Anecdote*, Foulis, 1912

MACTAGGART, JOHN, *The Scottish Gallovidian Encyclopaedia*, Cluny Press in assoc. with the E. A. Hornel Trust, 1981

MCCALLUM, NEIL, *A Small Country*, James Thin, 1983

MCLAREN, MORAY, *Return to Scotland*, Duckworth, 1930

— *The Scots*, Penguin, 1951

MILLER, KARL (ed.), *Memoirs of a Modern Scotland*, Faber & Faber, 1970

MUIR, EDWIN, *Scottish Journey*, Heinemann, 1935

— *Collected Poems*, Faber & Faber, 1976

POWER, WILLIAM, *My Scotland*, Faber & Faber, 1934

RAMSAY, DEAN, *Reminiscences of Scottish Life and Character*, Edmonston & Douglas, 1861

— *Scottish Life and Character*, Edmonston & Douglas, 1861

ROYLE, TREVOR, *The Macmillan Companion to Scottish Literature*, Macmillan, 1983

SCOTT, WALTER, *The Minstrelsy of the Scottish Border*, James Ballantyne, 1806

SMITH, G. GREGORY, *Scottish Literature*, Macmillan, 1919

SMOUT, T. C., *A History of the Scottish People*, Collins, 1969

— *A Century of the Scottish People*, Collins, 1986

STEEL, TOM, *Scotland's Story*, Collins, 1984

STEVENSON, ROBERT LOUIS, *The Collected Works of Robert Louis Stevenson* (Tusitala Edition), Heinemann, 1924

THEROUX, PAUL, *The Kingdom by the Sea*, Hamish Hamilton, 1983

THOMSON, C. W., *Scottish School Humour*, Robert Gibson, 1936

URQUHART, SIR THOMAS, *The Life and Death of the Admirable Crichtoun*, The Pleiad, 1927

WATTS, CEDRIC and DAVIES, LAURENCE, *Cunninghame Graham: A Critical Biography*, Cambridge University Press, 1979

WEBB, KEITH, *The Growth of Nationalism in Scotland*, Molendinar, 1977

WITTIG, KARL, *The Scottish Tradition in Literature*, Oliver & Boyd, 1958

Index